CW00793690

THE PIED FLYCATCHER

THE
PIED FLYCATCHER

ARNE LUNDBERG AND RAUNO V. ALATALO

Illustrated by
TOMAS PÄRT

T & A D POYSER

London

© *T & A D Poyser 1992*
ISBN 0-85661-072-0

First published in 1992 by T & A D Poyser Ltd
24–28 Oval Road, London NW1 7DX

United States Edition published by
ACADEMIC PRESS INC.
San Diego, CA 92101

A catalogue record for this book
is available from the British Library

Text set in Bembo
Typeset by Paston Press, Loddon, Norfolk
Printed and bound in Great Britain by
Mackays of Chatham PLC, *Chatham, Kent*

This book is printed on acid-free paper

ISBN 0-85661-072-0

Contents

Acknowledgements   xi

1   The Pied Flycatcher: Background   1

2   Taxonomy and Distribution   7

3   Migration, Moult, and Age and Sex Determination   15

4   Nesting, Habitat, and Breeding Densities   37

5   Foraging Techniques and Diet   54

6   Breeding Time and Clutch Size   60

7   Egg-Laying, Incubation and Caring for Young   88

8   Longevity, Age at First Breeding, and Dispersal   111

9   Song   125

10   Male Plumage Colour and its Variation   138

11   Pair Formation and Female Choice   156

12   Mating Systems   180

13   Hybridization   213

14   Breeding in Natural Cavities   223

Appendices

1. Morphology of the Collared Flycatcher and Four Subspecies of the Pied Flycatcher   238

2. Diet of the Pied Flycatcher   239

3. Breeding Data for the Pied Flycatcher   240

4. Return Rates in Different Parts of Europe   241

5. Plumage Colour of Pied Flycatcher Males   242

6. Polyterritorial Bird Species in Europe   243

7. Polyterritoriality Distances   244

8. Frequency of Polygyny   245

9. List of Latin Names   246

References   248

Index   264

List of Photographs

1. *Breeding habitat in Sweden* 42
2. *Breeding habitat in Sweden* 42
3. *Breeding habitat in northern England* 43
4. *Breeding habitat in Tunisia* 43
5. *The male has attracted a female* 158
6. *The male shows the nest site* 158
7. *The male is calling from inside* 159
8. *The female inspects the nest site* 159

List of Figures

1. The forehead of a Pied Flycatcher male   3
2. Linnaeus' drawing of a Pied Flycatcher   8
3. Pallas' description of a Pied Flycatcher   9
4. Song differences in flycatchers   11
5. The Palaearctic distribution of Pied and Collared Flycatchers   12
6. Wintering areas in tropical Africa   16
7. Afrotropical ringing recoveries of the Pied Flycatcher   17
8. Autumn passage of Pied Flycatchers in southeast Sweden   19
9. Autumn recoveries of Swedish ringed Pied Flycatchers   20
10. Finnish recoveries of older Pied Flycatchers   21
11. Finnish recoveries of one-year old Pied Flycatchers   22
12. Spring recoveries of Swedish ringed Pied Flycatchers   25
13. Spring arrival of one-year old and older males   26
14. Spring arrival time in central Sweden   28
15. Outer greater coverts of one-year old and older Pied Flycatcher males   31
16. Relationship between wing length and first primary length   34
17. Design of a song play-back experiment   45
18. Arrival time to new and old nest box areas   46
19. Fledging success at different breeding densities   49
20. Types of foraging sites   56
21. Laying date plotted against altitude   62
22. Laying time in relation to temperature at two sites in Finland   63
23. Time from female arrival to start of laying   64
24. Onset of egg-laying in relation to temperature   65
25. Laying time in relation to temperature at Uppsala, Sweden   66
26. Laying pattern during a cold spell   67
27. Start of laying by one-year old and older females   68
28. Laying time of individual females in consecutive years   68
29. Resemblance between mothers and daughters in laying time   69
30. Clutch size plotted against latitude   71
31. Clutch size plotted against altitude   71
32. Clutch size in relation to habitat   72
33. Clutch size and number of fledged young in relation to start of egg-laying   75
34. Breeding performance in relation to start of egg-laying   76
35. Clutch size of one-year old and older females   78
36. Variation in clutch size with female tarsus length   79
37. Breeding performance in relation to clutch size   81
38. Reproductive success in manipulated broods   83

39. *Reproductive success in manipulated broods in different years*   84
40. *Clutch size of the same female in successive years*   85
41. *Resemblance in clutch size between mother and daughters*   86
42. *Body mass changes in females during breeding*   92
43. *Hatching success in relation to temperature*   95
44. *Weight increase of nestlings*   96
45. *Feeding rates of males and females*   98
46. *Broods fed by two parents in relation to season*   100
47. *Male contribution to the feeding of nestlings*   101
48. *Feeding rates in different categories of nests*   103
49. *Breeding success in deciduous and coniferous forest*   105
50. *Fledging success in relation to temperature*   106
51. *Fledging weights in Sweden and England*   107
52. *Return rate in relation to fledging weight*   107
53. *Fledging weight of surviving and non-surviving birds*   108
54. *Survival rate in relation to age*   113
55. *Age at first breeding*   115
56. *Survival rates of males and females*   116
57. *Fledging weight of surviving males and females*   122
58. *Sonogram of a song strophe*   126
59. *Examples of simple and complex song*   127
60. *Repertoire size between years*   129
61. *An example of song copying of other species*   129
62. *Song rate at different temperatures*   131
63. *Song rates of fed and unfed males during bad weather*   132
64. *Experimental design of a song attraction experiment*   134
65. *Sonograms of a song strophe in primary and secondary territory*   135
66. *Distribution of dark- and brown-coloured Pied Flycatcher populations*   140
67. *Male coloration in relation to age in Sweden*   141
68. *Male coloration in relation to age in England*   142
69. *Change in male plumage colour from one year of age to the age of two*   142
70. *Change in male plumage colour from two years of age to the age of three*   143
71. *Resemblance in male coloration between fathers and sons*   145
72. *Relationship between fledging weight and male coloration*   146
73. *Return rate in relation to coloration in Sweden*   149
74. *Return rate in relation to coloration in England*   149
75. *Male Pied Flycatcher coloration and breeding distance from a Collared Flycatcher male*   151
76. *Correlation between male arrival and mating order*   162
77. *Correlation between male darkness and mating order*   167
78. *Design of a laboratory experiment on female choice*   169
79. *Female mating order in relation to leaf damage*   175
80. *Design of a male–male competition experiment*   176
81. *Mate choice in relation to male plumage colour of males arriving at the same time*   178

82.   *The polygyny threshold model   183*
83.   *The mating system of the Pied Flycatcher   185*
84.   *Male mating status in relation to arrival time   187*
85.   *Singing intensity of unmated and already-mated males   189*
86.   *Female nest-site preferences in relation to nest-hole density   193*
87.   *The timing of copulations   195*
88.   *Distance between males and females after pair formation   195*
89.   *Males attempting extra-pair copulations   196*
90.   *Relative breeding success of secondary females   199*
91.   *Yearly variation in breeding success   200*
92.   *Utilization of different territories   205*
93.   *Female choice of already-mated and unmated males   206*
94.   *Number of females leaving their territory after next box entrance size had been changed   209*
95.   *Sonograms of pure and mixed Pied Flycatcher song, and of Collared Flycatcher and hybrid song   218*
96.   *Breeding failures in conspecific and heterospecific pairings   221*
97.   *Forest types in our natural study area   225*
98.   *Nest bottom area in natural cavities   226*
99.   *Nest volume in natural cavities   227*
100. *Clutch size in relation to bottom area in natural cavities   229*
101. *Height of successful and predated nests   231*
102. *Hole quality of natural cavities   232*
103. *Polyterritorial distances in a natural forest   235*

List of Tables

1. *Shape of the white forehead patch in Pied Flycatcher males* 3
2. *Arrival times of Pied Flycatchers in breeding areas in spring* 27
3. *Spring passage of migrating Pied Flycatchers in the Mediterranean and in southern Sweden* 27
4. *Wing length in relation to age of Pied Flycatcher males* 33
5. *Morphometry of Pied Flycatcher males and females in different habitats* 47
6. *Degree of reduction in clutch size and number of fledged young with progress of season* 75
7. *Parental return rate in a clutch size manipulation experiment* 83
8. *Fledging success at Uppsala, Sweden* 104
9. *Male dispersal distances* 118
10. *Female dispersal distances* 119
11. *Natal dispersal distances* 122
12. *Male plumage colour at different ages* 143
13. *Influence of male characteristics on female choice* 163
14. *Time to attract a female in a field experiment* 168
15. *Reproductive success of females mated to one-year old and older males* 171
16. *Male feeding intensity in relation to age and morphology* 172
17. *Outcome of male contests over a free nest box* 177
18. *Back colour of Pied Flycatcher males in conspecific and heterospecific pairs* 216
19. *Breeding success of pure, heterospecific and hybrid flycatcher pairs* 220
20. *Type of nest-hole and predation rate* 230
21. *The quality of natural cavities* 233
22. *Entrance size of natural cavities* 234
23. *The mating status of males breeding in natural cavities* 235

Acknowledgements

In many ways the results of the studies on the Pied Flycatcher described in this book are a joint effort. Our mutual investigations started in 1978 with the arrival at the Department of Zoology in Uppsala of Professor Staffan Ulfstrand, who brought about the first contact between the present authors. Rauno Alatalo arrived at Uppsala in 1979 and left his position there in 1986, when he moved to the University of Jyväskylä in Finland. After our spatial 'divorce' we have continued to work on joint projects, though in different countries. On Staffan's suggestion, under his supervision, and using his money, we started a study of the Pied Flycatcher in 1979. Our first aim was to test Fretwell's (1972) idea of 'ideal free' and 'despotic' distributions by comparing reproductive success across habitats (Lundberg et al., 1981). However, by 'rediscovering' Lars von Haartman's old observations of polyterritorial polygyny in the Pied Flycatcher, and after having proposed an adaptive explanation for this behaviour (Alatalo et al., 1981), we later shifted our focus towards the breeding behaviour of the Pied Flycatcher, and we found this so interesting and rewarding that we immediately became hooked on the species. For this we also have to thank our friends in other countries who have never failed to object to our interpretations. Although we disagree with many of their alternative interpretations concerning the Pied Flycatcher's breeding biology, we gratefully acknowledge the 'scientific pressure' they have imposed on us, thus forcing us to continue the studies for many years beyond what we planned in the beginning. Another source of inspiration has been our field studies in England, where the study areas are beautifully and strategically located in the Cumbrian mountains in between the Kirkstile Inn and the Wheatsheaf, both of which serve excellent food and local ale. It was by pure chance that in 1985 we met the enthusiastic amateur bird ringer Alan Old, who told us that Pied Flycatcher nestlings return to their natal area in Cumbria (which they do not do in Sweden or Finland), and he allowed us to work with the birds that used his nest boxes. Alan Old has also actively helped us in the field and collected many of the Cumbrian data presented in this book. Subsequently, several other local Cumbrian bird ringers (listed below) have also put their boxes at our disposal.

A vast number of people have helped us in the field or in the laboratory, as amateurs, students, or professional scientists. With apologies to anyone we might have forgotten, they are in alphabetical order: Susanne Åkesson, Klas Allander, Mats Björklund, Ingegerd Borg, John Callion, Allan Carlson, Peter Davies, Reija Dufva, Dag Eriksson, Torbjörn Fagerström, Jackie Foot, Richard Fredriksson, Hans Gelter, Carolyn Glynn, Karin Gottlander, Lars Gustafsson, Matti Halonen, Lars Hillström, David Holloway, Matti Hovi, Esa Huhta,

Margareta Hultquist, Jukka Jokimäki, Berit Martinsson, Juan Moreno, Alan Old, Karin Olsson, Päivi Palokangas, Osmo Rätti, William Searcy, Pirkko Siikamäki, Bob Spencer, Jukka Suhonen, Jan Sundberg, Staffan Thorman, Staffan Ulfstrand, Susanne Venhuizen, Lars Wallin, Björn Westman and Liisa Widell. We also very much appreciate all discussions and valuable suggestions given to us by colleagues at our respective departments. We owe a considerable debt to Richard Heijkenskjöld and Astrid Ulfstrand who drew the figures for this book, which were later reproduced into glossy prints by Lars-Erik Jönsson. Staffan Ulfstrand read almost the whole book in draft, while Dag Eriksson, Anders Pape Møller, Markku Orell, Tomas Pärt, Jan Pettersson, Osmo Rätti, William Searcy, Lars Wallin and David Wiggins commented on many chapters. All of them suggested lots of improvements. A special thank-you goes to the head secretary at our department in Uppsala, Marianne Heijkenskjöld, who, as well as turning all bureaucratic problems into pleasure, also voluntarily read several chapters of this book as a representative of the category of non-enthusiast bird-watchers. Nils-Erik Persson and Mats Ekström are qualified for a citation in the *Guinness Book of Records* because they have probably made more nest boxes than anyone else in the world – thank you both. In recent years Antti Sirkka and his colleagues at Konnevesi Research Station in Finland have become serious competitors for this award. Rauno Alatalo is in debt to the research station at Konnevesi for supporting the field studies in many other ways. Last, but not least, our studies would not have been possible without the financial support obtained from the Swedish Natural Science Research Council and from the Academy of Finland, and support in other forms provided by our respective families.

The authorship of almost all of our joint research publications has been in alphabetical order although we have, on average, equally shared the responsibility for field work, data analyses, and writing up. In this book we try to rectify this by reversing the usual order of authorship.

ARNE LUNDBERG and RAUNO ALATALO

CHAPTER 1

The Pied Flycatcher: Background

This book about the Pied Flycatcher is primarily based on our own experiences and information we have gained during a 12-year-study period (1979–90) in Sweden, Finland and England. We have paid special attention to the remarkable variation in male plumage coloration both within and between populations and on the polyterritorial mating system of the males. Another feature adding excitement to this research is the hybridization between the Pied and the Collared Flycatcher. In our own research we have also collected substantial amounts of data on habitat preferences, timing of breeding, clutch size, breeding success, and cues for mate choice. In collaboration with students and other colleagues we have studied such aspects as the function of vocalizations, dispersal and hatching patterns. We have comparatively little research experience of our own concerning moult, migration, courtship feeding, foraging techniques and diet, but fortunately, there is a rich literature on these elements of the biology of the Pied Flycatcher. Topics less fully treated in this book are endocrinology and the seasonal development of reproductive organs, despite the many studies made in this field, e.g. by Bengt Silverin; and the possible influence of parasites on male coloration and breeding success. We have scanned the numerousness of blood parasites in male Pied Flycatchers, but the results are not yet fully analysed, and therefore not presented here.

Like the Great and Blue Tits, the Pied Flycatcher has become somewhat of a European equivalent of the North American Red-winged Blackbird in attracting an extraordinary amount of research interest. During the writing of this book we have made use of about 300 publications about the Pied Flycatcher, but have probably overlooked many. We have found it impossible to relate and evaluate the contents and conclusions of all these publications. Thus, we have not tried to review everything that has been written about Pied Flycatchers, but have deliberately emphasized our own research though at the same time considering current research on relevant general ecological questions. Where our interpretations differ from those of other people we have given prominence to our own views, although we have also, as objectively as possible, tried to present the merits of alternative explanations. We have tried to make this book appeal to enthusiastic amateurs as well as professional scientists, although a certain admixture of references, descriptions of methodology and statistics has been judged inevitable.

EARLIER RESEARCH

Ecological research in Europe on the Pied Flycatcher was started in the early 1930s by Gerhard Creutz, W. Trettau and F. Merkel in Germany. The main focus of their work was directed towards population dynamics, although their extensive capturing and ringing activities also provided new and useful insights into individual variation. These pioneering studies were continued in the early 1940s by Lars von Haartman at Lemsjöholm near Turku in southwestern Finland. Through his work over almost half a century von Haartman stands out as one of the founders of modern ornithology and, among many other achievements, laid the foundations of our knowledge of the Pied Flycatcher. He was the first to propose an evolutionary explanation of polyterritorial polygyny, which is one of the most fascinating components of the biology of this species. Lars von Haartman was soon followed by Bruce Campbell who in the late 1940s studied the Pied Flycatcher in the Forest of Dean in Gloucestershire in southwest England. The German tradition of Pied Flycatcher research has been continued to the present day by such workers as Rudolf Berndt, Eberhard Curio, Hans Löhrl, Helmut Sternberg and Wolfgang Winkel. In the last twenty years the many advantages of the Pied Flycatcher for research on evolutionary biology have also been recognized by research groups in Sweden and Norway.

THE PIED FLYCATCHER AND WHY TO STUDY IT

The Pied Flycatcher is a small (12–13 g) passerine bird, which breeds in many forested areas of the Palaearctic region. It only stays in the north for the spring and summer, spending the rest of the year on migration or in the wintering areas in tropical West Africa. Virtually nothing is known about the species from the

Fig. 1.   The three most common types of forehead patches in the male Pied Flycatcher.

wintering grounds and very little from the migration periods. Thus, most of our knowledge derives from the short period of breeding in the north.

The Pied Flycatcher breeds naturally in holes in trees, most often those that have been excavated by woodpeckers or that have arisen when a branch has fallen off the trunk. However, if good quality nest boxes are provided, they are strongly preferred over natural cavities, making it possible to attract almost the whole breeding population within a woodland to boxes. This is one of the main reasons why the Pied Flycatcher has become such a popular object of research.

We have been studying problems of general scientific interest, and have found the Pied Flycatcher a suitable organism for that purpose. In fact, few species are more amenable to field experimentation. Another reason for using this species is its abundance: the total Swedish population has been estimated at about 2 million pairs (Ulfstrand and Högstedt, 1976), which ranks it among the 15 most abundant bird species in Sweden. Additional features making Pied Flycatchers suitable for research include their relative tameness which makes them easy to catch, their reluctance to abandon a breeding attempt after having been caught and handled, and the variable plumage of the males which makes them individually recognizable in the field by plumage characters, even if one should fail to catch them. One of these individually variable features is the shape and size of the white forehead patch, which usually takes one of three different forms: rectangular, divided into two dots, or a combination of both (Fig. 1). In Sweden males seem to be equally likely to belong to any type whereas rectangular forehead patches seem to be less common in Britain (Table 1). Since Pied Flycatchers are

Table 1.   Frequency distribution (%) of the shape of the white forehead patch in Pied Flycatcher males at Uppsala Sweden, and Cumbria, England. (1) Denotes two separate dots, (2) two fused dots and (3) a rectangular forehead patch. See Fig. 1 for further details.

	Type of forehead patch			
	1	2	3	*n*
Sweden	32.2	35.3	32.5	329
England	39.7	41.8	18.5	509

normally easy to catch in the nest boxes, most individuals in a study area can be individually marked and thus made identifiable, which is an enormous advantage, for example, in behavioural studies. Yet, one has to admit that even Pied Flycatchers have certain disadvantages from a researcher's point of view: they are small and spend much time hidden in the canopy, which makes them difficult to follow and identify on an individual basis.

STUDY AREAS AND METHODS

Our studies of the Pied Flycatcher have mainly been carried out at Uppsala, central Sweden (59°50′N, 17°40′E), from 1979 to 1990, in Cumbria, northwest England (54°35′N, 3°23′W) from 1985 to 1990, and at Konnevesi, central Finland (62°14′N, 25°44′E) from 1986 to 1990. In collaboration with colleagues at the Department of Zoology in Uppsala, especially Lars Gustafsson and Dag Eriksson, we have also been closely involved in starting up research on Pied and Collared Flycatchers breeding in sympatry on the Baltic islands of Gotland (57°10′N, 18°20′E) and Öland (57°10′N, 16°58′E). Much of our knowledge about interspecific relationships derives from their continuing studies.

The surroundings of Uppsala are very flat and are dominated by farmland interspersed with deciduous, coniferous and mixed woodlands. Many broad-leaved tree species have their northern limit in Sweden just north of Uppsala, while further north the land is largely covered by extensive areas of coniferous forest. Up to 1986 our main focus in the studies on the Pied Flycatcher was on reproductive success, particularly in relation to the mating status of birds, habitat and breeding density. These studies were generally carried out in a number of deciduous and coniferous woodlands around Uppsala, and the total number of nest boxes available each year was about 500–600. Usually boxes were provided in excess of the number of pairs utilizing them; other bird species commonly using these boxes were Great and Blue Tits, and occasionally also Marsh and Coal Tits, Redstarts, Tree Sparrows and Wrynecks. Since deciduous forests, which are preferred by Pied Flycatchers, make up only a small fraction of the land area at the latitude of Uppsala, we have been limited in our efforts to collect data more by the availability of suitable woodlands than by the number of boxes we could control. From 1985 onwards we directed our research more towards problems concerning mate choice by females. These studies required large-scale nest-box manipulations with the consequence that data of reproductive success from recent years are not always comparable with previously collected data. At Uppsala we have also collected breeding data on the Pied Flycatcher for three years from a semi-natural deciduous forest where all pairs bred in natural cavities.

Konnevesi is situated in the Finnish 'lake district' (Järvi-Suomi in Finnish) and apart from all the lakes the landscape is dominated by coniferous forest interspersed with patches of silver and downy birch in wetter places. Here we have mainly carried out nest-box experiments in order to examine various aspects of male polyterritoriality, female choice and competition between males. This means that rather few data have been collected by us in Finland on reproductive success in unmanipulated situations.

In Cumbria, England, in the 'real' Lake District, the study sites are mainly situated on steep hillside slopes. The small woodlands are dominated by sessile oak and are often grazed by sheep, leaving little scope for dense understorey vegetation, apart from bracken. For many years nest boxes have been provided in these woodlands by local bird ringers who have also checked laying dates and clutch size and ringed the nestlings; our task has been to catch, measure and ring all males, and also to weigh and measure the young at 13 days of age (up to 1989). The main advantage of this study is that the birds in Cumbria are severely limited by habitat, and therefore most surviving individuals return to their natal area or their previous breeding site. This has made it possible for us to look in more detail at resemblance in morphology and behaviour between parents and offspring, and within individuals between successive years.

In central Sweden, the first Pied Flycatchers usually turn up in the first week of May, and as in most migratory passerines, males arrive ahead of females and older birds before younger ones. On their arrival we have caught and ringed the males, mainly using 'nest-box traps' (Fig. 64) in combination with play-back song. Males were measured, weighed, scored in plumage darkness and aged as yearlings or older (Fig. 15). In Cumbria, many individuals had been ringed in a previous year, either as nestlings or one-year old, and we could thus assign them an exact age. In several cases active nests were found before we were able to catch and identify the male. Several of these males could be trapped in their boxes later when feeding young. In yet other cases, however, no male was observed during the nestling stage. In some cases, he might have died although usually he was probably an already-mated male with another territory and another female elsewhere. Females were usually caught during incubation or when feeding nestlings. From the day the female arrived each nest box was checked at least twice a week to determine the start of nest-building, the laying time and the clutch size. From these observations we were able to estimate the hatching date, which was to be verified later by direct observation. When they were 13 days old we ringed and weighed the young and also measured their tarsus length.

Much of the material in this book has already been published in a series of scientific papers; this is especially the case for the data collected in Sweden and Finland, though most data from England are so far unpublished. However, we have combined all information on a particular subject under the same heading, wherever it was, and whether it was previously published or not; thus it is possible to draw general conclusions and indicate possible sources of variation. Unfortunately repetition between chapters has proved inevitable, and certain topics such as breeding success, pair formation, male plumage coloration and polygyny have been dealt with more than once.

CHAPTER 2

Taxonomy and Distribution

This chapter we devote to the taxonomy and nomenclature of the Pied Fly-catcher. This means that we will present its subdivision into geographic subspe-cies, its relationship to other species and its supposed postglacial history in Europe. We also relate the story of how the Pied Flycatcher eventually got its currently valid scientific name – a story with numerous complications and a lesson in nomenclaturial procedure.

7

OLD WORLD FLYCATCHERS

Flycatchers belong to the family Muscicapidae, which contains 9 subfamilies and 107 species, breeding from Africa and Europe in the west through Asia to Japan in the east (Howard and Moore, 1991). The genus *Ficedula* is one of the most species-rich in this subfamily, having 26 species, which occur from North Africa and Europe all the way to southeast Asia. Many of the species occur on islands in the East Indies, where some of them are endemic or have endemic subspecies on particular islands. The species with the smallest range is probably the Damar Flycatcher which only occurs on the tiny island of Damar in the Banda Sea. In many *Ficedula* species, males are conspicuously coloured in black and white, black and red/orange, black and yellow, or blue and red/orange. Yet other species have a duller brown or olive-brown plumage, sometimes with a rusty tinge on the breast. Females of most species are brownish. Strong sexual dimorphism is thus a frequent feature in this subfamily.

NOMENCLATURE

The Pied Flycatcher was first scientifically described by Linnaeus in 1746 in his book *Fauna Svecica* (Fig. 2). At that time he had not yet invented binominal nomenclature and had loosely assigned the species, together with many other passerines, to the 'genus' *Motacilla*. Linnaeus most certainly had not seen the Pied Flycatcher himself but probably relied on a description given to him in 1744 by a researcher in anatomy and medicine at Lund in southern Sweden (Johan Leche, 1704–64). In his book Linnaeus failed to match the text (no. 230) with the drawing (no. 229), and the latter actually accompanied the text on the Blackcap. This came to cause even worse confusion in later publications by Linnaeus. Thus,

Fig. 2.   Linnaeus's drawing of male and female Pied Flycatchers in his book Fauna Svecica *published in 1746.*

in the next edition of *Fauna Svecica* (1761), now with binominal Latin names, the original drawing was still present (now no. 256), while the accompanying text was removed. However, in the description of the Whinchat (*Motacilla rubetra* according to Linnaeus's nomenclature) he referred to the text on both the Whinchat and the Pied Flycatcher given in the first edition, while the original text on the Pied Flycatcher was now incorporated in the new text about the Blackcap. Similarly, in the 10th edition of his *Systema Naturae* (1758), the text and the drawing of the Pied Flycatcher were mixed up with those of the Whinchat and the Blackcap. It is possible that Linnaeus believed the Pied Flycatcher and the Blackcap to be the same species (an idea probably dating back to Aldrovandi; see below), and that the Pied Flycatcher in autumn changed its plumage into that of a Blackcap. Therefore, in an effort to tie up the loose ends, he had to hide the original Pied Flycatcher text and included it with the description of the Whinchat.

Finally, in 1766 (in the 12th edition of *Systema Naturae*), Linnaeus got it right and named the Pied Flycatcher *Muscicapa atricapilla*, the genus name (which means precisely 'flycatcher') being probably taken from Brisson (1760). Unfortunately he had by then been preceded by Peter Simon Pallas (a Berlin-born medical doctor and naturalist, and later, professor of Natural History at St Petersburg) who had correctly described the species two years earlier. Pallas gained his doctor's degree at Leiden University in 1760, and travelled extensively in the Netherlands to visit hospitals and museums (Mearns and Mearns, 1988). During these travels he probably came in contact with Dutch bird collections, one of which, containing 322 bird species and including a catalogue published in 1764, was brought together by a Mr A. Vroeg, who had probably also prepared the specimens. The author of the catalogue is unknown, but it has been argued that Peter Simon Pallas and not Vroeg was the author of the new names in a separate outline at the end of the catalogue (the 'Adumbratiunculae'), in which the Pied Flycatcher, *Motacilla hypoleuca*, is no. 156 (Fig. 3). When the catalogue was rediscovered early this century (van Oort, 1911) the species name *atricapilla* was replaced with *hypoleuca* for priority reasons, though van Oort argued that the names in the 'Adumbratiunculae' were pre-occupied by the names in the main catalogue, the author of which is unknown. Also, the new names in the 'outline' must, according to van Oort, be rejected as this part was written anonymously.

N. 156 MOTACILLA (*hypoleuca*) fufca fubtus alba, remigibus intimis, rectricibufque tribus lateralibus exterius albis. Magn. fere Lufciniæ. Supra nigro fufca femina, mas nigrior. Frons prima, fubtufque tota alba. Remiges 2, tectricefque intimæ maximam partem albæ. Rectrices utrinque 3. exterius longitudinaliter verfus bafin albæ.

Fig. 3. The description of the Pied Flycatcher in the Adumbratiunculae of Vroeg's catalogue of birds published in 1764. It has been claimed that Peter Simon Pallas was the author of the new names, among them that of the Pied Flycatcher.

Thus, it seems that Linnaeus's species name for the Pied Flycatcher (*atricapilla*) should have priority over *hypoleuca*, but this cannot be changed because of the fifty-year rule, which states that a name that has been out of use for fifty years or more cannot be allowed.

The Pied Flycatcher was again described as a new species, and named *Emberiza luctuosa*, by Scopoli (1769), who had used specimens described in Linnaeus's 10th edition of *Systema Naturae* (1758) as his reference. Later still the species was described by the Norwegian naturalist Hans Ström (1774) who named it *Motacilla leucomelas*. Obviously these names cannot be accepted since the Pied Flycatcher had already been given a proper scientific name. Charles Darwin used the Pied Flycatcher as an example in his book *The Descent of Man* (1871) when he discussed the different colours of males and females. In the context of nomenclature, however, it is worth noting that he used the genus name of Linnaeus but the species name suggested by Scopoli – *Muscicapa luctuosa*.

The genus name *Ficedula* probably dates back to Aristotle (384–322 B.C.) who in his *Historia Animalium* named certain insectivorous passerines *Sycalis* (i.e ≈ 'possible to catch when figs are ripe' in Greek). *Sycalis* later became translated by several authors into Latin as *Ficedula* (= fig-eater) and was so used by the Italian naturalist Ulyssis Aldrovandi (1522–1605). Both Aristotle and Aldrovandi used this name not only for the Pied Flycatcher but also for the Blackcap and possibly the Marsh and Sombre Tits. Both obviously knew that Pied Flycatchers change plumage in autumn, and may have believed that they turned into one or the other of the above mentioned species, most likely into a Blackcap. (A much more detailed account of old descriptions of flycatchers is given in Swedish by Rosvall, 1982.) The present use of *Ficedula* instead of *Muscicapa* as the generic name for several flycatcher species is probably based on a review of the Pied Flycatcher by Dunajewski (1938).

SUBSPECIES AND DISTRIBUTION OF THE PIED FLYCATCHER

The Pied Flycatcher breeds in northern Africa and right across Europe to western Siberia and southwest Asia (Fig. 5). Howard and Moore (1980) divide it into five subspecies; *Ficedula h. hypoleuca, F. h. iberiae, F. h. speculigera, F. h. semitorquata* and *F. h. tomensis* (= *sibirica* in Vaurie, 1959; *sibirica* will pre-occupy *tomensis* if *Ficedula* is not maintained). The status of *semitorquata* is under lively debate. Stresemann (1926) and Vaurie (1959) considered it a subspecies of the Collared Flycatcher, while it is sometimes suggested that it is a true species (Curio, 1959a), and most modern bird field guides follow this opinion (often calling it the 'Semicollared Flycatcher'). It resembles the Pied Flycatcher in plumage while the alarm call sounds like that of the Collared Flycatcher (Curio, 1959a). The song, however, is intermediate between the Pied and Collared Flycatchers, or slightly more similar to that of the Pied Flycatcher (Fig. 4). *F. h. iberiae* was not accepted as a subspecies on its own by Vaurie (1959), while Curio (1960a) after a closer examination of 23 individuals from Spain argued that it

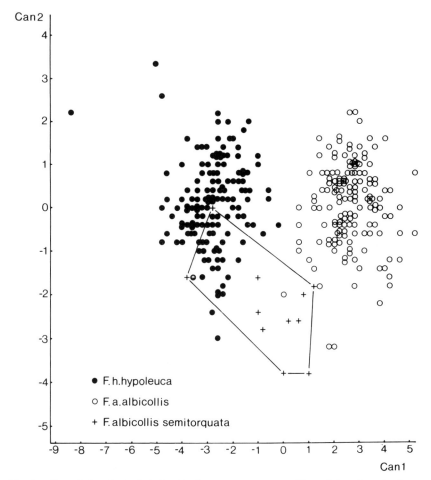

Fig. 4.   *Canonical analysis of relationships between nine song variables and three flycatcher forms:*
F. h. hypoleuca (●), F. h. semitorquata (+) *and* F. a. albicollis (○). *The polygon encloses*
plots of semitorquata. *Each symbol represents one phrase. Canonical discriminant analysis is a*
dimension-reduction technique by which two variables are derived from linear combinations of a set of
quantitative variables. From Wallin (1986). The nomenclature in the figure follows the original
source.

should either be regarded as a subspecies or be combined with *speculigera*, which it
most resembles.★

We have measured individuals of some Pied Flycatcher subspecies and of the
Collared Flycatcher at museums in Europe and the USA, and these measurements are presented in Appendix 1. The Collared Flycatcher clearly differs from

★ In the second edition of Howard and Moore (1991), which became available during the production
of this book, *semitorquata* has been transferred to a subspecies of the Collared Flycatcher and *iberiae* has
been completely removed as a subspecies.

all subspecies of the Pied Flycatcher in having a white collar and more white on the rump. Some *F. h. semitorquata* individuals may have a trace of an incomplete collar, thus partly resembling hybrids between Pied and Collared Flycatchers (see Chapter 13). In other morphological characters, *hypoleuca* and *semitorquata* most resemble each other, e.g. males of both subspecies are duller and more variable in back colour, and the white patch on the forehead is rather small and variable in shape, as opposed to *albicollis, iberiae* and *speculigera* which are dark and have a large rectangular forehead patch. With regard to the amount of white on the primaries, however, *semitorquata* most resembles the Collared Flycatcher while *hypoleuca* deviates most (Appendix 1). Within *F. h. hypoleuca*, central European populations are browner in plumage than northern and eastern populations (see Chapter 11) and were in the past sometimes considered a separate subspecies called '*muscipeta*' (Dunajewski, 1938).

With regard to the ranges of the subspecies of the Pied Flycatcher, and following the nomenclature of Howard and Moore (1980), *F. h. hypoleuca* breeds over large parts of northern Europe east to the Urals; *tomensis* from the Urals eastwards; *iberiae* in Spain and Portugal; *speculigera* in the Atlas mountains in Morocco, Algeria and Tunisia; and *semitorquata* in southeastern Europe, Asia Minor and Iraq. The distribution ranges are shown in Figure 5 together with that of the closely related, and partly sympatric, Collared Flycatcher.

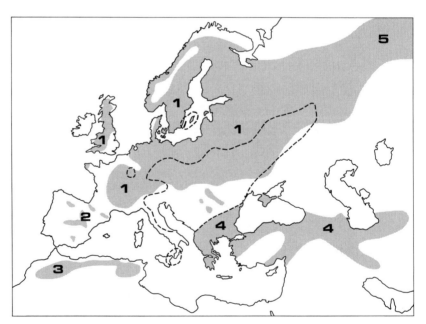

Fig. 5.   The Palaearctic distributions of the subspecies of the Pied Flycatcher. (1) F. h. hypoleuca, (2) F. h. iberiae, (3) F. h. speculigera, (4) F. h. semitorquata and (5) F. h. tomensis. The range of the Collared Flycatcher F. albicollis is indicated with a dotted line. The map is based on European atlases, handbooks, field guides and miscellaneous reports and the nomenclature follows Howard and Moore (1980).

Historical information on the Pied Flycatcher in Sweden suggests that it has spread across Europe from the southwest towards the northeast, mainly during the last two centuries. For example, Linnaeus probably never saw the species during his journeys in Sweden in the middle of the 18th century, and it was at that time only known from the most southerly part of the country. In the late 18th and early 19th centuries, however, the Pied Flycatcher seems to have become established in central Sweden, and towards the middle of the 19th century some naturalists even reported it as common (e.g. Tengmalm, 1783; Ödmann, 1792; Nilsson, 1824; Mesch, 1845), and even in Swedish Lapland it was found breeding (Nilsson, 1858). This relatively rapid increase in population size and range was probably quite independent of the practice of providing nest boxes for small passerine birds in Scandinavia. Nest boxes have been used in Sweden at least since the 16th century, though mainly for larger species like waterfowl and the Starling, from which eggs or nestlings could be collected for food consumption. Nest boxes for small passerine birds did not become popular in Sweden until the second half of the 19th century, at which time the Pied Flycatcher was already rather common. The rationale for putting up boxes at that time was to prevent insect damage to orchards and nurseries, and the practice probably spread from Germany (Karlsson, 1984). Nowadays people put up boxes more for pleasure or to replace the loss of natural cavities in modern managed forests.

Von Haartman (1949) also favoured the view that the Pied Flycatcher has spread from the southwest. His scenario, partly based on Stresemann (1926) and Huxley (1942), is approximately as follows. The distribution range of the ancestral black and white flycatcher became split into eastern and western parts during the last glaciation, and the population in the west became the present *F. h. hypoleuca*, *iberiae* and *speculigera*, and that in the east became *semitorquata*. After the glaciation *hypoleuca* spread towards the northeast while *semitorquata* expanded towards the northwest, there forming *F. a. albicollis*, probably at the secondary contact zone with *hypoleuca*. Some support for this hypothesis comes from the location of wintering areas. All subspecies of the Pied Flycatcher, apart from *semitorquata*, seem to winter in tropical West Africa (Chapter 3), while *semitorquata* probably winters in East Africa (Lynes, 1934). Wintering areas of the Collared Flycatcher are located east of that of the Pied Flycatcher, but reach farther south (Vaurie, 1959; see Fig. 6). Thus, *albicollis* and *semitorquata* seem to have partly overlapping wintering areas, possibly suggesting that both have an easterly origin. An alternative scenario, however, could be that the ancestral form had already split during some earlier glaciation than the last one, and that *speculigera* and/or *iberiae* could be the original western forms. After both an eastern and a northeastern expansion they have become *F. h. semitorquata* and *F. h. hypoleuca*, while *F. a. albicollis* should be the eastern form, which has expanded towards the northwest. We do not know what actually happened, but the resemblance in plumage is striking between *hypoleuca* and *semitorquata*, and apart from the collar, also between *albicollis*, *speculigera* and *iberiae*. The calls of *hypoleuca* and *speculigera* are similar (Wallin, unpublished) while the song of *semitorquata* is intermediate between *hypoleuca* and *albicollis*. However, *hypoleuca* also has a more *albicollis*-like song in areas of sympatry with the Collared

Flycatcher (see Chapter 14). Whether or not *semitorquata* originates from the east or west, it is highly probable that *hypoleuca* has expanded towards the northeast. The data from Sweden (see above) support this proposition, and a northwesterly expansion of the Collared Flycatcher is supported by the probably quite recent colonization of the islands of Gotland and Öland in the Baltic (Rosvall, 1982).*

SUMMARY

Flycatchers belong to one of the most species-rich families of birds, and Old World flycatchers breed from Africa and Europe through Asia to Japan. The Pied Flycatcher was first described by Linnaeus in his book *Fauna Svecica* (1746), but in later editions and in other books he confused it with the Whinchat and the Blackcap. Consequently Peter Simon Pallas is credited with the first correct scientific description of the species (in 1764). The ancestor of the black and white flycatchers now found in Europe probably became split into western and eastern populations during one of the ice ages, the western line giving rise to the Pied Flycatcher and the eastern to the Collared Flycatcher. The Pied Flycatcher is divided into five subspecies, and probably spread rapidly during the 18th century from southwestern Europe and/or northwest Africa towards the northeast where it has come into secondary contact with the Collared Flycatcher.

*After having completed this book we have been informed (Boudjema Samraoui, pers. comm.) that *semitorquata*-like flycatchers breed in Algeria in sympatry with *speculigera*. If they are indeed *semitorquata*, this might have further implications as to whether it should be considered a subspecies or a true species, and on the ancestry of black and white flycatchers.

CHAPTER 3

Migration, Moult, and Age and Sex Determination

In this chapter we deal with the migration and moulting patterns of the Pied Flycatcher and how to age and sex individuals. The reason for treating these subjects together is that they are in several ways interrelated. Moulting is in part a preparation for migration because it involves a renewal of the flight feathers, while conversely migratory habits influence moulting patterns. During the winter, males moult into a more conspicuous breeding plumage. First-year and older birds do not moult in exactly the same way and this makes it possible for us to determine their age; in the Pied Flycatcher first-year and older birds can be separated by their moult patterns during the breeding season. Indeed, under-standing the moulting pattern is a prerequisite for a correct age determination. After the summer moult, not only age but sex determination can be difficult, and we therefore also give some hints how this can be done.

MIGRATION

The winter quarters of northern and central European Pied Flycatchers are presumed to be in tropical West Africa (Fig. 6). Moreau (1972) and Grimes (1987) report the species as occurring in gallery forest, woodland savanna and citrus groves from Guinea, the Ivory Coast and Ghana (*c.* 10°N) down to the equator. However, so far only seven ringing recoveries confirm this (Dowsett *et al.*, 1988; Fig. 7). Out of over 400 000 Pied Flycatchers ringed in Sweden none has been recovered south of the Sahara. It has been suggested, based on ringing recoveries in winter, that some Pied Flycatchers might spend the winter as far north as the Iberian peninsula (e.g. Österlöf, 1979). This has, however, turned out to be probably incorrect; and these recoveries can instead be better explained by illegal hunting and subsequent falsification of catching dates (Ojanen, 1982).

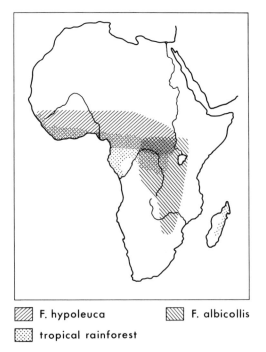

F. hypoleuca   F. albicollis
tropical rainforest

Fig. 6.   Presumed wintering areas of the Pied and Collared Flycatcher in tropical Africa. Map based on Moreau (1972) and Curry-Lindahl (1981).

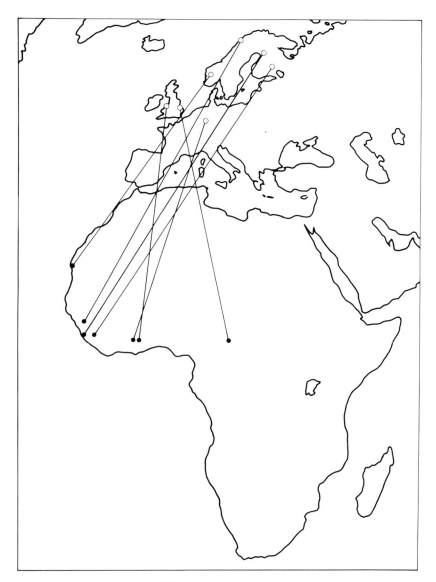

Fig. 7. Ringing recoveries of Pied Flycatchers from the presumed wintering areas in tropical West Africa. Lines join ringing and recovery sites. From Dowsett et al. *(1988).*

AUTUMN MIGRATION

The Pied Flycatcher leaves its breeding areas in late summer. Trapping throughout the summer in a forest in the Hoge Veluwe area in The Netherlands showed that almost all breeding birds were gone by the end of July, while the occurrence of unringed birds, presumably immigrants, peaked in the first half of August (van Balen, 1979). Among locally born birds all recoveries were made within 10 km up to the age of about 45 days (a month after fledging). But by some 10 days later the majority of young birds had already left the natal area and were found between 70 and 200 km away (Dutch ringing recoveries). At the age of 70–90 days, i.e. mainly in August, most recoveries were from 800–2700 km from the birthplace. At Signilskär Bird Observatory in the Åland archipelago in the Baltic, the autumn passage occurred from early August to late September, with a peak in late August (Hyytiä and Vikberg, 1973). Likewise, the autumn passage at British bird observatories peaked in the period from mid-August to mid-September (Hope Jones *et al.*, 1977). In Figure 8 we show the timing of autumn migration at Ottenby Bird Observatory, on the island of Öland in southeast Sweden, between 1980 and 1989. The first birds appear in late July while the latest pass by in mid-September. An analysis between age and sex classes reveals that yearling males and females peak about the same time (median, 26–7 August), but older males are clearly earlier and older females somewhat later than yearlings. Young birds of both sexes probably grow their flight feathers at the same rate during the nestling and post-fledging stages, and so both sexes should be ready to start autumn migration at about the same time as indicated by the data in Fig. 8. The earlier passage of older males compared to older females, however, is more difficult to explain, though it is in agreement with the earlier onset of moult in males than in females (see below). However, the reason that males start their summer moult earlier than females is as yet unknown. We know that birds are territorial at stopover sites during autumn migration (see below) but we do not know whether they also hold territories on the wintering grounds (though presumably they do).

Scandinavian birds migrate towards the southwest, and most Swedish ringing recoveries during autumn migration are from Denmark, Belgium, France, Spain and Portugal down to Morocco (Fig. 9). Also German and British ringing recoveries are concentrated in the Iberian peninsula, with Portugal being the most important stop-over area (Drost and Schilling, 1940; Hope Jones *et al.*, 1977), and there are even records from this area of birds from as far east as Moscow. We ourselves saw many migrating Pied Flycatchers on stop-over in the Toulouse area of southern France during the last week of August 1985.

Older birds that have previously made at least one autumn migration seem to hit the target areas on the Iberian peninsula more accurately than young and inexperienced birds performing their first migration (Rabøl, 1978). This is illustrated in Figures 10 and 11 which show autumn recoveries of Finnish ringed birds. Many of the young birds were found in the Alps and thus off the course to Spain and Portugal, while very few older birds had strayed so far east. This finding has been supported by recent autumn release experiments, where it was

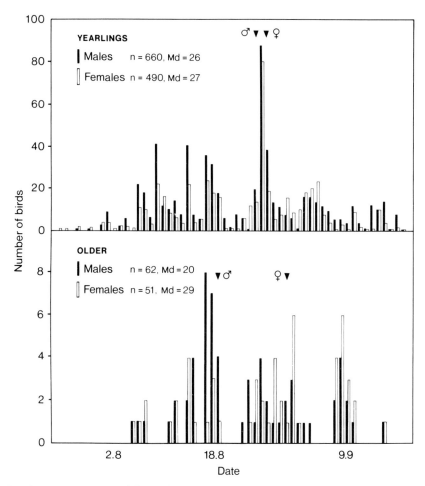

Fig. 8.   Autumn passage of older and yearling Pied Flycatcher males and females at Ottenby Bird Observatory, southwest Sweden. ▼, Median passage date. Reproduced with permission from the Bird Observatory.

found that inexperienced birds had larger angular dispersion than experienced birds (Sandberg *et al.*, 1991). Alerstam and Högstedt (1983) kept nestling Pied Flycatchers from southern Sweden in indoor cages until autumn migration restlessness was well developed, and then tested them in orientation cages for take-off directions during the night. They found that if following the magnetic compass Pied Flycatchers would migrate towards the west (mean 289°). The authors suggested that a magnetic compass system is probably used as a basis for determination of position during migration, while celestial compass cues may be used for flying in the appropriate southwesterly direction.

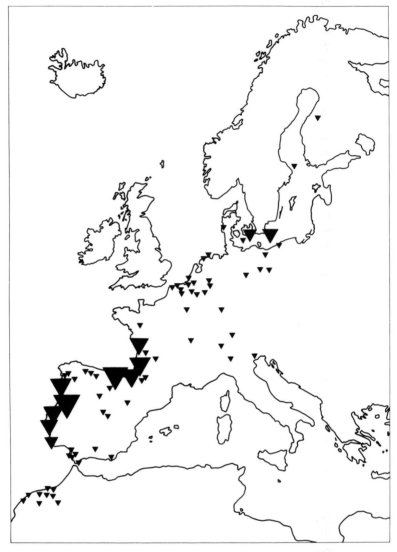

Fig. 9.   Recoveries of Swedish ringed Pied Flycatchers (1960–8 and 1980–8) during autumn migration. The size of triangles is proportional to the numbers found (small triangles = one individual). Reproduced with permission from the Swedish Bird Ringing Office.

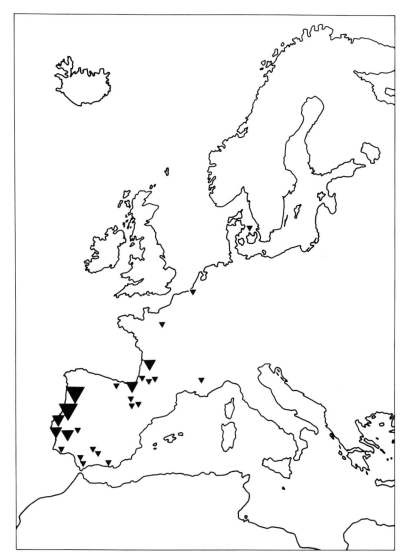

Fig. 10.   *Autumn recoveries of Finnish ringed adult Pied Flycatchers (1948–67). These birds have successfully performed at least one previous autumn migration. Redrawn from Rabøl (1978).*

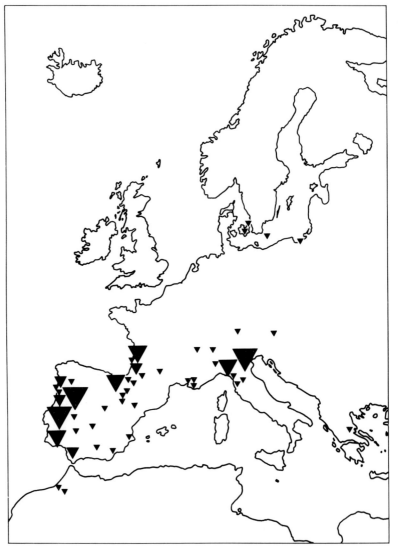

Fig. 11. *Recoveries of Finnish ringed yearling Pied Flycatchers (1948–67) during their first autumn migration. Redrawn from Rabøl (1978).*

At stop-over areas, high densities (1.25–4.25 birds/ha) have been recorded, for example in cork oak forests in September near Lisbon, where birds are territorial and stay for several days. At departure they are up to 40% heavier (16.8 g) than during breeding because they have built up stores of fat as fuel for a possibly direct crossing of the Mediterranean and the Sahara (Bibby and Green, 1980). At an oasis in the Sinai desert Pied Flycatchers were found to stop over for an average of three days (Lavee *et al.*, 1991). This crossing, however, has other obstacles besides food shortage. Many islands in the Mediterranean Sea and along the Atlantic coast of northwest Africa hold colonies of Eleonora's Falcon, which breeds during autumn and at that time feeds mainly on migrating birds passing through these islands. From prey remnants collected between 26 August and 23 September at two colonies, one in the Aegean sea and one off the coast of Morocco, Walter (1968, 1979) found the Pied Flycatcher to be one of the ten most common species in the diet of Eleonora's Falcon; it made up 4.2% and 5.1% of the total number of birds caught at each site, respectively. The birds caught in Morocco probably came from northwest Europe while those in Greece most likely had a more easterly origin.

In trying to trace the timing of migration through Africa, it seems that most Pied Flycatchers pass Morocco in September and early October (Smith, 1965), with one late observation on 15 November. In Vom in Nigeria, 1963/4 and 1964/5, the autumn peak was recorded in mid–October, with the first bird caught on 18 September (Smith, 1966). A few birds stayed at that site throughout the whole winter though the majority apparently proceeded further south. In northern Ghana, near the border with Burkino Faso, Hedenström *et al.* (1990) counted Palaearctic migrants along a line transect, and saw a few Pied Flycatchers up to 11 November. Based on these observations, it seems likely that most Pied Flycatchers probably reach their wintering grounds in October and November. There are no published reports (known to us) on densities of Pied Flycatchers on the wintering grounds, but Staffan Bensch and co-workers (pers. comm.) made a line transect on 1 and 2 January 1990 in central Ghana. They came up with a density estimate of 10 birds per km^2, though this was probably a clear underestimate since the birds were usually silent and therefore difficult to find.

The speed of autumn migration was calculated to be about 70 km/day by Drost and Schilling (1940). Their estimate was based on nine individuals ringed on southward migration in Germany and later retrapped elsewhere. Based on a much larger data set ($n = 296$ birds) from Signilskär Bird Observatory in the Baltic, Hyytiä and Vikberg (1973) estimated the speed of autumn migration as about 120–170 km/day. They further found no differences in speed of migration between adults and yearlings. This is a bit surprising since adults seem to migrate faster than one-year-old birds during spring migration. Moreover, in most passerine long-distance migrants adults seem to migrate faster than yearlings during autumn (Jan Pettersson, pers. comm.). With a speed of 120–170 km/day a Pied Flycatcher should be able to make the journey, for example, from our study areas in central Sweden to some place just north of the equator – a straight-line distance of about 6500 km – in approximately 45 days. Thus, if they leave in mid-August they should be able to reach their winter quarters in early October. Since the birds do not in fact follow a straight line the expected arrival on the wintering grounds is probably later, and this also fits the available data on passage times. From theoretical calculations (e.g. Pennycuick, 1975) the estimated flight speed for a bird of the size of a Pied Flycatcher would be about 15–20 km/hour if power is to be minimized or about 30 km/hour if distance travelled per unit time is to be maximized. Observed flight speeds of migrating birds more often correspond to the maximum range estimate than with that expected from a minimum power speed (Alerstam, 1982), which means that flying from dusk to dawn it should be possible for a Pied Flycatcher to cover about 250 km per night.

Spring Migration

There are less ringing recoveries from spring than from autumn. But they do indicate for Scandinavian birds that a more easterly route is taken on their way back to the north than during autumn migration (Fig. 12). The reason for this is not fully known, but it may be that the birds are in a greater hurry in spring, and more follow the great circle arc on their way to the breeding grounds than from them. A more likely explanation, however, may be that the important fattening areas in Iberia are unsuitable in spring. These areas experience quite cold and wet weather conditions during winter and spring, and therefore are almost totally hostile to birds on spring migration (Chris Mead, pers. comm.). This finding of a more easterly route during northward migration is supported by the analyses of Rendahl and Vestergren (1961) who found the same pattern among ringing recoveries before 1960 from all the Nordic countries. The same pattern of a more straight-line spring migration has also been reported from Germany (Berndt and Winkel, 1979).

It is as yet unknown how early the birds start their spring migration from Africa back to the breeding grounds in the north, but Smith (1966) caught Pied Flycatchers in Nigeria between mid-March and mid-May with a peak in the third week of April. Captures of spring migrating birds in northern Tunisia (1989 and 1990) showed the median passage time to be 26 April (males: 20 April, females: 28 April, $n = 69$ birds; Jan Pettersson, pers. comm.). Rosenfeld and Fagerström (1980) compared the passage of mist-netted Pied Flycatchers at Örskär in the northern Stockholm archipelago with figures for birds killed at Danish light-houses (Hansen, 1954). In 1966 and 1967 the median arrival times at Örskär were 18 and 13 May for males and 24 and 17 May for females, respectively. Median passage time for birds killed at Danish lighthouses (not the same years) was 3 May for both sexes combined. Based on these figures Rosenfeld and Fagerström (1980) estimated the speed of spring migration to be about 100 km per day. Spring records from British bird observatories are scanty apart from those from Fair Isle (Hope Jones *et al.*, 1977). The main passage there occurs in the first half of

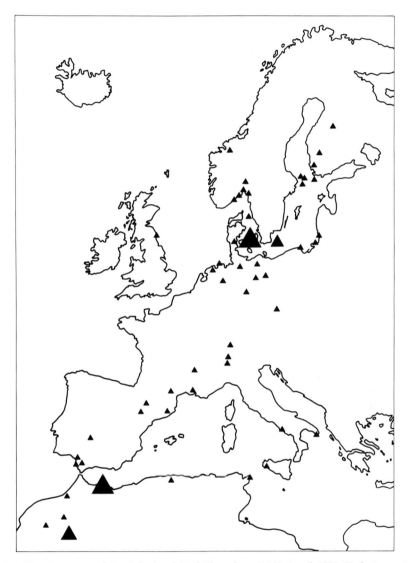

Fig. 12. Recoveries of Swedish ringed Pied Flycatchers (1960–8 and 1980–8) during spring migration. The size of triangles is proportional to the numbers found (small triangle = one individual). Reproduced with permission from the Swedish Bird Ringing Office.

May, and these birds are probably heading for northern Scandinavia rather than Britain.

Arrival Time on the Breeding Grounds

Older males arrive at the breeding grounds before yearling males (Table 2, Fig. 13). However, it is not known whether older males start spring migration before yearling males or if all start simultaneously but some travel faster. Recent studies (1986–9) from the bird observatories at Capri, Italy and Ottenby, Sweden indicate that older Pied Flycatchers migrate much faster than one-year-old birds (Table 3), possibly suggesting that older birds do not start much earlier than yearling birds but that they migrate faster. The mean passage date for both older and yearling males at Capri was 27 April but at Ottenby older males were five days ahead. The same pattern, though less pronounced, was found among females: older females were three days ahead on Capri but six days at Ottenby. These data also suggest that males migrate faster than females: at Capri older males were five days in advance of older females while at Ottenby they were ten days ahead; one-year-old males were eight days ahead of females of the same age at Capri while the difference was eleven days at Ottenby. The reason why older birds arrive earlier might be that they are more experienced, and can therefore accumulate energy reserves faster at their stop-over sites. Alternatively it may be due to the fact that older birds have longer wings than yearlings (see Table 4), and can thus fly faster (likewise females have shorter wings than males and arrive

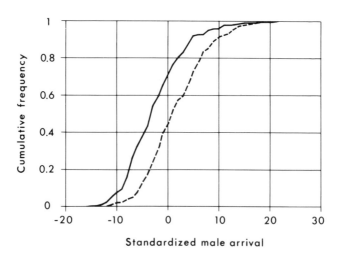

Fig. 13.   Cumulative distribution of one-year old (dotted line; $\bar{x} = +2.3$ days, n = 185) and older males (solid line; $\bar{x} = -1.9$, n = 226) at Uppsala, Sweden. Based on data from the years 1982–86. Arrival dates have been standardized by the mean arrival of each year.

Table 2.   *Mean arrival time (±SD) for older and yearling Pied Flycatcher males at Uppsala in 1982–6 (1 = 1 April, i.e. 31 = 1 May).*

	Older	n	One-year-old	n
1982	42.1 ± 9.2	17	46.5 ± 8.2	27
1983	35.9 ± 7.8	17	41.0 ± 6.0	17
1984	40.2 ± 5.7	82	46.0 ± 6.3	49
1985	44.4 ± 4.9	49	48.5 ± 6.3	26
1986	41.7 ± 5.1	63	44.5 ± 4.5	52

Table 3.   *Mean passage time during spring migration at Capri (Italy) and Ottenby (Sweden) Bird Observatories. 5 = hatched last calendar year, 6 = hatched before last calendar year (Euring code). The data were kindly put at our disposal by Ottenby Bird Observatory.*

Age	Sex	Capri	n	Ottenby	n
6	Male	27 April	34	5 May	58
5	Male	27 April	329	10 May	201
6	Female	2 May	87	15 May	24
5	Female	5 May	294	21 May	222

later). Males in our Swedish study areas arrive at the breeding grounds about a week before females (Fig. 14).

It is advantageous to arrive early (but not too early), because the earliest birds can take the best territories. It may, on the other hand, be favourable for females to arrive later than males, as is the normal pattern among migratory bird species, since this might reduce their search costs for finding a good nest site or a good quality male. Females can then inspect singing males and their nest sites rather than having to pay the cost of searching for good nest sites themselves (see also Chapters 4 and 11). This scenario may explain the frequent occurrence among migratory birds of males preceding females at the breeding sites. Also, since in most bird species males take up and defend territories and females choose between males, not vice versa, there is little reason for females to arrive before males.

The first Pied Flycatchers normally arrive in northern Germany in mid-April. The median arrival of first males ($n = 18$ years) at Dresden (Creutz, 1955) was 22 April with the earliest observation on 12 April, while in Curio's (1959c) study near Berlin the median arrival time for all males was 25–26 April and that for females only one to two days later. Rendahl and Vestergren (1961) compiled Swedish records of first sightings in spring from 1879 to 1940 ($n = 1730$ birds) and found median first arrival time to be 6–10 May in the southern part (55–60°N) while it was 11–15 May for the northern part of the country (data mainly from 60–62°N). In our study areas at Uppsala the first birds appear in late April or early May, with the median for all males being 13 May and for all females 18 May (Fig. 14). Our earliest record ever was 14 April 1989, in a spring that was much warmer

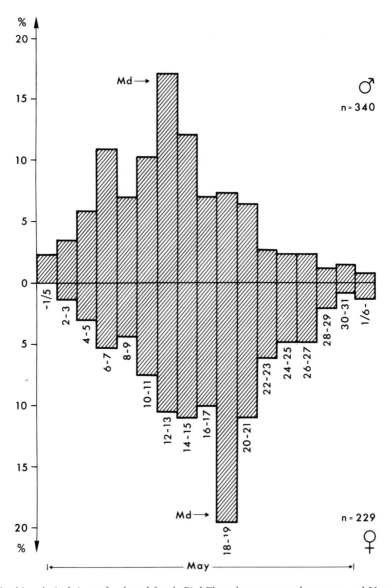

Fig. 14.   Arrival times of male and female Pied Flycatchers at our study areas around Uppsala, central Sweden.

than average. However, most birds that year arrived at the normal time and, in fact, the mean laying date for 1989 was a few days later than for an average year. In Sweden, as in other countries, people commonly note spring arrival dates for first individuals seen of migratory species, and compilations of such observations from areas around our study sites at Uppsala show that the mean first arrival of males was 2 May for 1941–50 while it was four days later in 1965–79 (Lundberg and Edholm, 1982); in fact springs also seem to have been warmer in the 1940s than they are now. Tropical migrants must have difficulties in forecasting the weather conditions at the breeding sites. Therefore, larger changes in arrival times at the breeding grounds are probably affected by long-term changes in climate while short-term changes probably reflect the weather conditions encountered during migration more than the actual weather at the breeding sites.

At Trondheim (63°N) in Norway the first males start to arrive at the end of April and females in the first week of May (Slagsvold and Lifjeld, 1988a); and the median arrival time for all males was 11–12 May and that for females was 17–18 May.

In Spain, Pied Flycatchers (subspecies *iberiae*) arrive relatively late, being only a few days earlier than in our study areas. In one study site northeast of Madrid median male arrival was 7 May and female arrival 17 May (Potti and Montalvo, 1991b). This study area was situated at an altitude of about 1300 m, and bad weather often occurred well into May. It is possible that birds breeding at lower altitudes arrive earlier.

Pied Flycatchers breeding in the Atlas mountains in northwest Africa (subspecies *speculigera*) seem to arrive at their breeding grounds at the same time or even later than Scandinavian birds. We (A.L., Dag Eriksson and Lars Wallin) made a visit to the breeding grounds near Ifrane, at about 1500 m altitude, in the Moyen Atlas between 19 and 24 April 1985, but no birds had arrived at that time. Near the Atlantic coast, however, we saw several foraging male and female Pied Flycatchers, probably on northward migration. On a subsequent trip between 16 and 22 May 1987 to northwestern Tunisia (altitude about 500–1000 m; by Staffan Thorman and Lars Wallin) several singing males were found in mixed oak forest. Since males were still singing at that time, breeding had obviously not started although some females were seen.

MOULT

The Pied Flycatcher exhibits the moult pattern most frequent among European passerines. This means that adults perform a complete summer moult and a partial winter moult while young birds have both partial summer and winter moults (Svensson, 1984). In adults, the complete summer moult, which involves the replacement of all the primaries (10), secondaries (9, a few may remain unmoulted) and rectrices (12), starts during late breeding or just after breeding (June to July) and goes on until August. As soon as the moult is finished, birds are ready for their autumn migration. The moult starts, as in almost all European passerines, in descending order of each feather group (away from the body), usually with the two innermost primaries and the outermost greater wing coverts being the first to be replaced. In general males start moulting before females, and many males begin to moult in June while the nestlings are being fed. Some females delay the start of moult until the end of July or early August, which is just before autumn migration (Ginn and Melville, 1983). The duration of the post-breeding moult is about 50 days (Ojanen and Orell, 1982), but late moulting birds probably have to moult more rapidly. During the complete summer moult males lose their conspicuous breeding plumage and then become more like females. At this stage it is quite difficult to separate the sexes (Svensson, 1984). Before migration, i.e. about July and August, the young birds undergo a partial post-juvenile moult and replace their nestling body feathers, changing into a female-like plumage; they also moult the lesser and median wing coverts, and sometimes one or two of the inner greater coverts (Karlsson *et al.*, 1986).

In the African winter quarters, and before spring migration, birds of all age groups undergo a pre-breeding partial moult, when they renew, for example, the inner secondaries (tertials) and five to six of the inner greater coverts, and a variable number of the lesser and median coverts (Karlsson *et al.*, 1986; Ojanen, 1987). This moult also includes most of the body feathers and as a result males change into their conspicuous pied breeding plumage. The exact timing of this moult is unknown but it is thought to occur in January and February (Ginn and Melville, 1983), though Smith (1966) found a few Pied Flycatchers still in moult as late as mid-March. The birds seen by Staffan Bensch and co-workers (pers. comm.) on 1 and 2 January in Ghana were all ($n = 15$) still in their brown autumn plumage.

All the primaries, primary coverts, outer greater coverts, and tail feathers are the same on return in spring as those carried during the autumn migration. The feathers grown by juveniles in their natal area, however, are of less durable quality than the feathers moulted into by the adults in autumn. Therefore, on arrival at the breeding grounds in spring the feathers of older birds are fresher and less worn than those of yearling birds.

AGE DETERMINATION

As suggested above, Pied Flycatchers can be separated into yearlings and older birds during spring on the basis of their moult patterns and feather quality. In our own research we have above all used a method of looking at the colour and wear of the outermost greater wing coverts, a method originally invented at the Ottenby Bird Observatory in Sweden and still accepted as very reliable (Karlsson *et al.*, 1986; Ojanen, 1987). However, additional characters like feather wear and shape can also be used, as well as the colour of the inside of the upper mandible (Karlsson *et al.*, 1986; Ojanen, 1987).

For males in spring, differences in the colour of feathers that young birds have kept but adults have moulted during the summer or winter may serve as a good character for ageing (Karlsson *et al.*, 1986; Ojanen, 1987). Adults lose their outer greater coverts during the summer, but not the winter moult. Young birds retain their original outer greater coverts whereas the inner greater coverts are replaced in Africa. In general the feathers become darker with age of the bird, which creates a colour difference between the unmoulted outer and the moulted inner greater coverts, and this difference is more pronounced in young birds than in older ones. The position of the moult edge, however, might be variable. In Scandinavia it often seems to lie between feathers 4 and 5 (counted towards the body) while in England it often falls between feathers 2 and 3 or 3 and 4. In young birds (Euring age code 5) the three outermost coverts are most often brown with a small yellow-brown spot on the tips (which becomes larger towards the base of the wing), while the fourth has a distinctly larger triangular spot on the tip of the outer web (if unmoulted – see Ojanen, 1987). These light-coloured tips may in many cases be lost due to wear and are replaced by a notch. If the outermost greater coverts are dark, the male should be older than one year (age code 6). If the coverts are brown, the bird could be old if the tips have no spots but do have a light edge. The tips are also most often more rounded and less worn in older than in yearling birds (Fig. 15). It becomes increasingly more difficult to age a bird using these criteria as the breeding season progresses, because birds will have already started moulting the outer greater coverts during breeding. Looking at the colour difference at the moult edge and the shape of the tips of the four outermost greater coverts also allows ageing of females, though with more

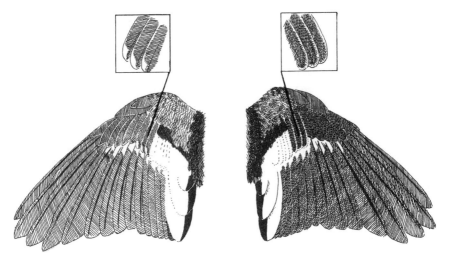

Fig. 15.   Form and colour of outer greater coverts of one-year old (left) and older (right) Pied Flycatcher males in spring. In one-year old males unmoulted outer coverts are pale, and usually worn or tipped with white on the outer web; in older males they are often dark and more rounded.

difficulty than for males. We can confirm the reliability of this ageing method in males from studies in Cumbria, northwest England, where Pied Flycatchers are restricted by habitat and most surviving offspring return to their natal area. Most breeding birds have been ringed as nestlings so we know their exact age. Among 80 breeding males of known age in 1989, we could assign 90% of the birds correctly as yearlings or older on the basis of colour and wear of the greater coverts; for 4 males (5%) we could not tell and for another 4 males we were wrong in the age determination. So far we have no corresponding data for females because the object of that study was to look at colour variation of males.

Additional characters for ageing Pied Flycatchers are the shape and wear of the tail feathers, the primaries and the primary coverts, which should preferably be looked at in that sequence according to Ojanen (1987). Yearling males have worn and pointed tips to the rectrices while older males have rounded tips with little or no wear. The same applies to the wear and shape of remiges and primary coverts, though less clearly than for the rectrices. As with the previous method, it becomes increasingly more difficult to age the birds as the breeding season progresses. During incubation (females only) and feeding of nestlings, tail and wing feathers will become even more worn. Using only the rectrices Karlsson *et al.* (1986) claimed that they could easily assign 88% of the birds caught at Falsterbo Bird Observatory, in southwest Sweden, to age group (5 or 6), while the corresponding figure was 93% if only checking the outermost greater coverts. Difficulties mainly occurred in older males.

Another possible method to use for ageing in spring is to look at the colour of the inside of the upper mandible. In general older birds have dark mandibles while some one-year-old birds have light beaks (Karlsson *et al.*, 1986; Ojanen, 1987). This method seems to be more useful in females than in males. The upper mandible colour for females also seems to be more variable between ages than it is for males.

Yet another ageing method, suggested by Alatalo *et al.* (1984b), is to measure the difference between total wing length and the length of the first primary. In general, older birds have longer wings but shorter first primaries than yearling birds. The original data illustrating this were collected on Collared Flycatcher females. In that species males can easily be aged on the colour of the primaries. Females with a difference between maximum wing length and first primary length of less than 43 mm turned out in most cases to be one-year old while those with a larger difference were older. This method is also applicable to the Pied Flycatcher. In Table 4 we show the mean total wing length and mean first primary length for Pied Flycatcher males of different ages in our study areas in Cumbria and at Uppsala. The mean difference between wing and first primary length for older birds is around 43 mm but is only 40–41 mm for yearlings (Table 4). Note, however, that the individual variation is quite large (Fig. 16), so not every individual can be aged using this method. An adaptive explanation for young birds having shorter wings and longer first (outermost) primaries than older birds may be that more rounded and slotted wings (the first primary serves as a wing slot) increase manoeuvrability and thus help inexperienced young birds

Table 4. *Wing length, first primary length, and the difference between these two measurements for Pied Flycatcher males of different ages in Cumbria, England and Uppsala, Sweden. Only birds of known exact age are included.*

Age (years)	Measurement	Cumbria Mean ± SD (mm)	n	Uppsala Mean ± SD (mm)	n
1	Wing length	77.5 ± 1.7	188	78.8 ± 1.6	83
	Primary length	37.3 ± 1.6	183	37.6 ± 1.4	83
	Difference	40.3 ± 1.8	129	41.2 ± 1.5	83
2	Wing length	78.9 ± 1.4	122	79.8 ± 1.6	13
	Primary length	36.1 ± 1.4	119	36.4 ± 1.3	13
	Difference	42.8 ± 1.5	119	43.4 ± 1.2	13
3	Wing length	79.3 ± 1.6	53	80.0 ± 1.3	9
	Primary length	36.0 ± 1.6	52	36.6 ± 1.1	9
	Difference	43.3 ± 1.4	52	43.4 ± 1.5	9
>4	Wing length	78.7 ± 1.5	18	80.9 ± 1.5	7
	Primary length	35.5 ± 1.5	18	36.9 ± 2.0	7
	Difference	43.2 ± 1.2	18	44.0 ± 0.9	7

to avoid predators and to find food. Adult birds may compensate by their greater experience, and benefit from longer wings by being able to fly faster, which is probably important during migration. Support for the view that differences in wing length between adult and young birds are adaptive comes from a study of individually marked Blackbirds (Leverton, 1989), though young birds in that case were considered to benefit from a shorter wing only during the first few weeks or months of life.

All the above methods for ageing refer to the breeding season. We have no experience in ageing Pied Flycatchers in autumn, but according to the literature several characters could be used. According to Svensson (1984) the most useful differences are in the amount of white on the outer web of the central tertial (more broadly tipped in young birds; the best method according to Jan Pettersson at the Ottenby Bird Observatory in Sweden), the colour of the inside of the upper mandible, and skull ossification. The upper inner mandible in autumn, in contrast to spring, is light in most juvenile individuals but dark in the majority of older birds. Karlsson *et al.* (1986) also showed that in autumn, young birds (age code 3) have their unmoulted greater coverts tipped with a triangular white spot on the outer web while older birds (age code 4) are narrowly tipped brownish white (as in spring). Also, as in spring, the tip edges of primary coverts and tail feathers are more rounded and fresh in older than in yearling birds. As an additional ageing character Karlsson *et al.* (1986) were able to show that older birds have a more or less brown-coloured iris compared to a 'dark graphite grey' in yearlings.

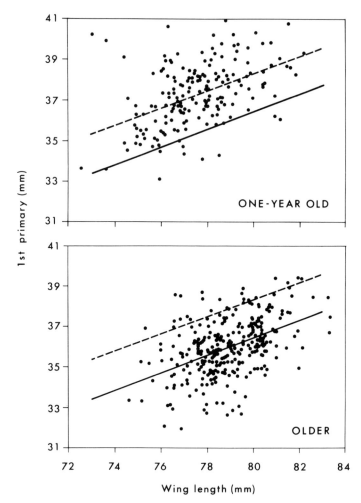

Fig. 16.   *The relationship between wing length and first primary length in one-year old (dotted line, n = 182) and older (solid line, n = 298) Pied Flycatcher males in Cumbria, England. Based on data from the years 1986–90. One-year old individuals above the dotted line and older individuals below the solid line can be aged quite reliably using this method.*

SEX DETERMINATION

Sexing in spring is normally easy since males during the winter moult change into a conspicuous black and white breeding plumage, while females, though they also change most of their body feathers, stay mainly brown. A few males in spring, however, can be very female-like in plumage, especially in populations in central Europe (for details see Chapter 10), and therefore they are difficult to sex.

In spring, males most often also have a white patch on the forehead and more white on their tertials than have females.

In autumn sexing is more difficult because adult males have then moulted into a female-like plumage. With some experience, however, most birds can, according to Karlsson *et al.* (1986) also be sexed in autumn. As a first step, they suggested trying to determine the age of the bird. The next step is to look at the colour of the longest upper tail coverts and of the tail feathers. Both should be darker in males (see also Drost, 1951; Busse, 1984), although some females may be male-like (doubts about using this method were raised by Svensson, 1984). If, after this examination, the bird still cannot be sexed, the pattern of white on the outer web of the second outermost tail feather (no. 5) and/or on the inner web of the outermost tail feather (no. 6) may be used. In males the demarcation line between white and dark colours is usually distinct while in females it is diffuse (for more detailed information see the figures and tables in Karlsson *et al.*, 1986).

SUMMARY

The Pied Flycatcher overwinters in tropical West Africa where it can be found in gallery forests and savanna woodlands. Most birds leave northern Europe in August and probably reach their wintering grounds in October and November. An important stop-over area is the western part of the Iberian peninsula where birds build up fat stores for a possible direct crossing of the Mediterranean and the Sahara. The northward migration in spring probably starts in March, and ringing recoveries indicate that the birds take a more easterly route on their way north than on autumn migration. Older birds seem to migrate faster than one-year-old birds, and males faster than females, and when arriving on the breeding grounds in Scandinavia in early May males are about a week ahead of females.

Adults perform a complete summer moult and a partial winter moult whereas young birds have partial summer and winter moults. During the summer moult males lose their conspicuous breeding plumage and resemble females. In spring Pied Flycatchers can be separated into yearlings and older birds on the basis of

these differences in moult pattern. The best character for ageing is the colour and shape of the outer greater coverts, but the shape and wear of tail feathers, primaries and primary coverts should also be looked at. Additional characters are the colour of the inside of the upper mandible and the difference between total wing length and the length of the first primary. In autumn sexing can be difficult because males have lost their breeding plumage, though with some experience one can separate the sexes on the colour of tail coverts and tail feathers.

CHAPTER 4

Nesting, Habitat and Breeding Densities

How and where an individual bird should settle and take up a territory for the breeding season has been the topic of many empirical and theoretical studies. Nest predation is common among birds and it is therefore important to choose as safe a nesting site as possible; even the design of the nest itself may affect the risk of predation. It is also important that the territory is located in a good feeding area so that there is enough food to meet the demands of the nestlings. However, although food abundance in itself is important for a bird's decision of where to take up a territory, so also is the number of potential competitors both of the same species and of other species with similar ecological niches.

In this chapter we describe types of nest-sites used by the Pied Flycatcher, what they prefer if different alternatives are available, and how they build their nests. We also give details of breeding densities in different types of habitats, how numbers of conspecifics and other species might affect reproductive success, and how an increase in Pied Flycatcher density might affect other species.

NEST-SITES AND NEST-BUILDING

The Pied Flycatcher is a cavity-nesting bird. Predation is the most important factor reducing reproductive success, and so birds prefer nest-sites with low predation risks. To achieve this, Pied Flycatchers tend to use holes with rather narrow entrance holes (about 30 mm) and situated high up in trees. Natural tree holes of good quality are probably quite scarce so if nest boxes are provided they are most often used in preference to natural nest-sites. In fact, almost all the Pied Flycatchers in a woodland can be attracted to boxes if high quality boxes are provided in excess. This is in contrast to tits, where usually many individuals breed in natural sites even if nest boxes are provided in abundance. This might be due to the fact that tits start breeding earlier than flycatchers and can therefore choose the best natural cavities, which might be of even higher quality than nest boxes. The most common predators of Pied Flycatcher nests are stoats and weasels which, however, might be likely to overlook or be unable to climb to holes high up in trees. Other important predators are woodpeckers which cannot enter narrow entrance holes without first enlarging them. Nest boxes often suffer less predation than natural holes (see Chapter 14), especially during the first years after erection. Mammalian nest-cavity predators, like weasels and martens, probably have a long-term memory and may learn that nest boxes contain bird nests and certainly also remember the locations of nest boxes and holes from year to year (Sonerud, 1985). Thus predators might inspect many boxes each year, and if a predator develops a search image for nest boxes, these might be attacked at an even higher rate than natural cavities, though in our experience this seems to happen only rarely.

The Importance of Nest Height and Entrance Size

In 1984 we performed an experiment where we put up groups of nest boxes with different sizes of entrance holes. Each group consisted of three boxes, 40 m apart, in the corners of a triangle. Entrance sizes in the three boxes were 30 mm, 35 mm and 40 mm. In other respects the boxes were as identical as possible, and they were put up at the same height in deciduous forest. Boxes were so close together that one male could monopolize all three boxes. In total we put up seven groups. Thus, prospecting females had the choice of three nesting sites within each male territory. In five cases the female first chose the box with the smallest entrance size, in two cases the second smallest opening and in no case the largest entrance size. This clearly indicates that females prefer small entrance openings for their nesting sites.

In another experiment, in 1986, we erected groups of four boxes, each with a different combination of height (1.6 or 4 m) and entrance hole size (30 or 35 mm). Boxes were about 50 m apart, and each box had a different male defending it. However, the boxes were close enough that prospecting females had the opportunity to visit and inspect each male and his box. We arranged five such groups. In this situation males with boxes high up in trees attracted females significantly earlier than males with boxes lower down (see also Fig. 86), while entrance size did not seem to influence mating order for males if boxes at the same height were compared (Alatalo *et al.*, 1988a). The conclusion from this experiment is that females prefer nest-sites high up in trees (see also Chapter 14).

Other Factors Influencing Nest-Site Preferences

Experiments comparing large with small, upright with tilted, and dry with wet nest boxes have demonstrated (Slagsvold, 1986a, 1987; Slagsvold and Lifjeld, 1988b) that Pied Flycatchers prefer larger over smaller, upright over tilted, and dry over wet. These preferences might be related to avoidance of predation and of nest-sites with unfavourable microclimate or insulation. In our experience in Sweden Pied Flycatchers also seem to prefer new boxes to old ones. The reasons for this are unclear, but we can think of several explanations. One is that new boxes are often more visible from a distance and therefore may be easier to find. Other explanations are that new boxes contain fewer cracks, and no old nesting material. Old nest boxes, even if the old nest has been removed, may house parasites. To our knowledge no published studies, so far, have been designed to find out whether or not flycatchers avoid previously used or parasite-infested nest-holes. In one recently started study, however, Karin Olsson (pers. comm.) found a preference for new nest boxes containing an old nest (put in by her) over new and clean boxes. Maybe the presence of an old nest indicates that the nest-hole is a good breeding site, since it seems to have been used before. In another study, Alerstam (1985) could not find a preference from one year to the next for previously empty boxes compared to boxes containing old nests, which means that a clean nest box is not the primary criterion for the choice of a nesting site.

In conclusion, for people interested in attracting Pied Flycatchers to boxes, we recommend new boxes with an entrance of about 28 mm, not only because they prefer this size but also because it excludes many Great Tits. Although Pied Flycatchers prefer nest-sites higher up in trees it is of course much more convenient to put them rather low down (1.5–2.0 m) because they are then easier to put up, inspect and clean out. If only low boxes are available, the birds will still prefer them over natural sites higher up in trees.

NEST-BUILDING

Nest-building is done exclusively by the female. When the male has attracted a female, she soon starts building the nest. Nest building mainly takes place from early morning until midday. According to Curio (1959b) in Germany it takes about 5 (range 2–9) days to complete a nest while Stjernberg (1974) found it to take on average 8 days (range 6–11) in Finland. Replacement nests were more quickly built (average 4 days) than first nests. Early arriving females, even if bringing a few pieces of bark or a few leaves into the nest box at mating, will often wait several days before starting nest-building, while late females often start immediately they arrive. Likewise, early females have more time available for nest-building than late females; thus the range of egg-laying dates is shorter than the range of female arrival dates.

The nest of the Pied Flycatcher basically consists of two layers, an exterior, bottom one of packing material and an inner, interior one of more fibrous material (Meidell, 1961; Stjernberg, 1974). The nest material used varies considerably according to what is available. However, the bottom layer is commonly made up of such material as pine and birch bark, dry pine and heather twigs, and dead leaves (often oak or birch). The inner layer and the nest cup are almost always composed of dry grass, animal hair, root fibres, and shafts of moss. The nest greatly resembles that of the Redstart except that Redstart nests often have some feathers in the nest cup.

HABITAT PREFERENCES, BREEDING DENSITY AND TERRITORY SIZE

Pied Flycatchers breed in most types of forest habitats provided nest-sites are available. Natural nest-cavities are more abundant in deciduous than in coniferous forests, and the birds are also more abundant in the former habitat. Even if nest boxes are provided in excess in both habitats, Pied Flycatchers still reach higher densities in deciduous than in coniferous forest (Lundberg *et al.*, 1981). Some typical breeding habitats in different countries are shown in the photographs on pages 42–43.

There are very few data on breeding densities of Pied Flycatchers in forests without nest boxes. In a deciduous woodland north of Uppsala, central Sweden, with a large proportion of southern deciduous trees like pedunculate oak, small-leaved lime and Norway maple, we found about 0.6 pairs/ha (Alatalo and Lundberg, 1984a), with a maximum density of about 1 pair/ha in the most natural parts. In unmanaged deciduous habitats in southern Sweden, Nilsson (1979), by mapping territories, found 0.25–0.40 pairs/ha, and Enemar and Sjöstrand (1972), using the same method in unmanaged subalpine birch forest in northern Sweden, found about 0.1 pairs/ha. Palmgren (1930) and Soveri (1940), using parallel line transects, found breeding densities to range between 0.1 and

0.48 pairs/ha in deciduous and mixed forests in Finland. In natural forests in Poland the breeding densities (based on territory mapping) ranged from 0.01 to 0.3 pairs/ha (Tomialojc *et al.*, 1984); the lowest figure refers to oak–hornbeam and pine–bilberry coniferous forest while the highest was found in ash–alder stands. However, in this area in Poland Pied Flycatchers had to compete for territories with Collared Flycatchers, which attained natural breeding densities of up to 0.7 pairs/ha.

In coniferous forest in southern Sweden, Nilsson (1979) estimated breeding density at 0.15 pairs/ha on the basis of territory mapping, while Olsson (1947) found 0.05 pairs/ha in a similar habitat in central Sweden. Palmgren (1930) and Soveri (1940), and Alatalo and Alatalo (1979) found only 0.01–0.03 and about 0.05 pairs/ha, respectively, in coniferous and mixed forests in Finland; both studies used parallel line transects. This latter method, however, probably underestimates the size of the true breeding population (Helle and Pullianen, 1983).

In areas provided with nest boxes, breeding densities can rise well above the level in 'natural' habitats. The maximum breeding density we know of is 21 pairs/ha, recorded from coniferous forest in Finland (Tompa, 1967; calculated from his Fig. 1 and Table 2). In that study 30 boxes were put up at a spacing of 12.5 m in a rectangularly shaped plot. Tompa obtained 10 nestings with a mean nearest-neighbour distance of 18 m. There were probably no other potential nesting sites available nearby, and many or most pairs must have foraged outside the nest-boxed area. In Germany, Pfeifer and Ruppert (1953), probably in deciduous forest, found a breeding density of 16 pairs/ha. In this case also the nest box area was small (1.25 ha) and the result was probably influenced by that small area or by edge effects. We have provided nest boxes in excess (40 m apart) over a number of years on a small island (10.5 ha) with mixed deciduous and coniferous forest in the Baltic archipelago, thus making edge effects unimportant, and here we have found a maximum breeding density of 3.2 pairs/ha.

One reason why high breeding densities can be attained is that the Pied Flycatcher defends a rather small territory and as a result population density is restricted by the number of available nest sites rather than by territorial behaviour (von Haartman, 1956a). Most territorial fights take place near the defended nest site (median 10 m; von Haartman, 1956a), while foraging can take place far away from the nest, and foraging areas often overlap with those of neighbouring pairs (see e.g. maps 6–8 in von Haartman, 1956a).

Few studies have provided data on breeding densities of Pied Flycatchers in the same area before and after providing a surplus of nest boxes. In one such study, however, performed in subalpine birch forest in northern Sweden, Enemar and Sjöstrand (1972) found an increase from about 0.1 pairs/ha before to about 2.4 pairs/ha after nest boxes were provided. By supplying nest boxes in forests on mountain slopes in southwestern Norway, Meidell (1961) attained a threefold increase in the breeding density of Pied Flycatchers, and after erection of the nest boxes very few pairs bred in natural sites.

Open oak forest with nest boxes at Uppsala, central Sweden. This is one of the most preferred breeding habitats for Pied Flycatchers. (Photo: A. Lundberg.)

Suitable breeding habitat for the Pied Flycatcher outside Uppsala. In this type of habitat, natural breeding density will be about 0.5 pairs/ha, but with boxes in excess the breeding density can be increased to about 3 pairs/ha. (Photo: Mats W. Pettersson.)

Typical breeding habitat on a hillside in northern England. (Photo: A. Lundberg.)

Breeding habitat in Tunisia, N. Africa. In this area the birds breed in natural cavities. (Photo: L. Wallin.)

In our nest box areas around Uppsala we have provided boxes in excess, and most often with an inter-box distance of about 50 m in deciduous forest and 100 m in coniferous forest. The size of deciduous woodlands, which we have filled with boxes, has ranged from 5 to 25 ha, and actual breeding densities have ranged in different areas and years, from 0.4 to 3.1 pairs/ha, with an average of 1.8 pairs/ha (Alatalo *et al.*, 1985). In coniferous forest, where nest box areas have ranged between about 8 and 30 ha in size – though the forests have been much larger – breeding density has varied between 0.2 and 1.3 pairs/ha, with a mean of 0.6 pairs/ha. These breeding densities are probably more 'normal' for nest box areas than the maximum densities cited above. Thus, for example, Creutz (1955) reported breeding densities from 0.15 to 4.9 pairs/ha in different forests in Germany, though boxes were probably not in excess in all areas. In a long-term study (1957–88) in Lower Saxony, Germany, Winkel (1989) found a mean breeding density of 2.8 pairs/ha (range 1.5–3.9) in oak–hornbeam forest, and 2.5 pairs/ha (1.8–3.5) in mixed deciduous and pine forest. In deciduous woodland in southern Sweden, Källander (1975) found 1.0–2.3 pairs/ha, and Alerstam (1985) 2.6–3.8 pairs/ha, while in subalpine birch forest in northern Sweden Enemar and Sjöstrand (1972) found 1.4–3.3 pairs/ha. In a long-term study (16 years) in the Forest of Dean in England, Campbell (1968) found 2.3–4.2 pairs/ha while in a deciduous wood in North Yorkshire, Follows (1982) recorded 1.5–2.1 pairs/ha in a three-year study.

In nest box areas in coniferous forest Källander (1975) attracted 1.1–1.8 pairs/ha in southern Sweden and Askenmo (1977a) 0.44–0.75 pairs/ha near the Swedish west coast. In coniferous forest in Finland with an admixture of birches, Virolainen (1984) attracted 0.3–0.8 pairs/ha in an area with one box per ha and 0.9–2.1 pairs/ha in an area with four boxes per ha. In pure pine forest in Germany, 1957–88, Winkel (1989) found on average one pair per ha with a variation between 0.6 and 1.3. Thus, the breeding density data support the idea that deciduous habitats are preferred to coniferous.

However, if nest boxes are put up in excess, both in deciduous and in coniferous forest, nearby boxes are often used at a lower frequency than expected by a random distribution while somewhat more distant boxes are occupied more often than expected (Alatalo *et al.*, 1982b). Similarly, in a study of nest distribution in a 23 ha forest area in southern Finland containing about 500 nest boxes, Tiainen *et al.* (1984) found that on a finer scale Pied Flycatcher nestings were over-dispersed but on a larger scale were clumped. The interpretation is that territorial behaviour probably prevents males from occupying nest-sites too close to one another. The reason why nestings are clumped might depend on habitat heterogeneity but also on the tendency of males to settle in one another's vicinity. The mechanism behind the clumping is unknown though it probably has something to do with the singing of other males (see below).

On arrival, early males often defend many nest-sites within quite a large area, but as population density builds up males restrict their singing activity and nest-site defence to one or a few nearby nest-holes. Males probably use the song of other males as a cue for finding nest-sites; the presence of a singing male might

3 / 4   **0 / 4**

Fig. 17. Design of a song play-back experiment in which we tried to attract males to groups of boxes where male song was broadcasted or not. Three out of four groups with song play-back became occupied while none of the 'silent' groups attracted any male. This experiment was performed in a coniferous forest area with few, if any, natural holes, and which previously lacked nest boxes.

indicate that several potential nest-sites exist in the neighbourhood. As an example, we put up nest boxes in groups of four in a coniferous forest with few natural holes, where there had previously been no boxes, and where accordingly, Pied Flycatchers had been very scarce. In half the groups ($n = 4$) we put up a loudspeaker broadcasting Pied Flycatcher song. Three out of four groups with broadcast song became occupied while none of the 'silent' groups attracted any Pied Flycatchers (Fig. 17), indicating that males actually use the song of other males to locate suitable breeding areas (Alatalo *et al.*, 1982b). All in all, then, breeding density usually becomes higher in deciduous than in coniferous forest even though nest boxes are provided in excess in both, suggesting that factors other than the existence of nest-holes are also important. The most likely factor is difference in food abundance (see Chapter 5).

Other support for the preference for deciduous compared to coniferous forest comes from the timing of settlement. In 1979, the year we started our studies, all nest boxes were newly erected and put up in woodlands previously lacking nest boxes. We had five deciduous plots and two coniferous ones; one coniferous plot was situated close to one of our deciduous areas while the other was far away from any deciduous vegetation. We found that the deciduous areas and the coniferous plot adjacent to deciduous forest became occupied first and at approximately the same time. In the remote coniferous plot settlement was delayed by one week (Lundberg *et al.*, 1981; Alatalo *et al.*, 1985), suggesting that birds first started to look for nest-sites in deciduous forest or in its surroundings.

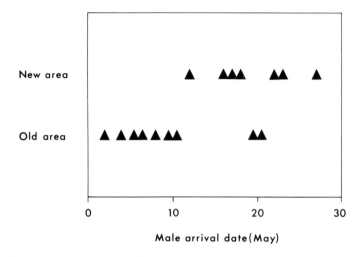

Fig. 18.   Male arrival time to an old (Md = 8 May, n = 9) and a new (Md = 17 May, n = 7) nest box area in coniferous forest at Uppsala, Sweden in 1983. The earlier settlement in the old area suggests that previous knowledge of nesting facilities plays a role for time of settlement.

However, in later years (1981 and 1982) when some of the birds could return to their previous breeding sites (Chapter 8), there was only a very slight difference in the timing of habitat occupancy, though breeding density in the coniferous plots never attained the level in deciduous forest (Alatalo *et al.*, 1985). In 1983 we put up boxes in a new coniferous area about 1 km from an old one (the one situated far away from deciduous forest). In this case median male arrival was delayed by 9 days in the new area compared to the old (Fig. 18), female arrival by 6 days, and date of laying of the first egg by 4 days (Table III in Alatalo *et al.*, 1985), suggesting that previously acquired experience of nesting facilities played a role in the speed of settlement. First-year breeding males colonizing a new area probably use the song of other males, which have returned to their breeding area of the previous year, as a guide to finding potential nest-sites (see also above), and therefore areas previously lacking nest-sites will become inhabited later than previously inhabited areas.

MORPHOLOGY AND AGE OF BIRDS IN DIFFERENT HABITATS

There are two main hypotheses accounting for morphometric variation in birds between habitats. In the first, individuals inhabiting different habitats have different morphological adaptations for optimally exploiting those environments: either they select habitats according to their morphology, or birds in different habitats belong to different subpopulations. According to the other hypothesis, social dominance may affect habitat distribution of individual birds, with larger and hence dominant individuals being found in the preferred habitat and smaller birds in less preferred habitat(s). The characters most likely to differ between birds in different habitats are bill dimensions which probably influence foraging skills on different substrates. Relatively longer and more pointed bills suitable for searching for food among needles could be expected among birds in the coniferous habitat (e.g. Snow, 1954; Lack, 1971; Grant, 1979), if there is a direct adaptive response between foraging conditions and bill dimensions.

In the first year of our study (1979) we found that bill length and wing length were slightly shorter and that weight was significantly lower in Pied Flycatcher males in the coniferous as compared to the deciduous habitat, while we found no such differences among females (Lundberg *et al.*, 1981). In subsequent years we added tarsus and tail length and colour type to the features compared. We found that only the wing length and weight remained significantly lower in the coniferous habitat. No difference in female size was found between habitats in the extended data set (Alatalo *et al.*, 1985; Table 5). Wing length in passerine birds increases with age (see Chapter 3), which suggests that the birds in the coniferous habitat were younger than those in the deciduous forest. This might have been true in the first year, when all our study areas were new, but the age structure turned out not to be significantly different in subsequent years (when we had learned to age the birds, see Chapter 3). The proportions of one-year-old and

Table 5. *Morphometric measurements of Pied Flycatcher males and females in deciduous and coniferous forest.*[1] *From Alatalo et al. (1985).*

| Characteristics | Measurements | | | | | | t-test | P |
| | Deciduous | | | Coniferous | | | | |
	$\bar{x}$	SD	n	$\bar{x}$	SD	n		
Males								
Wing (mm)	79.42	1.49	172	78.81	1.88	70	$t = 2.70$	<0.01
Tarsus (mm)	19.49	0.51	132	19.50	0.49	51	$t = 0.12$	NS[2]
Bill (mm)	13.57	0.42	173	13.55	0.39	71	$t = 0.34$	NS
Tail (mm)	53.02	1.46	131	52.80	1.40	51	$t = 0.92$	NS
Weight (g)	12.49	0.59	134	12.22	0.55	69	$t = 3.12$	<0.01
Colour type	3.24	1.29	130	3.51	1.33	51	$t = 1.26$	NS
Females								
Wing (mm)	77.58	1.55	158	77.48	1.46	93	$t = 0.50$	NS
Tarsus (mm)	19.58	0.49	140	19.57	0.46	68	$t = 0.14$	NS
Bill (mm)	13.61	0.43	184	13.53	0.41	94	$t = 1.49$	NS
Tail (mm)	52.27	1.49	141	52.16	1.31	68	$t = 0.52$	NS
Weight (g)	12.95	0.96	156	12.90	0.87	83	$t = 0.40$	NS

(1) Because weight varies through the breeding cycle, we have included only data from the nestling period for males and from the last week of the nestling period for females. A lower value for colour type indicates darker colour.
(2) NS, not significant.

older Pied Flycatcher males and females did not differ between deciduous and coniferous forest (see Tables V and VI in Alatalo *et al.*, 1985), but males still had shorter wings and were of lower weight in coniferous as compared to deciduous habitats. In another study, in southern Sweden, Gezelius *et al.* (1984) found Pied Flycatcher females to be younger in coniferous than in deciduous forest. Females also had shorter wings in the former habitat, though that might simply be an effect of age. We want to conclude that the morphological adaptation hypothesis (see above) is unlikely to explain the size variation found between birds breeding in different types of forest habitats since.

In an often cited model Fretwell and Lucas (1969) and Fretwell (1972) suggested that birds occupy habitats in either an 'ideal free' way or in an 'ideal despotic' distribution. In the first case, birds should distribute themselves, on the basis of habitat quality, so that on average all individuals achieve the same reproductive success. Under the second model, some birds are forced, by males already in possession of territories, into less suitable habitats; and the fitness of birds in less preferred habitats will become lower than that of birds in preferred habitats. Birds forced into the less favourable habitat should also be of inferior competitive ability, for example, as a result of their smaller size. We found no significant differences in reproductive success between deciduous and coniferous forest – a finding that tended to support the 'ideal free' settling model. However, the fact that males had shorter wings and were of lower weight in coniferous forest suggests that larger, older and more dominant males may force younger and smaller males out of the preferred habitat, and thus that the distribution of males follows a despotic rather than an ideal free settlement pattern. Since no size differences were found between females, we would reject the hypothesis that birds settle according to their morphology (e.g. for optimally exploiting the resources). Gezelius *et al.* (1984) interpreted their data on Pied Flycatchers as supporting the hypothesis that dominance interactions affect habitat occupancy rather than the alternative that birds settle in an ideal free way.

BREEDING DENSITY OF PIED FLYCATCHERS IN RELATION TO BREEDING SUCCESS

Food for Pied Flycatchers is probably more abundant in deciduous than in coniferous forests (see Chapter 5). Even so, food can be depleted if there are too many individuals to share it, and hence reproductive success could be expected to drop as the density of birds increases. At high breeding densities clutch size might decrease, more eggs being infertile, while nest predation may increase and, thus, the number of fledglings would be reduced; all these effects have been established in Great Tits (Kluijver, 1951; Perrins, 1965, 1979; Lack, 1966; Krebs, 1970; Dhondt, 1977; Dhondt and Eyckerman, 1980).

In one of our first papers on the species (Lundberg *et al.*, 1981) we found, by the use of regression methods, that clutch size decreased both seasonally and with increasing breeding density of Pied Flycatchers. However, regression methods do not reveal causation and may be misleading for ecological reasons: for example, in years of high breeding density there might be a higher proportion of young individuals. In the Pied Flycatcher yearling birds often lay smaller clutches than older birds (Berndt and Winkel, 1967), and then an observed lower clutch size or breeding success under high density may depend not so much on breeding density as on the age structure of the population. To circumvent these problems in 1981 and 1982 we performed an experiment in luxuriant deciduous forests around Uppsala, where we provided nest boxes at two densities, one resulting in high (two pairs/ha) and the other low breeding densities (less than one pair/ha). Confounding variables in this type of experiment are parental age and laying date, and also in the case of the Pied Flycatcher the frequency of polygyny. However, none of these variables differed in our experiment between high- and low-density areas (Alatalo and Lundberg, 1984b), so we could directly compare breeding data between the two different densities. In neither year did we find any effect of breeding density on clutch size or hatching success. However, in 1981, nestling weight at 13 days of age and number of fledged young were both significantly reduced at high densities as compared to low-density areas (Fig. 19).

Low   **High**

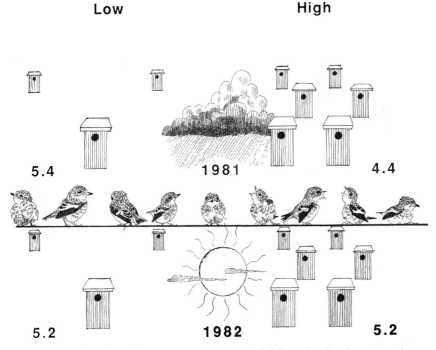

Fig. 19. *Number of fledged young in an experiment with different breeding densities. In the year with bad weather (1981) pairs breeding at high densities produced fewer young than pairs breeding at low density.*

That year there was some very bad weather with heavy wind and rain, and the temperature dropping near to freezing on 12 June. This occurred at about the time of hatching of the earliest clutches, and almost certainly had an adverse effect on feeding. In the second year the weather was more normal and we found no differences in nestling weight or fledging success between the two breeding densities, though nestlings in high-density areas had shorter tarsi than nestlings in low-density areas. Thus the experiment supported the idea that breeding success can be negatively affected by the breeding density of conspecifics, especially if the weather is bad. Note, however, that our high-density areas in this experiment had about twice the breeding density to be found among birds breeding in natural cavities, and so intraspecific competition for food is probably less intense in natural situations.

In other studies on the effects of breeding density, Tompa (1967) and Virolainen (1984) in coniferous forests in Finland, came to somewhat different conclusions. In Tompa's study there was no relation between breeding density and clutch size while Virolainen, using data from 13 years, found clutch size to be higher if breeding density was lower. On the basis of his nest-box experiment, Tompa (1967) argued that breeding density did not affect fledging success either. However, a reanalysis of his data (he arranged his boxes with different regular distances, viz. 200 m, 100 m, 50 m, 25 m and 12.5 m, respectively) shows that if the first three groups are pooled and compared with the last two groups (or the first two with the last three), then pairs in high-density areas indeed produced fewer offspring than pairs in low-density areas (for statistics see Alatalo and Lundberg, 1984b). As in our study, density dependence was more pronounced in the year (1965) when the weather was adverse. Also Virolainen (1984) found a slight but significant density-dependent effect on fledgling numbers during his 13-year study in Finland. Alerstam (1985) compared two deciduous woodlands in southern Sweden with different breeding densities of Pied Flycatchers and found that clutch size was almost identical in the two areas while fledging success was lower in the wood with the higher density. This result is not necessarily due entirely to the competition with other flycatchers since habitat differences may also be important.

BREEDING DENSITY OF OTHER SPECIES IN RELATION TO BREEDING SUCCESS OF THE PIED FLYCATCHER

The Pied Flycatcher competes for nesting sites mainly with tits and Nuthatches. There are also close similarities in breeding ecology and food between tits and flycatchers (Lack, 1966), so that the breeding density of potential competitors might influence reproductive success of flycatchers. Slagsvold (1975) looked for such effects by analysing published data from the Forest of Dean in England and from Lemsjöholm in southwest Finland. He found a significant negative correlation between the clutch size of the Pied Flycatcher and the breeding density of Great Tits at Lemsjöholm ($n = 14$ years), while there was a slight positive effect of Great Tit density on the clutch size of the Pied Flycatcher in England. The data from Finland could be interpreted in the following way: in years when Great Tits were very abundant there was a tendency for the Pied Flycatchers to lay late, and in this species clutch size decreases with time of season (see Chapter 6). However, as Slagsvold (1975) also pointed out, the negative correlation between clutch size and density of Great Tits could be due to other factors than competition. He further found that the total number of Pied Flycatcher young raised in the Forest of Dean was negatively related to the total number (adults and young) of Great Tits present in the summer.

These analyses suggest that interspecific competition with Great Tits may influence the breeding performance of Pied Flycatchers. The studies referred to above were conducted in nest box areas where boxes were provided in excess. In the natural situation, where nest–sites are more limited, the situation may be different. Also, correlative studies, where one compares two variables between different years, normally give weaker conclusions than experimental approaches. We are not aware of any conclusive study on interspecific competition involving the Pied Flycatcher, but there is one on the closely related Collared Flycatcher. In an experiment in nest box areas Gustafsson (1987) greatly reduced the number of breeding tits in half of his study plots while in the other half there were breeding densities of Collared Flycatchers and tits that closely corresponded to the natural situation. He then found that in plots with few tits the number and mass of Collared Flycatcher nestlings increased. Also, flycatcher pairs with few tit competitors contributed more recruits to the next breeding population than did pairs breeding in areas with more tits. The reason why flycatchers with few tit neighbours did better was probably that they had better access to food. The study also showed that competition with tits affected the reproductive success of Collared Flycatchers more than did intraspecific competition.

EFFECTS OF INTRODUCTION OF PIED FLYCATCHERS ON OTHER PASSERINE BIRD SPECIES

In 1966 to 1970 Enemar and Sjöstrand (1972) compared the bird communities in plots with and without nest boxes in a rich subalpine birch forest in Swedish Lapland. The experiment was designed to find out whether the introduction of Pied Flycatchers influenced the composition and density of the passerine bird community. In areas without nest boxes the commonest species were Willow Warbler, Redwing and Brambling; the Pied Flycatcher was the most numerous hole–nesting species, followed by the Redstart and the Willow Tit, and it was the ninth commonest species in the birch forest community. In areas provided with nest boxes the total passerine bird community increased by about 76% in number of individuals due to the immigration of Pied Flycatchers. However, this introduction of Pied Flycatchers did not cause any demonstrable change in the population numbers of the other species. Unfortunately, Enemar and Sjöstrand (1972) only measured bird densities and fluctuations between years, and not breeding success. They offered two explanations for the lack of response in other passerine birds to the introduction of Pied Flycatchers: first that the Pied Flycatcher is ecologically fairly separate from the other species in the community, and second that the rich subalpine forest is greatly underpopulated by birds in relation to its capacity. Personally, we support the second explanation. Enemar *et al.* (1972) also made another study of the effects of the introduction of Pied Flycatchers, this time in a riverine woodland in southern Sweden. The valley, covering 13 ha, was censused each year between 1959 and 1970. In 1963 to 1966 nest boxes were put up in excess, which considerably increased the number of breeding Pied Flycatchers (and Great Tits). The abundances of open-nesting passerine birds was compared before and after the 'nest box period' with their numbers during the period when nest boxes were available. Again, the introduction of Pied Flycatchers did not influence the numbers of other passerines. A third study was made by Alerstam (1985) who put up nest boxes in two years in a south Swedish woodland (12 ha). From having been an uncommon breeder in that woodland, the Pied Flycatcher became the second most common species in the whole passerine bird community. Again no effects on the numbers of other species could be established.

SUMMARY

The Pied Flycatcher is a cavity-nesting bird which prefers nest boxes, if they are provided, rather than natural cavities. If given a choice between different types of boxes the birds seem to prefer new ones over old, those high up in trees over low ones, and those with narrower entrance sizes over larger. These preferences might be related to risks of predation. Pied Flycatchers breed in most

types of forest habitats if there are holes available, but prefer deciduous over coniferous forest. In unmanaged natural forests breeding density can locally be up to 1 pair/ha while if boxes are provided in excess the density can be much increased, most often to about 3 pairs/ha. If breeding density is high fledging success becomes slightly reduced, particularly in seasons when the weather is bad. High densities of competing species may have the same effect, while the introduction of Pied Flycatchers to woodlands by putting up boxes seems to have no effect on the numbers of other species.

CHAPTER 5

Foraging Techniques and Diet

For birds about to start breeding it is important to be able to collect enough food and nutrients for the formation of eggs and to provide energy reserves to cover the costs of incubation. After that it is of great importance to find and collect abundant and nutritious food both for the nestlings during their period of dependence, and for the parents themselves while caring for the young and later for carrying out migration. In this chapter we describe how Pied Flycatchers search for food, and what kinds of prey items they eat. We give separate treatment to what males give females during incubation, what adults eat during the breeding season and during migration, and what kinds of food are given to the nestlings.

FORAGING HABITS

Flycatchers feed mainly on insects, and of course have been given their name because of the habit of flying from a perch to catch flying insects in the air. However, insects and other arthropods are also taken from trunks or branches of trees and from the ground. On the basis of more than 300 food captures during the breeding season, von Haartman (1954) found that in southern Finland about 65% of food catches were made on the ground, 20% in the air and 15% on trees. This preference for ground-dwelling prey was also reported by Silverin and Andersson (1984) who examined the stomach contents of more than a hundred adult Pied Flycatchers, mainly from coniferous forest, and were able to assign the prey items to different microhabitats. Among identified prey items, 50% could be classified as strictly ground living and 25% as either living in the vegetation or having been caught in the air. It was not possible from this study to estimate the proportion of prey caught from trees, but several of the species identified were known to live almost exclusively on tree trunks. Alatalo and Alatalo (1979) compared the foraging sites of the Pied Flycatcher in different habitat types (mainly coniferous forests) and in different stages of the breeding season in northern Finland. They found, for all habitats combined, that 43% of the food captures were made on trees, 38% on the ground and 19% in the air. However, in spruce forest, ground feeding was much more frequent (57%) than in pine or mixed forests of birch and conifers. They also found that over the season, airborne prey was taken more in the early part (May–June) than later (August–September), while the opposite was true of prey from trunks, branches and twigs. Also, ground feeding was uncommon in autumn. In a study of Pied Flycatchers on temporary territories during migration in Portugal, Bibby and Green (1980) found that of 547 capture attempts, 77% were made in the air, only 9% on the ground, and 14% involved snatching items from trunks or branches. Thus, in the breeding area, the Pied Flycatcher seems less often to catch food in the air as suggested by its name, than to forage from the ground or on trees. Flycatching, however, seems to be the major foraging technique used at resting areas during migration. Foraging techniques used in different microhabitats are summarized in Figure 20.

In European woodlands the most abundant other species with similar foraging techniques are the Collared Flycatcher, the Spotted Flycatcher and the Redstart. Alerstam *et al.* (1978) compared the foraging tactics of Pied and Collared Flycatchers on the islands of Gotland and Öland in the Baltic (see also Chapter 13), and found a very great overlap in the mode of feeding. The slight interspecific difference observed was mainly due to a somewhat higher proportion of ground feeding by the Pied Flycatcher while the Collared Flycatcher fed more in the canopy. In comparison with the Pied Flycatcher, Alatalo and Alatalo (1979) found the Spotted Flycatcher to take more food in the air (*c.* 65%) while the Redstart more often fed on the ground (59%). Thus, the species are partly separated with regard to the source of their individual prey items. These authors also found that the foraging niche overlapped more with the Redstart

Fig. 20.   Proportion of foraging sites (in trees, air, or on the ground) used by the Pied Flycatcher according to four different studies. 1, von Haartman (1954); 2, Alatalo and Alatalo (1979); 3, Edington and Edington (1972); 4, Bibby and Green (1980). The last study refers to temporary territories during migration.

than with the Spotted Flycatcher. The same large overlap in foraging technique between these three species was also found in a broad-leaved woodland in Wales (Edington and Edington, 1972) though both the Pied Flycatcher and the Redstart fed aerially more frequently in Wales than in Finland. The diet of the Pied Flycatcher also overlaps with that of other species, such as tits. Edington and Edington (1972), however, found that, during the breeding season, tits much more than Pied Flycatchers specialized in taking food from leaves of trees and took airborne and ground-living prey to a much lesser extent.

COURTSHIP FEEDING

In many bird species the male feeds the female during the pairing and egg-laying stages and during incubation. This behaviour has been called 'courtship or incubation feeding'. A classical interpretation is that it strengthens the pair bond between the mates (e.g. Lack, 1940). Later hypotheses have advanced other functions: for example, that courtship feeding may serve as a cue for female choice, allowing a hen to assess the quality of potential male partners on the basis of their capacity to feed her (Nisbet, 1973), or that feeding the female may improve reproductive success (Royama, 1966). The pattern of courtship feeding differs between bird species. Thus, in some species it mainly occurs during the early stages of reproduction while in others it is mainly later in the cycle. Therefore the various hypotheses given above might each apply to different species. In the Pied Flycatcher courtship feeding is rare during the mating period but more prevalent during incubation (Lifjeld and Slagsvold, 1986) and, thus, most likely serves to improve female nutrition rather than influence female choice. With respect to the Pied Fly-catcher we therefore prefer to refer to the feeding of the female by the male as 'incubation feeding'.

In a study in 1980 (Alatalo *et al.*, 1982c), we recorded male incubation feeding, but during 6 hours of nest watches we only saw six of these feedings, and could not find any positive effects of it on female incubation behaviour. Females whose mates were removed did not leave the nest for foraging for longer periods than monogamous females. In a more detailed study near Trondheim in Norway, Lifjeld and Slagsvold (1986), however, in two successive years (1983 and 1984) found the mean rate of incubation feeding to be about 3 and 6 feeds per hour, which agrees quite well with Curio's (1959b) observations of 2.7 food deliveries per hour and von Haartman's (1958) estimate of about 100 feedings per day. The highest feeding rate in the Norwegian study was observed in the colder of the two years (1983), when food was probably more difficult to find and of greater value to the female. They also found that feeding positively influenced female body weight, and that females with high body weights produced offspring of higher fledging weight. These findings support the idea that incubation feeding has been selected for in order to improve female nutritional status and hence breeding success. In another study, near Oslo, Lifjeld *et al.* (1987) again found that incubation feeding dropped with increasing air temperature, but they also discovered that males that were heavier on arrival fed their females more diligently than did males of lower weight. Polygynous males (see Chapter 12) fed their mates at approximately the same rate as did monogamous males but divided their efforts between the two females, often with a slight bias in favour of the primary female, resulting in each polygynously mated female on average receiving less food than comparable monogamously mated females. The reduced aid given to polygynously mated females resulted in their spending more time off the nest (about 5 min more per hour), which in turn led to a prolongation of the incubation period by about half a day (see also Chapter 7). In another study Lifjeld and Slagsvold (1989b) gave extra food to the primary female. Then the male shifted his efforts spent on incubation feeding towards the secondary female and gave her most of the food.

DIET OF ADULTS

The Pied Flycatcher is an almost completely insectivorous species. Very few studies, however, have studied the diet of adults, mainly because of methodo-logical problems. We are aware of only one such study from the breeding season, where an analysis of stomach content was performed on birds collected for other reasons (Silverin and Andersson, 1984). The results were presented in the form of diagrams so that exact figures cannot be quoted. However, the study did show that Hymenoptera (ants, bees and wasps) and Coleoptera (beetles) were the main prey. Among the Hymenoptera, and even in total numbers, ants were the prey species eaten most, and it was even suggested that 'anteater' could be a more appropriate name than 'flycatcher'. This predilection for ants was corroborated by a study on the diet of birds occupying temporary territories during migration (Bibby and Green, 1980). This showed, by analysis of faeces, that almost 25% of total food items eaten were ants and that other major prey groups were sphecid wasps (Hymenoptera) and beetles (Coleoptera).

FOOD GIVEN TO NESTLINGS

There is much more information in the literature on food given to nestlings than on what is eaten by adults. This is because data on food given to nestlings are easier to collect. The most common methods involve the use of neck collars on nestlings (preventing them from swallowing the food), or the removal of beak-loads from parents immediately after they have entered the nest box (if trapped they often keep the food in the beak), but analyses of stomach contents have also been used. The studies uniformly show (Appendix 2) that Aranea (spiders), Lepidoptera (butterflies and moths), Diptera (flies and mosquitoes), Hymenop-tera (ants, bees and wasps) and Coleoptera (beetles) are the most common prey categories (Mansfeld, 1942; Creutz, 1953; von Haartman, 1954; Meidell, 1961; Bösenberg, 1964; Dornbusch, 1981; Silverin and Andersson, 1984; Alatalo *et al.*, 1988b; Lifjeld and Slagsvold, 1988a). Among Lepidoptera and Hymenoptera, larvae seem to be eaten much more than adult insects while it is the other way around for the other groups (e.g. von Haartman, 1954).

The proportions of imagines and larvae, and of different prey species, how-ever, varies between habitats. According to the literature compilations made by Slagsvold (1975) the proportion of caterpillars in the diet of nestlings may vary between 15% and 65% in deciduous forest while it is considerably lower in coniferous forest (6–29%). Accordingly, insect imagines on average make up a larger proportion in coniferous as compared to deciduous forest (55% and 40%, respectively). In a comparison between habitats in Germany, Bösenberg (1964) found that in beech forest larvae made up 77% while the corresponding figures for pedunculate oak and Scots pine forest were 56% and 31%, respectively.

Though there is little data on the diet of adult Pied Flycatchers, it does seem that they eat somewhat different prey types from those given to nestlings.

Silverin and Andersson (1984) found that significantly more nestling than adult stomachs contained spiders and butterfly and moth larvae, whereas ants were more frequent in adults than in nestlings. Thus, nestlings are probably given softer prey items than those eaten by the parents, and according to Pruska (1980; cited in Silverin and Andersson, 1984) this difference may be even more pronounced if one compares small nestlings with adults than if one compares fully grown nestlings and their parents. Support for the idea that smaller nestlings are given softer food than larger nestlings comes from the study of Meidell (1961) in mountain forests in western Norway. He analysed the stomach contents of small, medium and large Pied Flycatcher nestlings and found that small nestlings were given large amounts of Lepidoptera larvae and spiders while the dominant food items provided to older nestlings were Lepidoptera larvae and ants.

SUMMARY

The Pied Flycatcher is almost exclusively insectivorous and of course got its name from its habit of catching flying insects in the air. However, when we look in more detail at the foraging technique and the food items captured, it turns out that many prey are also caught from the ground. Among prey species eaten by adults ants predominate and it has even been suggested that 'anteater' could be a more appropriate name than flycatcher. The food given to nestlings is dominated by caterpillars, which are probably also the most nutritious food items, though the proportion of insect larvae as compared with imagines in the diet varies between habitats.

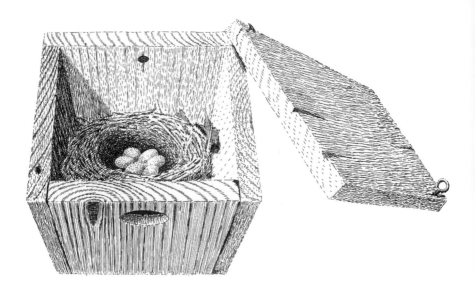

CHAPTER 6

Breeding Time and Clutch Size

The determination of clutch size has been a subject of major interest in ornithological studies. In particular, David Lack (1947, 1948, 1954, 1966) was deeply
interested in the question why each species and population has its own typical
clutch size. The Pied Flycatcher was one of the first species chosen for research
aiming to solve the problem of variation in clutch size. The early works of von
Haartman (1951a) in Finland, Creutz (1955) in Germany and Campbell (1955) in
England had already been directed at the 'family size' problem. Since then many
more studies have been devoted to the Pied Flycatcher as documented in the
recent review by Järvinen (1989) on the geographical variation of brood size. His
compilation includes no less than 103 different study sites in Europe and North
Africa, for which data exist on the clutch size.

In this chapter, we simply ask why a Pied Flycatcher female lays a certain
number of eggs, no more, no less. Lack's (1954, 1966) answer was that the clutch
size of altricial birds is limited above all by the amount of food that parents can
bring to their nestlings; birds lay the number of eggs that maximizes the number
of surviving offspring. The many studies of Pied Flycatchers allow us to test this
hypothesis in a detailed way. Before going on to this question, we first need to
describe the natural variation of clutch size in relation to geographical area,

habitat, type of nest site, population density, breeding time, age of the female, and her mating status. Since clutch size is closely related to breeding time, however, we will first examine the factors determining the onset of breeding.

BREEDING PHENOLOGY

GENERAL HYPOTHESES

Basically natural selection should cause birds to start their breeding at a time that maximizes their lifetime reproductive success, that is, the number of offspring recruited into future breeding populations. Perrins (1970) made this point quite clearly, although at that time the emphasis was often put on short-term benefits and costs of each behavioural action, while concepts such as 'lifetime' and 'recruits' were neglected. It is necessary to take into account that current reproduction may impose costs for parents in terms of reductions in future reproduction. Therefore the crucial parameter is lifetime reproductive success. Furthermore, the number of fledged young need not necessarily reflect the number of recruits, since a large proportion of the young will die before their first potential breeding opportunity.

Perrins (1970) emphasized two main factors constraining the start of breeding, namely (1) the resources required by females to start egg-laying, and (2) the resources required by parents to feed the nestlings. In the first case, such environmental factors as the availability of suitable food for the female while she is forming the eggs, are critical. A female starting too early may suffer increased risk to her life, or may simply be unable to form many and high-quality eggs. The fact that during adverse weather the birds fail to lay an egg each morning (see below) shows that resources for egg-laying may indeed be critical. Another constraint is that the vicissitudes of weather may punish females in travelling north and arriving on the breeding grounds too early. The second hypothesis emphasizes the need for breeding birds to match the time when the offspring need most food with the time when the abundance of food is at its maximum. Later we will demonstrate that in Pied Flycatchers, as in most altricial birds, the brood size is limited above all by the provisioning capacity of the parents, and therefore it is easy to imagine that birds generally try to match their breeding phenology with the time of maximum food availability for the nestlings. Therefore, it is likely that both of the constraints mentioned above influence the start of breeding in the Pied Flycatcher.

VARIATION IN BREEDING PHENOLOGY

Invariably, Pied Flycatchers raise only one brood each summer. The breeding season is short, and only early nest losses lead to renesting. Appendix 3 lists typical starting dates of breeding in different populations. Unsurprisingly, the

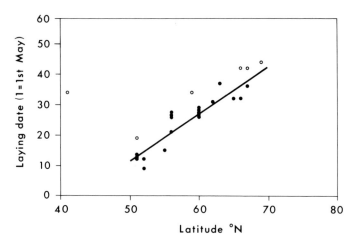

Fig. 21.   Average (or median) laying date plotted against latitude of the study site. Open circles are for high altitude sites and solid discs for low altitude sites (<300 m). The line indicates the regression for low altitude sites (Date = 1.55 × Latitude − 65.7, n = 20, P < 0.001). Data are from Appendix 3 and Berndt and Winkel (1967); von Haartman (1969); Haverschmidt (1973); Pasanen (1977); Alatalo (1978); Järvinen and Lindén (1980).

start of breeding is related to the time of the local rise in the ambient temperature, with birds breeding far north and at high altitudes starting relatively late in the spring or early summer (Fig. 21). Across study sites at low altitudes, the average or median laying dates are delayed by 1.5 days with each degree of poleward displacement. In Germany and in England most of the females start laying in the middle of May, while in the northern parts of Scandinavia and Finland, laying begins approximately one month later. Zang (1980) studied Pied Flycatchers on the Harz mountains in Germany up to a height of 1000 m, and reported laying time to be delayed by 1.7 days per 100 m of increased altitude. Thus 100 m of altitudinal change is approximately comparable to 100 km of northward displacement. As far south as Spain, at the high-altitude (1750 m) study site of Potti *et al*. (1987), laying did not start until early June, that is, at the same time as at low-altitude sites in northern Scandinavia.

Von Haartman (1990) has collected data about his nest box area in Lemsjöholm in southern Finland from 49 years, and over that time period the date of laying the first egg remained remarkably constant. In the 1940s the average date of laying the first egg was 20.6 May, and in the 1980s it was 21.0 May, corresponding to an average difference of eight hours. On the other hand, there are yearly variations depending on the weather conditions. For instance, in von Haartman's (1990) data the median egg-laying date, i.e. the date when half of the females in the population have laid their first egg, has varied by eleven days, viz. between 23 May to 3 June.

DETERMINATION OF LAYING TIME

Little is known about the phenology of food availability for the Pied Fly-catcher. The fact that all over Europe brood size decreases with the progress of the season without any initial increase, together with the shortness of the breeding season, suggests that the start of laying is always somewhat late with respect to food availability for nestlings. While the diet of flycatchers is quite diverse (Chapter 5), one of the most abundant and nutritious foods for nestlings is caterpillars. Caterpillars have a brief peak period in early summer, and fluctuations in timing and abundance have been shown to affect the breeding success, for example, in tits (Perrins, 1979). In our study areas in Uppsala and Cumbria, not only did the clutch size of the Pied Flycatcher decrease with laying date, but so also did the likelihood of an egg producing a fledgling, or of a fledgling being recruited into the population (see below, and Figs 33 and 34). The probability of an egg producing a recruit was also found to be quite low for the latest broods in Campbell's data from the Forest of Dean (Lack, 1966), suggesting that early broods are reared at a more favourable time in terms of food availability.

Slagsvold (1976) and Järvinen (1983) compared the start of breeding with vegetational phenology and with air temperature. As an example, Figure 22 shows the egg-laying times in southernmost Finland and in northernmost Finnish Lapland. The northern populations start their breeding earlier with respect to vegetational phenology and to air temperature than do populations further south. In the south females started to lay eggs after the leafing of birch

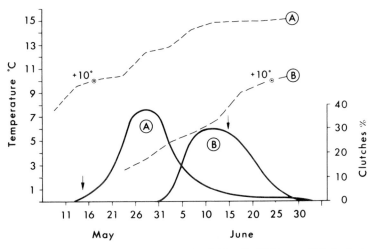

Fig. 22. Laying of first eggs in southern Finland (A, 60–62°N, n = 392 clutches) and in northernmost Finland (B, 69°N, n = 371) in relation to the mean daily air temperature. Arrows indicate time of birch leafing. Modified from Järvinen (1983).

trees, while most females in the north started to lay before birch leafing. Likewise the mean daily air temperature at the peak starting time was about +12°C in the south and only +6°C in the north. This suggests that females in the south ought to be able to start breeding earlier, and the start of breeding cannot be explained solely by the constraints set by the resources required by females to form the eggs. In the north the summer is very short, and females are likely to be in a hurry to lay their eggs so as not to miss the chance of breeding altogether. Therefore, the benefits of laying while the weather is still cold are relatively high and outweigh any increase in the risks involved in laying at an early phenological stage. The start of breeding with respect to vegetational phenology is also relatively late at high altitudes and in years when spring comes late (Slagsvold, 1976).

After female arrival on the breeding grounds and the formation of pairs it takes at least another five days for the eggs to develop in the oviduct so that they are ready for laying (von Haartman, 1951b, 1990). In fact, late arriving females start laying about five days after pair formation, whereas early females may wait several weeks (Fig. 23). Consequently, late arriving females are able to start their egg-laying as soon as they have paired up, the only delay being the five days it takes for the eggs to develop. The longer waiting times in early arriving females may indicate both difficulties in forming eggs in early spring and the need to time the hatching of the brood to the most suitable period for feeding the nestlings.

Slagsvold (1976) found that the start of egg-laying in a population can be predicted from the weather conditions in the preceding month, and the median laying date by the weather in the preceding two weeks. According to our experience in central Sweden and Finland, egg-laying in the population started at the earliest in mid–May, about five days after particularly warm and sunny days

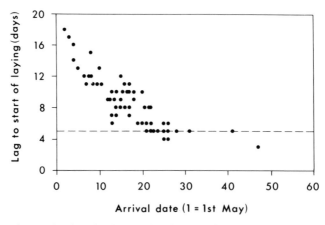

Fig. 23. *The time lag from female arrival to the start of egg-laying in a study site at Uppsala 1982–3 (see Alatalo et al., 1984c). The broken line indicates a lag of five days, which is the time needed for the final rapid growth of oocytes (von Haartman, 1990). The correlation between the variables is* $r_s = -0.87$, n = 61, P < 0.001.

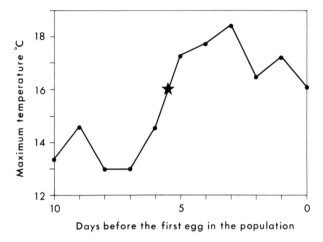

Fig. 24. *The average maximum temperatures during the ten days preceding the laying of the first egg in the population. Based on six years of data (1979–84) at Uppsala and eight (1971–8) at Oulu, Finland (65°N, Rauno V. Alatalo, unpublished data). The star indicates a significant increase (t = 3.00, n = 14, P < 0.05) in air temperature from the previous day.*

(for similar data see also Järvinen, 1983; von Haartman, 1990). In Figure 24 we have compiled data from the six summers of 1979 to 1984 at Uppsala (this study) and the eight summers of 1971 to 1978 in Oulu, northern Finland (Rauno Alatalo, unpublished data). There was a significant increase in daily maximum temperature on the fifth day before the laying of the first egg in the population. The lag of five days fits nicely with the time needed for the final rapid growth of oocytes in the oviduct. Weather may thus be the proximate factor triggering the start of egg-laying. In many birds the hormonal control of the breeding cycle is geared to annual photoperiodicity, modified by weather conditions, and this is likely to be the case in the Pied Flycatcher too.

If the weather continues to be favourable, more and more females will soon start laying, and the peak laying date is reached in a few days' time. A normal distribution curve is followed in the beginning of laying, but because of renestings there will be a tail with some late breedings (Fig. 25). In our study site in Uppsala the latest clutches are started at the end of June. Often colder and rainier periods occur causing delays in the start of laying. As an example, Figure 25 illustrates the distributions of the starts of laying in two summers at Uppsala. In 1980, the warm weather around 15 May triggered the first females to start to lay on the 19th. However, by that date the weather had already turned to a colder period that lasted about a week. This caused a prolonged period with only a few new females starting each day, and many did not start to lay until the first days of June. In 1981, the weather was continuously warm after mid-May, and most of the females started to lay within four days between 20 and 23 May.

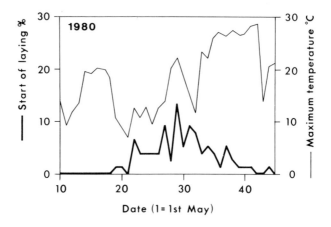

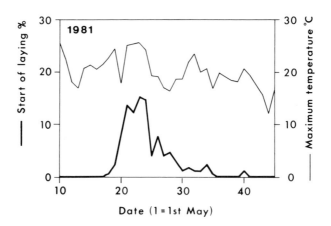

Fig. 25.   *The distribution of dates for laying of the first eggs in two summers (1980, n = 76; 1981, n = 171) in Uppsala in relation to variation in daily maximum temperature.*

Usually a female lays one egg each day until the clutch is completed, but during periods of particularly adverse weather females seem to be unable to gather enough resources for egg formation, causing a gap of a day or two between the laying of consecutive eggs. Von Haartman (1990) reported such a situation for his study site in 1944 in late May during a cold spell with snow cover. A similar situation happened in 1990 in our study site at Konnevesi, central Finland (Fig. 26). In that year the first females started laying on 17 or 18 May after unusually warm weather which lasted from 10 to 15 May. Just as laying started, however, the weather turned very cold and there was a slight snowfall. On 19 May no new

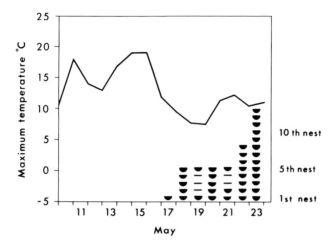

Fig. 26.   *Laying pattern of the first 13 nests at Konnevesi, central Finland in 1990 when a cold spell with some snow on 17–19 May caused interruptions in the laying sequence (marked by −) on 19 and 21 May.*

females started to lay, and three of the five that had already started did not lay any eggs on that day. There were also gaps on 21 May. New females did not start laying until 22 May, though their laying also had probably been triggered by the warm weather prior to 15 May.

FEMALE CHARACTERISTICS

Many studies have demonstrated that the age of a female influences her time of laying (Berndt and Winkel, 1967; von Haartman, 1967a; Harvey *et al.*, 1985; Järvinen, 1991), and in Figure 27 we have compiled the data for our study site in Cumbria. With the help of records made by Alan Old since 1985, we will be able to use that data here and elsewhere in this chapter. We shall consider only females that were ringed as nestlings, whose age is therefore known exactly. We have excluded repeat clutches, and all clutches started more than 20 days after the yearly median dates for the start of laying. The median laying date for yearling females is three days later than that for older females, which corresponds well with the typical 2–3-day difference observed in other studies (see the review by Järvinen, 1991). Such a difference may be due to the inexperience of yearling birds, their shorter wings which may delay migration, or the possibility that yearling birds avoid high risks if this improves their chances of breeding more successfully later in life.

In the Cumbrian population we can also look at the constancy of laying date for a single female from year to year. Any correlation would indicate heritability for

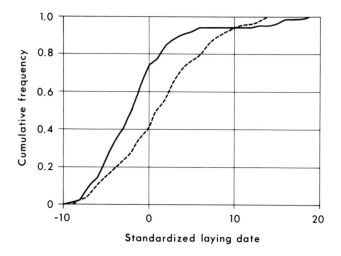

Fig. 27.   *Cumulative distribution of the start of laying by one-year old (dotted line; Md = +1, n = 47) and older females (solid line; Md = −2, n = 84, U-test, z = 3.27, P < 0.01) in Cumbria, England based on the years 1986–9. In each year the laying dates have been standardized to account for yearly differences in median laying dates. Clutches laid more than 20 days after the median date have been excluded.*

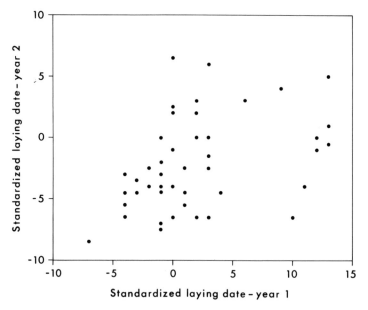

Fig. 28.   *Correlation between laying dates of the same female in consecutive years in Cumbria, England. Laying dates are standardized in relation to yearly population medians and late repeat clutches have been omitted. The correlation is r = 0.41, n = 51, P < 0.01).*

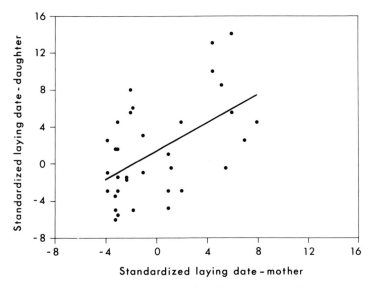

Fig. 29.   *Resemblance in laying time (standardized from yearly population medians) between mothers and their daughters in Cumbria, England. Regression line: Daughter's laying date = 0.76 × Mother's date + 1.33, n = 34, P < 0.01.*

the timing of the start of laying and/or that some females are phenotypically in better condition and are always able to start earlier than the others. Such a correlation does exist (Fig. 28), notwithstanding a great deal of variation. To check whether females inherit from their mothers genes that influence the timing of laying, we can also compare daughters' laying times with those of their mothers. There is, in fact, quite a high resemblance which indicates high heritability (Fig. 29), even though there may also be factors other than inheritance causing a resemblance between mothers and daughters. In particular, maternal effects are possible in the way that early-breeding females have the best chance of raising their young under good conditions, and therefore their offspring will be in better condition and capable of early arrival and laying next year.

VARIATION IN CLUTCH SIZE

GEOGRAPHICAL VARIATION

A major geographical pattern in avian clutch-size variation is that species in the tropics have small clutch sizes, while the size tends to increase the further one moves from the equator towards subtropical and temperate zones. For instance, in the Old World Flycatchers, the typical clutch size in Africa south of the Sahara is 2–3 eggs, while in Europe it is 5–7 eggs (Lack, 1947, 1948). This general pattern of clutch size increasing towards the north was one of the first problems tackled by ornithologists trying to apply evolutionary thinking to their research problems. Lack (1947, 1948, 1954, 1966, 1968) suggested that the increase in day-length towards the north during the breeding season may allow birds to raise larger broods. At about the same time, Skutch (1949) proposed that high predation pressure in the tropics should select for small broods.

At present it seems that a major part of the differences in clutch size between the tropics and the temperate zone can be explained in terms of an idea advanced by Ashmole (1963) and later favoured by Lack (1966, 1968; see also Ricklefs, 1980). According to this scenario, in temperate areas food is abundant for only a short time in summer, while even including the migrants there are relatively few birds. Therefore the amount of food per individual bird is high, allowing parents to raise large broods. In the tropics, with less variable food supplies, bird populations are more saturated, and the high density of birds means that parents cannot find enough food to raise a large brood. Yet other factors, such as day-length, nest predation, costs of reproduction, and adult mortality may also contribute to the large-scale geographical variation in brood sizes. The possible impacts of predation and of costs of reproduction on Pied Flycatcher clutch size will be discussed later in this chapter, but in general they are unlikely to be very important. That day-length may be of importance is supported by a recent experiment in Finland, in which a reduction of the daily activity time of Pied Flycatcher parents resulted in a reduction of their breeding success (Matti Halonen and Markku Kuitunen, pers. comm.).

While recognizing the clutch-size differences between the tropics and the temperate zone, it is also of interest to see whether there is intraspecific geographical variation in clutch size. Pied Flycatchers have been studied in many parts of Europe, and the resulting data have been subjected to several tests of latitudinal and longitudinal variation (Berndt and Winkel, 1967; von Haartman, 1967a; Berndt et al., 1981; Järvinen, 1989). Berndt et al. (1981) reported a tendency for clutch size to increase northwards and eastwards across 39 sites in Europe. Recently Järvinen (1989) made a multivariate analysis based on 103 study sites, and found no clear pattern with respect to latitude or longitude. Instead there was a clear effect of altitude. We have included part of the clutch-size data in Figure 30, but have used only the average value from each study project, to avoid the interdependency in data that can arise when data from several adjacent sites are each regarded as independent observations. This analysis shows no latitudinal trend in the clutch size of the Pied Flycatcher. The clutch size is largest on the British Isles and smallest in high-altitude sites in northern Scandinavia, Germany, Spain and North Africa (see also Appendix 3). Despite the general tendency among birds of increasing clutch size from the tropics to the temperate zone, there is no reason to expect that this would also apply on a finer scale to a single species. Different populations face different local conditions, for instance with respect to habitat, and these may easily override any general changes in the environment due to latitude.

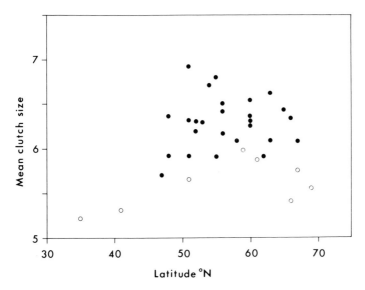

Fig. 30. Average clutch size plotted against latitude. Solid discs refer to low altitude (<300 m) study sites and open circles high altitude sites. Based on Appendix 3, references mentioned in Fig. 21 and Haftorn (1971); Stephan (1961) and Lichatschev (1955) both cited in von Haartman (1967a); Glutz von Blotzheim (1962) and Isenmann and Moali (1987). The correlation between latitude and clutch size among all sites is r = 0.08 *(n = 37, P > 0.10) and for the low altitude sites it is* r = 0.03 *(n = 29, P > 0.10).*

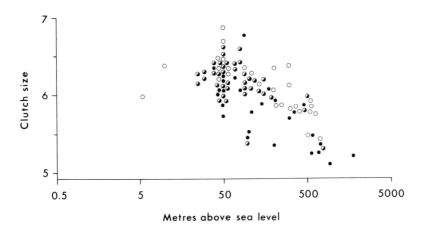

Fig. 31. Mean clutch size plotted against the altitude of the study plot. Open symbols are deciduous, solid symbols coniferous and half-filled circles are mixed habitats. Modified from Järvinen (1989).

While latitudinal changes are absent among European Pied Flycatcher populations, there is a clear reduction in clutch size with respect to increasing altitude (Fig. 31). This reduction is found in both coniferous and deciduous habitats, and is not confounded by latitude or longitude (Järvinen, 1989). At altitudes of 50 m or less, the average clutch size is typically between 6 and 6.5 eggs, while at altitudes of 500 m or higher clutches are about one egg smaller, normally between 5 and 5.5 eggs. This corresponds closely with the reduction of 0.14 eggs per 100 m rise in altitude found in the Harz mountains in Germany by Zang (1980). There was even a difference in clutch size between the northern and southern mountain slopes, such that the latter have a higher clutch size (Zang, 1985). All these differences are likely to reflect differences in the availability of food in the harsh environment at high altitudes with colder weather.

Habitat and Density

There are differences in average clutch size between habitats within the same study areas (Berndt and Winkel 1967; Källander, 1975; Alatalo *et al.*, 1985; Källander *et al.*, 1987). In general these inter-habitat differences in clutch size are slight (see Table 8) and, for instance, in our study areas in Uppsala clutch size in deciduous forest dominated by pedunculate oak was 6.53 eggs while in coniferous forest with Norway spruce and Scots pine as dominating tree species it was 6.31. Figure 32 is a compilation of average clutch sizes in a number of studies for

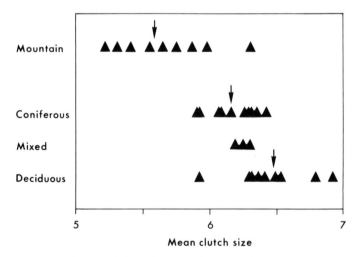

Fig. 32.   *Mean clutch size in different habitats. The average for each habitat is indicated by an arrow. Based on data in Appendix 3 and references mentioned in Figs 21 and 30. A variance analysis indicates a significant variation between all habitats (F = 20.5, n = 32, P < 0.001), which is true also when excluding the mountain sites (F = 4.38, n = 24, P < 0.05).*

different habitats. High-altitude sites are listed separately from low-altitude ones, since both coniferous and deciduous habitats high up in mountains differ in many ways from similar habitats at low altitudes. In this comparison the average clutch size in deciduous forests was about 0.3 eggs larger than in coniferous forests. Since there is frequently a difference of about two days in laying dates between habitats and since clutch size is negatively correlated with laying date, this may explain part of the difference.

Järvinen (1989) compared the effect of habitat on clutch size in a multivariate analysis using altitude as a covariate. He was able to confirm that even at the same altitude, Pied Flycatchers nesting in deciduous forests lay more eggs than do birds nesting in mixed or coniferous forests (Fig. 31). The difference, amounting to about 0.5 eggs, can probably be ascribed to a difference in availability of food. Although the difference is small it is in agreement with the much higher population density of Pied Flycatchers in deciduous habitats even if nest boxes are provided in excess in both habitats (see also Chapter 4).

Population density has at most a very slight impact on clutch size. In an experiment where we manipulated breeding density in deciduous forests by providing boxes at different distances from each other, no significant difference in clutch size was obtained (Alatalo and Lundberg, 1984b). In deciduous forest with a high density of two pairs per hectare, the clutch size was 6.42 ($n = 155$) while at a low density of less than one pair per hectare it was 6.55 ($n = 94$). Breeding success, too, was only slightly influenced, indicating that intraspecific food competition does not significantly reduce the clutch size of densely nesting Pied Flycatchers.

NATURAL CAVITIES AND BOX SIZE

Using nest boxes is a very efficient way of studying birds, and since Pied Flycatchers always prefer boxes rather than natural cavities, most studies have been made under semi-natural conditions, a fact not to be ignored. For passerine birds breeding in boxes it has been suggested that clutch size may be limited by the area of the bottom of the cavity. Such a relationship has been documented for Pied Flycatchers nesting in boxes of various dimensions in southern Sweden (Gustafsson and Nilsson, 1985). In the smallest boxes, with a bottom area of 57 cm^2, the mean clutch size was 6.35 ($n = 35$), compared with 6.48 ($n = 60$) for an area of 87 cm^2, 6.57 ($n = 14$) for 104 cm^2, and up to 7.00 ($n = 8$) for 125 cm^2.

Providing boxes of different sizes and then measuring the corresponding variation in clutch size may not be adequate to evaluate the impact of bottom area alone. If birds are allowed to choose between boxes it is likely that better quality individuals will end up in the larger boxes, and that for that reason larger clutches are laid in those boxes, increasing the apparent effect of box size. For a final test one has to prevent birds from choosing their own box size, for instance, by allowing birds to settle in similar-sized boxes, and then changing the box size either randomly or systematically. This was partly achieved for the Collared

Flycatcher by Gustafsson and Nilsson (1985) who reported that clutch sizes still differed, which suggests that the size of the box really had some influence on the clutch size.

The next question concerns the relative importance of the impact of bottom area on clutch size: it is important to know how natural cavities vary in size and how clutch sizes differ between boxes and the natural holes. Nilsson (1984) found a significant difference ($t = 2.87$, $P < 0.01$) in average clutch size ($\pm$SD) between nest boxes (6.48 ± 0.80, $n = 108$) and natural cavities (6.00 ± 0.97, $n = 33$) in southern Sweden. However, in our study areas in central Sweden, clutch sizes in boxes (6.62 ± 0.77, $n = 194$) and natural cavities (6.45 ± 0.74, $n = 74$, $P > 0.10$) did not differ significantly (Alatalo *et al.*, 1988c). Nor was there any obvious correlation between the bottom area of natural holes and the clutch size (Fig. 100), in spite of the very great variation in bottom area. To sum up, the various features of the hole seem to have only slight effects on clutch size (see also Chapter 14).

It is quite unknown what the mechanism of any such effect might be, since there is usually no problem in having enough space for the chicks in the nest. Slagsvold (1989) manipulated the nest-cups within Pied Flycatcher nest boxes, and found that breeding success was reduced if the cup was made of a material that does not expand and if the diameter of the cup was as small as 6 cm, as it is when the female incubates. However, in natural situations the nest-cups are flexible and can expand to fill the whole bottom area of the cavity.

Breeding Time

In most birds breeding in the temperate zone the clutch size decreases with the progress of the breeding season (e.g. Klomp, 1970), and this is so for the Pied Flycatcher (Fig. 33A). In fact, the reduction is unusually rapid in this species, falling by 0.05–0.1 eggs for each successive day of delayed breeding. Why does clutch size decrease with breeding time?

An obvious explanation is that this is in response to gradually deteriorating conditions for breeding through the breeding season, and this possibility is supported by the fact that Pied Flycatchers have an uncommonly short breeding season. Alternative factors could be that birds that breed later are of lower quality, as indicated by the fact that they arrive late and are frequently yearlings. However, this explanation may not be very important since, broadly speaking, the same relationship between laying date and clutch size prevails in all years in a given population (Table 6, Fig. 33A). This is what von Haartman (1967b, 1982) called the 'calendar effect', and might reflect a mechanism of proximate control of clutch size that is linked with the absolute date. He compared years that nesting started particularly early with those when it started late. If in each year the first birds to begin breeding are of best quality and hence lay large clutches, the regression lines for the two types of years should have the same slope but differ in intercepts, as is the case for the Starling in Finland (von Haartman, 1982).

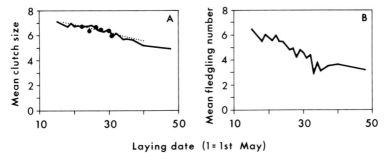

Fig. 33.   *Mean clutch size (A) and number of fledged young (B) plotted against date of start of egg-laying at Uppsala in 1979–84. In the laying date period 18–35 each day is presented separately, while for early and late clutches a few days have been pooled to attain a sample size of at least ten nests for each mean. In (A) the broken line shows the regression equation −0.071 × date + 8.34 (SE for the regression coefficient = 0.004, n = 849, P < 0.001), and the dots indicate yearly mean clutch sizes against mean laying date which follow the regression −0.066 × date + 8.19 (P < 0.05). The regression equation for fledged young in (B) is −0.131 × date + 8.40 (SE = 0.013, n = 818, P < 0.001).*

However, in Pied Flycatchers, the same regression line was followed in early and late years which suggests that it is the absolute date rather than the relative timing that matters. In our Uppsala data the 'calendar effect' is indicated by the fact that the yearly mean clutch sizes are lower for the years with late start of laying (Fig. 33A).

The calendar effect is likely to arise because the conditions for breeding may be related to the absolute date rather than to the relative timing of breeding in each year. Thus the absolute date may suit as the basis for a simple photoperiodic rule-of-thumb that birds use in their proximate control of clutch size. However, date does not explain all of the variation in clutch size, even if the regression slopes for early and late years are similar. In von Haartman's data (1967b, 1982) two years of similar median egg-laying date may have an average clutch size differing by more

Table 6.   *The yearly regression equations for clutch size and the number of fledged young in Uppsala including all nests.*

Year	Clutch size	Fledged young	n
1979	−0.075 × date + 8.27	−0.201 × date + 10.96	80
1980	−0.071 × date + 8.41	−0.071 × date + 7.29	74
1981	−0.084 × date + 8.43	−0.118 × date + 7.09	168
1982	−0.083 × date + 8.76	−0.201 × date + 10.56	154
1983	−0.072 × date + 8.33	−0.142 × date + 9.17	161
1984	−0.068 × date + 8.48	−0.148 × date + 8.74	181

than 0.5 eggs. Obviously birds are also able to employ other environmental cues for the proximate control of their clutch size.

The idea that clutch size decreases with the progress of the spring because of a deterioration in the food supply is supported by the relatively steep reduction in the numbers of fledglings against laying date (Fig. 33B). In Uppsala the average reduction per day was 0.13 while the corresponding reduction in clutch size was only 0.07 per day, indicating that nestling survival is lower for later start of breeding. A major part of the difference is a result of the higher frequency of secondary females among late nestings. However, even among monogamously mated females the reduction in fledgling number was as high as 0.095 per day (SE = 0.012, $n = 602$). While the reduction in clutch size against laying date is

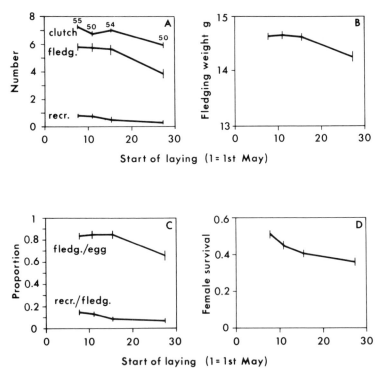

Fig. 34.   *Breeding data plotted against laying date in Cumbria, England during 1986–9. Laying time is divided into four approximately equal groups, and sample sizes are given above the category means in A. (A) Regression equations are: clutch size = $-0.069 \times$ date + 7.81 (P < 0.001), number of fledged young = $-0.098 \times$ date + 6.78 (P < 0.001), number of recruits = $-0.026 \times$ date + 1.01 (P < 0.001); (B) fledging weight at 13 days of age = $-0.020 \times$ date + 14.83 (P < 0.01); (C) fledged young per egg = $-0.008 \times$ date + 0.92 (P < 0.001), recruited young per fledgling = $-0.004 \times$ date + 0.17 (P < 0.001); (D) survival of the breeding female to the next year, which is not significantly related to laying date (logistic regression, P > 0.30, n = 126 in this case).*

rather constant over the years, the reduction in fledgling numbers is highly variable (Table 6). This variation reflects the effects of weather conditions on breeding success (see Chapter 7).

While numbers of recruits are typically small because most young disperse to breeding sites outside our Swedish study areas (see Table 11), there are enough data for us to consider relative recruitment at the Cumbrian study site (Fig. 34). The poor success of late broods becomes conspicuous as a reduction in the number of recruits to the breeding population. Similar results had earlier been obtained in the Forest of Dean (see Lack, 1966; Perrins, 1970). Not only does the probability of an egg producing a fledgling decrease for late breeders (Fig. 34C), but those offspring are also of relatively light weight (Fig. 34B). At the same time the likelihood of a fledgling becoming a recruit to the breeding population reduces from 14% in early nests down to 7% in the latest nests (Fig. 34C). While part of the difference may be due to the poorer quality individuals starting to lay latest in the season, it is likely that the reduction is even more due to the deterioration in the possibility of feeding the young late in the summer. Otherwise, it would be difficult to explain the calendar effect, under which it is absolute date rather than relative timing within each summer that determines the clutch size.

The survival of breeding females was not significantly related to their laying time, if anything the tendency is for higher survival among the early females (Fig. 34D). Therefore, the Cumbrian data supports the idea that clutch-size reduction with the progress of the spring is simply due to the poorer prospects of successful breeding later in the summer. At the same time, the results indicate the clear benefits for females to start breeding early because then the conditions for feeding the offspring will be best, as discussed on p. 61.

FEMALE CHARACTERISTICS

Traditionally, avian ecologists have been interested in the possible effect of the age of the female on her breeding performance. Recently, Järvinen (1991) summarized the data from his own and four other studies (Creutz, 1955; von Haartman, 1967b; Berndt and Winkel, 1967; Harvey *et al.*, 1985). The average clutch size of yearling females was from 0.5 to 0.9 eggs smaller than that of older females. In Cumbria, the corresponding difference was only 0.3 eggs and it disappeared if clutch sizes were standardized by the laying date (Fig. 35). In the large-scale study by Berndt and Winkel (1967) a difference remains even if one takes into account the small delay in the start of breeding by yearling females. Conceivably, the smaller clutch size of yearling females might arise from the avoidance of high reproductive costs at an early age, or from the poorer capacity of inexperienced yearling birds to raise offspring. Both these factors may operate in the Pied Flycatcher.

In addition to age, we found a slight dependency between the length of the tarsus and clutch size (Alatalo and Lundberg, 1986a). Females with tarsi slightly

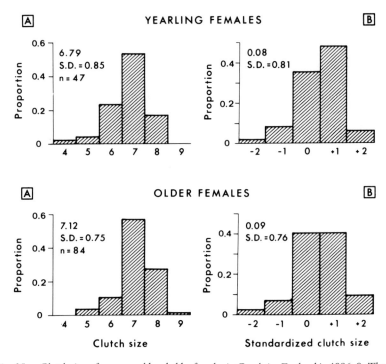

Fig. 35.   Clutch size of one-year old and older females in Cumbria, England in 1986–9. There is a difference in clutch size between age groups (= A), (t = 2.30, P < 0.05), which disappears if we standardize for laying date (= B), (t = 0.08, P > 0.90). The standardization is made as the deviation from the regression for the pooled data given in Fig. 34.

longer than average laid the largest clutches, while females with extremely long tarsi and in particular those with short tarsi laid smaller clutches (Fig. 36). This variation may reflect a weak stabilizing selection on tarsus length via clutch size, birds of average size being most capable of raising large clutches.

The condition of the laying female may well be a major factor influencing the size of the clutch. Females in poor condition may lay a small clutch because they would not be able to take care of a large brood, when we are speaking about condition as a proximate factor. Alternatively, or additionally, females in poor condition may ultimately be limited in their capacity to lay large clutches. One way to estimate female condition is to look at body weight. Askenmo (1982) found a clear positive correlation between the weight of the incubating female and the size of her clutch. Females weighing over 16 g had an average clutch size of 6.2–6.3, while those weighing less than 14 g had an average clutch size of 5.4–5.9. Likewise, in years when the average female weight was over 15 g the yearly average clutch size was 6.1–6.2, while in a year with average female weight of 14.4 g the average clutch size was down to 5.6. These correlations suggest that

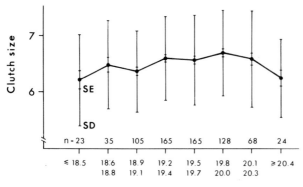

Fig. 36.   Variation in clutch size with female tarsus length. Data from Uppsala during 1980–4 (modified from Alatalo and Lundberg, 1986a). The regression equation is clutch size = 0.13 × tarsus length + 4.03, SE = 0.06, n = 713, P < 0.05.

female condition may be important, even though there may be alternative causes for such variation. A major confounding factor may be that the weight variation of the incubating female may partly reflect the necessity of early laying females to gather larger energy reserves. Early in the breeding season the probability of bad weather and consequent problems in incubation are higher.

An experiment by Slagsvold and Lifjeld (1988c) directly confirms that the condition of the female influences the clutch size. They handicapped females by removing some wing and tail feathers. In comparison to control females, the handicapped females laid smaller repeat clutches, the average difference being of the order of 0.5 eggs. Handicapped females had also reduced feeding rates. The authors implied that females were able to adjust their clutch size for their reduced working capacity during the period of feeding the nestlings. The conclusion of an ultimate determination of clutch size rather than of a proximate effect is based on the fact that handicapped females started to renest as quickly as the control females, suggesting that the handicapping did not constrain the laying capacity.

Also, the mating status of females has a slight influence on clutch size; monogamous females in Uppsala laying, on average, about 0.2–0.3 eggs more than simultaneously laying primary and secondary females (Alatalo and Lundberg, 1990). However, this reduction was not found for secondary females in a study in Norway (Stenmark *et al.*, 1988). In any case, the difference is slight, and may partly be related to a response of some females to the absence of their bigamous polyterritorial male. However, secondary females should lay much smaller clutches if they really were able to respond appropriately to the expected reduction in male help in feeding the nestlings. The slight reduction in clutch size may also be a consequence of harassment by other males at the nests of polyterritorial males when the territory owner is absent (Alatalo and Lundberg,

1984a). We have frequently seen males visiting other males' boxes in an attempt to take over the box. Once one egg was missing after such a visit, probably due to its breakage and subsequent removal by the female, the nest-cup being wet and yolky. In another case the female was seen on the ground fighting an intruding male for several minutes, and the next day no egg was laid in spite of good weather, suggesting damage of the forming egg.

OPTIMIZATION OF CLUTCH SIZE

A modern view of life-history theory (Stearns, 1976) predicts that animals set their reproductive effort on each breeding occasion at a level (optimum clutch size) such that the expected lifetime reproductive success of the individual in question is maximized. This is a more precise way of formulating Lack's (1954, 1966, 1968) notion that birds lay a clutch that maximizes the number of offspring that survive to breed, although Lack omitted the costs of reproduction that may decrease the optimum clutch size if there is any reduction in future survival of the female with increasing brood size (Charnov and Krebs, 1974).

Clutch Size and Reproductive Success

Lack (1947, 1954, 1966) expected that the modal clutch size in a population should be the most productive one in terms of number of offspring recruited to the breeding population. Von Haartman (1951a, 1967b) tested this idea on the Pied Flycatcher, and found that the larger the clutch size, the more fledglings were produced. The same pattern is also very obvious in our data from Uppsala (Alatalo and Lundberg, 1989) and Cumbria (Fig. 37). Numerous other studies have confirmed that in altricial birds the clutch size producing the largest number of fledglings is larger than the modal clutch size (for a review see Murphy and Haukioja, 1986).

One factor contributing to this discrepancy is the difficulty in most bird populations of measuring the true number of offspring surviving to breed. One can easily imagine that numbers of offspring produced do not closely reflect numbers of offspring recruited, if offspring quality is lower in larger broods or if brood-size-dependent mortality occurs after fledging. Von Haartman (1954) found a tendency for fledging weights to be higher in smaller broods, and in Great Tits offspring survival increases with fledging weight (Perrins, 1979). This was also the case in Collared Flycatchers breeding on the island of Gotland (Alatalo et al., 1990b), where offspring weighing less than 13 g at fledging were hardly ever recruited to the breeding population (Lars Gustafsson, pers. comm., see also Alatalo and Lundberg, 1989). In Pied Flycatchers similar data are much more difficult to collect, at least in Fennoscandia, because of the extensive natal dispersal. The few offspring from our study areas at Uppsala and on Gotland which were recaptured after two months or later, had a higher average fledging

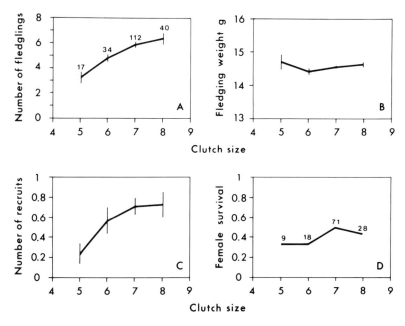

Fig. 37. Reproductive success and female survival plotted against the natural variation in clutch size. Data from Cumbria, England 1986–9. (A) Number of fledged young against clutch size (regression equation = 0.99 × clutch size − 1.20, P < 0.001). Sample sizes for A–C are given above the standard error bars in A. (B) Weight of offspring at 13 days of age did not vary significantly with brood size (P < 0.20). (C) Number of recruits increased with brood size (regression equation = 0.15 × clutch size − 0.38, P < 0.05). (D) Female survival rate did not vary significantly with brood size (logistic regression, P > 0.50, sample sizes indicated by numbers).

weight than the average fledging weight of all the offspring (Alatalo and Lundberg, 1989). However, the extensive data from Cumbria does confirm that in the Pied Flycatcher the offspring of less than 13 g do not survive to breed (Fig. 52).

Von Haartman (1967b) and Curio (1960b) found that among the few offspring that returned to breed in their study areas, the probability of returning was independent of brood size. In Uppsala the weight of offspring was not significantly related to clutch size (Alatalo and Lundberg, 1989; for Cumbria see Fig. 37B). It is possible to estimate indirectly the relative number of recruits on the basis of offspring weight and the relationship between weight and survival to breeding age using data from the Collared Flycatcher (see Alatalo and Lundberg, 1989). In spite of such indirect adjustments to approach the true reproductive success of Pied Flycatcher parents, there is a quite linear increase in the breeding outcome against the clutch size. In Cumbria we could directly estimate the recruiting success since nearly all the surviving offspring return to the study areas. Again, the number of recruits increased linearly with clutch size, although it seems that clutches of eight were no more successful than clutches of seven eggs (Fig. 37C). Survival rate of breeding females did not vary significantly with clutch size (Fig. 37D), suggesting that costs of reproduction were not higher for the females laying the largest clutches.

CLUTCH-SIZE MANIPULATIONS

The main problem with non-experimental studies is that all factors other than clutch size are assumed to be identical for all nests. This is obviously not the case, since environmental conditions and the condition of individual birds may vary greatly, affecting the potential of raising a brood of any given size (Högstedt, 1980). There is no single optimal clutch size for a population – rather the optimum is higher for individuals breeding under good conditions and lower if the conditions are poor. For instance, among flycatchers, early breeding birds are likely to have access to a richer food supply and hence may have a higher optimal clutch size as compared to late breeding birds.

Thus, experiments are needed to test whether individuals do in fact optimize their clutch size. This is easily done in species where brood size is mainly limited by the capacity of parents to feed nestlings. In Uppsala we manipulated brood size in a Pied Flycatcher population in two years by transferring one or two newly hatched young to another nest with offspring of a similar age (Alatalo and Lundberg, 1989). In control nests two young were switched between nests. The number of fledged young increased with the experimental increase in brood size, but these broods with extra young clearly suffered in that the offspring were of relatively low fledging weight (Fig. 38). Consequently, the estimated number of recruits only increased from reduced broods to the control broods, while broods with extra young did not produce more offspring likely to be recruited. It seems, therefore, that individuals optimize their clutch size with respect to their capacity to feed nestlings. Askenmo (1977b) and Källander and Smith (1990) have similarly manipulated brood sizes of Pied Flycatchers, and their results support the idea that parents are not able to increase their feeding capacity to match the needs of enlarged broods. In the Collared Flycatcher (Gustafsson and Sutherland, 1988), Magpie (Högstedt, 1980) and Great Tit (Pettifor et al., 1988), the direct measurement of offspring survival led to the conclusion that individuals optimize their clutch size to maximize the number of young they can feed successfully.

We did not find any evidence that the cost of reproduction in terms of reduced adult survival would constrain clutch size (Table 7), although in many other studies cost of reproduction in some form has been suggested (Lindén and Møller, 1989). Our data, however, are too few to detect any slight differences in adult survival since, because of dispersal, we could recapture only a proportion of the surviving adults. Once again we see that only experimental data can be used to check the cost of reproduction, since, if looking at natural variation, birds with

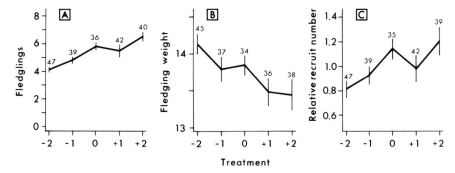

Fig. 38. *Reproductive success in manipulated Pied Flycatcher broods in 1983–4 at Uppsala (redrawn from Alatalo and Lundberg, 1989). A positive treatment indicates that one or two extra young were added to the nest while a negative treatment means that the same number of young were removed. In control nests we swapped one or two young between nests, thus keeping the brood size the same. Sample sizes are given above each standard error bar. (A) Number of fledglings increased with the size of treatment* $(r_s = 0.48, P < 0.001)$; *(B) the weight at fledging became reduced with treatment* $(r_s = -0.21, P < 0.01)$; *(C) the estimate of relative number of recruited offspring, based on fledging weight, increased with treatment* $(r_s = 0.25, P < 0.01)$, *but the estimate was not higher for broods with extra young compared with the control clutches (U-test,* $z = 0.29, P > 0.70$).

good breeding prospects will be the ones laying large clutches, and in addition parental survival may be improved by a more favourable environment (see Högstedt, 1981; Murphy and Haukioja, 1986).

Some indications of reproductive costs have been obtained for the Collared Flycatcher (Gustafsson and Sutherland, 1988). In the Pied Flycatcher Askenmo (1979) found a reduction in male survival after the brood size had been increased

Table 7. *Rates of return in the following year for parents of differently treated broods in a clutch-size manipulation experiment where we added (+) or removed (−) young (data from Alatalo and Lundberg, 1989).*

Treatment	Returned (%)	n	Chi-square test
Males			
−2	18.2	44	
−1	17.2	29	$\chi^2 = 1.04$
0	20.0	35	$P > 0.90$
+1	13.9	36	
+2	22.9	35	
Females			
−2 or −1	7.6	79	
0	7.9	38	$\chi^2 = 0.96$
+1 or +2	6.6	76	$P > 0.95$

to nine eggs. However, such a radical increase in brood size may not be relevant to the question of whether costs of reproduction really limit clutch size. For the cost to be relevant, one should be able to detect an effect by an increase of only one young. At the moment it seems that in small passerines, like the Pied Flycatcher, it is just the capacity of parents to feed nestlings that limits the clutch size. This is not to say that laying, incubation, and costs of reproduction are totally without influence. Rather, we believe that feeding of nestlings is the major determinant of clutch size, and the only one that is measurable in the Pied Flycatcher. In fact, there are indications that costs of incubation might have some effect, since experimentally enlarged clutches took one day longer to incubate than control or reduced clutches (Moreno and Carlson, 1989).

While arguing that flycatchers are able to optimize their clutch size, one should recall that optimization is possible only with respect to factors that are predictable by females at the time of laying. For example, an average reduction in food availability for nestlings over the breeding season might be a predictable factor. However, weather conditions during the nestling period are likely to have even more dramatic effects on the chances of raising a brood of a given size, but future weather is not predictable at the time of laying. We made our clutch-manipulation experiment in the summers of 1983 and 1984, and there was a clear difference in weather conditions between the two years. The average clutch sizes were practically the same in both years (1983: 6.82 eggs and 1984: 6.78 eggs) but the breeding success was much lower in 1984 (Fig. 39). Of the nine days when the majority of the nestlings were 10–13 days old, eight were rainy in 1984 compared to only one in 1983. It seems that in a good summer birds could actually raise larger broods than they do.

Low predictability of feeding conditions may allow some heritability to be

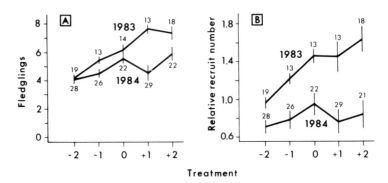

Fig. 39.   *Reproductive success in manipulated broods (see Fig. 38 for method) at Uppsala during two breeding seasons. (A) Number of fledglings (1983: $r_s = 0.74$, P < 0.001; 1984: $r_s = 0.32$, P < 0.001); (B) estimate of the relative number of recruited offspring based on fledging weight (1983: $r_s = 0.62$, P < 0.001; 1984: $r_s = 0.06$, P > 0.10). From Alatalo and Lundberg (1989).*

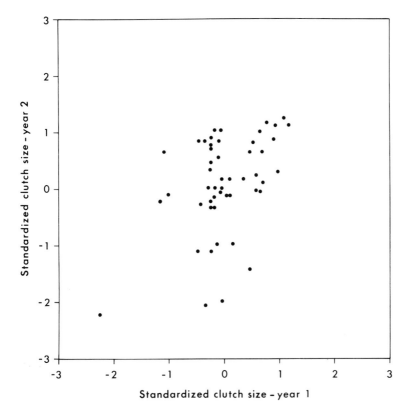

Fig. 40.   *The correlation of clutch size in individual females from one year to the next in Cumbria, England 1985–9. Clutch sizes have been standardized as deviations from the regression against laying date in the pooled data (see Fig. 34). The correlation is* r = 0.45 *(*n = 53, *P < 0.001).*

retained for clutch size, as has been demonstrated for the Great Tit (Noordwijk *et al.*, 1981). In the Collared Flycatcher the heritability of clutch size, estimated by mother–offspring resemblance, was 0.32 (Gustafsson, 1986). A similar heritability value may also be true for the Pied Flycatcher, since in the Uppsala data there is quite a high correlation of clutch size from year to year in the same female (*r* = 0.48, *n* = 48, *P* < 0.001, Alatalo and Lundberg, 1989). In the Cumbrian data the correlation is equally high (Fig. 40). There, we also have some data on mothers and their offspring (Fig. 41), which suggests there is little if any heritability for clutch size. However, the heritability estimate of 0.06 has a standard error of 0.20, indicating that before sampling a larger data set we cannot exclude the possibility of a mother–offspring resemblance that is as high as it is in the Collared Flycatcher.

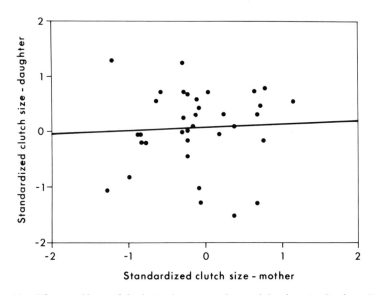

Fig. 41.   *The resemblance of clutch size between mothers and daughters in Cumbria, England. Clutch sizes have been standardized for laying date (see Fig. 40). The heritability estimate based on the mother–daughter regression is* $h^2 = 0.06$, $SE = 0.20$, $n = 35$, $P > 0.70$).

SUMMARY

Pied Flycatchers have a short breeding season with only one brood. The breeding success decreases rapidly with the progress of the spring, presumably because of a decline in food supply for nestlings. The timing of breeding is likely to be partly constrained by the capacity of females to lay early and partly explicable by the need to match the nestling period with the time in the summer when caterpillars are most abundant. The start of laying in the spring typically occurs about five days after the weather has turned favourable. The five-day lag corresponds well to the length of time needed for the final rapid growth of oocytes. On average, yearlings start laying a few days later than older females. From year to year each female tends to start at the same time in relation to other females, and there also is a resemblance in the laying dates of mothers and their daughters.

Clutch size does not vary with latitude, but it clearly reduces with increase in altitude, and it is somewhat lower in coniferous than in deciduous forests. Seasonal decline in clutch size seems to be due to the reduced possibility of producing recruits later in the summer. Female condition (age, size, weight) has an effect on clutch size. In general, larger clutches are more successful in producing recruits and there is no reduction in female survival with clutch size.

Experimental manipulations indicate that females tend to optimize their clutch size with respect to the possibilities of successfully feeding the young in the nest. Weather conditions during the nestling period have a clear effect on the chances of feeding the brood, but they are unpredictable at the time of laying, and this constrains the task of optimizing the clutch size.

CHAPTER 7

Egg-Laying, Incubation and Caring for Young

In Chapter 6 we asked why Pied Flycatchers lay a certain number of eggs. Here we will continue on the same theme, but give more detailed information on the behaviour of parents from the onset of incubation until the young leave the nest. We especially focus on the different roles of males and females during the various stages. Some Pied Flycatcher males are polygynous, having two (or three) females in separate distant territories (see Chapter 12) and therefore we also give information on parental investment and reproductive output in nests of different mating status. Thus, this chapter considers how parents should behave during the raising of offspring, given a clutch of a certain size, to optimize their reproductive success.

EGG-LAYING AND EGG SIZE

Each morning the female Pied Flycatcher lays one egg, which is light blue in colour. The exact timing of laying was followed in 13 clutches by Creutz (1955) in Germany, and he found that most eggs were laid between 05.30 and 07.00 hours. No eggs were laid after 8 a.m. After laying, the female stays in the nest for up to half an hour, but then very rarely visits the nest-hole during the rest of the day. However, she may spend the night in the nest (see below).

Egg size and composition have been studied in detail in northern Finland by Ojanen (1983). He found the mean length and breadth to be 17.8 and 13.4 mm, respectively, and by comparing different studies he further found very little geographical variation over Europe (volume was 1.56 cm^3). Ojanen also looked for a correlation between egg size and other traits. He found little or no correlation with clutch size, only a very weak correlation with female size, and a minimal effect of year. The only significant effect found was that egg size increased with laying sequence, though this effect was only present in large and early clutches, not in small or late clutches. This size increase was mainly due to the inclusion of water in the egg. Egg size was also affected by the temperature about one week before laying, so that in warmer weather conditions egg volume increased. This effect probably occurs because increasing ambient temperatures positively influence insect abundance, and thereby nutrition of the female. Most of Ojanen's findings were corroborated by a study in Finnish Lapland, though there it was found that during a very cold year egg size decreased with laying sequence. Also, at this high latitude larger females laid larger eggs which, in turn, produced more nestlings. This was mainly due to a greater hatching failure among small eggs, which may more easily become chilled during cold spells (Järvinen and Väisänen, 1983; Ylimaunu and Järvinen, 1987).

INCUBATION AND HATCHING

INCUBATION

Incubating birds regulate their eggs by direct heating. In the Pied Flycatcher the body temperature ranges between about 39.5°C and 42.5°C (Haftorn and Reinertsen, 1990), and incubating females can increase their body temperature so as to compensate for heat loss from the eggs to the nesting material at times of falling temperatures. This leads to relatively stable egg temperature levels during periods of fluctuating ambient temperatures. Another method of regulating egg temperature is through changes in nest attentiveness. Incubation in the Pied Flycatcher is done by the female alone and it normally starts when the last egg is laid. In more detail, the female actually starts incubation by gradually spending more and more time on the eggs during the period of laying. For example, Winkel and Winkel (1974) found that 25% of females spend the night on the nest prior to laying the third egg while 82% do so prior to the fifth egg. Full incubation normally begins when the last egg is laid (Haftorn and Ytreberg, 1988). However, in a few clutches full incubation can be postponed a few days; the above mentioned authors found one clutch that hatched after the female had waited six days before starting incubation. For further information on hatching success see a later section in this chapter (pp. 95–96).

The length of the incubation period is about 13–16 days, mainly depending on time of season, clutch size and weather conditions. At Lemsjöholm, in south-western Finland, von Haartman (1956b, 1969) found the incubation period for clutches completed in May to be on average 14.65 days and for clutches completed in June to be 13.98 days, the shortest incubation time observed being 12.25 days. Von Haartman measured the incubation length as the time period between completion of the clutch and hatching of half of the eggs. In a study at Trondheim in Norway, Slagsvold (1986b) found the duration of incubation to be 14–15 days for early clutches and about 13 days for late clutches (min.: 12, max.: 18 days) by measuring the time from the laying of the last egg to the time the last egg hatched. By defining the incubation period as the time between completion of the clutch (day 1 being the day the last egg was laid) and the first signs of hatching, Moreno and Carlson (1989) found the length of incubation to be on average 14.7 days near Uppsala, central Sweden. Using a similar definition of incubation length, Meidell (1961) estimated it to be 14.2 days in southwest Norway. Based on studies near Berlin in Germany, Curio (1959b) stated that the incubation lasted for 13–14 days with a range of 11.5–18 days. Järvinen (1990) compiled data on incubation length from seven sites in Europe, and found the mean period to range from 13.9 to 14.7 days, suggesting that, as a good rule of thumb, incubation normally lasts for 14 days.

Moreno and Carlson (1989) found, by manipulating clutch size, that enlarged clutches took about one day longer to incubate while reduced clutches hatched only slightly earlier than unmanipulated clutches. Furthermore, as in von Haartman's (1956b) and Slagsvold's (1986b) studies, late clutches were incubated for a shorter time than early ones. The reason why early clutches take longer to hatch could, in part, be that they are larger than late clutches. It is also possible that early breeding females delay the start of full incubation or that late breeders incubate their eggs more efficiently than early birds. Haftorn and Reinertsen (1990) found that one female, during bad weather conditions, left the nest for eight hours. The eggs nevertheless hatched successfully though hatching was clearly behind schedule. If the eggs are infertile or do not hatch for some other reason, the female may sit on the eggs for up to 20 days before abandoning the breeding attempt (Haftorn and Ytreberg, 1988).

On average, in Norway, Pied Flycatcher females spend about 75% of the active part of the day incubating the eggs (Haftorn and Ytreberg, 1988). The active day during incubation typically lasts for about 16.5 to 17.5 hours when females spend short periods of time both inside and outside the nest, while during the night they are resting inside the nest-hole. Haftorn and Ytreberg (1988) found that in southern Norway (*c.* 59°N) the active day started on average about 03.00

while in central Norway (*c.* 63°N) it started half an hour later. In northern Sweden (*c.* 66°N) the active day started at about 04.00 (Lennerstedt, 1969). According to these studies the active day of incubating females ended around 20.30 at both sites in Norway, while in northern Sweden females were active until half an hour later. Thus, start, end and length of the female's active day during incubation is very similar at different latitudes despite the longer day-length in the north at this time of the year. At both Norwegian sites female activity started after sunrise (a mean of 16 min after at 59°N and 96 min at 63°N) while it ended before sunset (64 min and 130 min, respectively), which was also the case at the site in northern Sweden where the sun is below the horizon for only about one hour during the incubation period of the Pied Flycatcher.

Mean periods on the nest in Norway ranged between 8 and 23 minutes (overall mean = 15.8 min), while periods off the nest lasted 4–8 minutes (overall mean = 4.8 min; Haftorn and Ytreberg, 1988). According to Curio (1959b) a Pied Flycatcher female in Germany typically incubates for about 12 and then leaves for about 5 minutes. By using artificial eggs Lennerstedt (1969) found that during active incubation the temperature in the egg is about 34°C and during periods when the bird is off it may drop to about 26°C, but seldom lower. By using real eggs and a thermistor placed about 1 mm beneath the upper surface of an egg, Haftorn (1988) found the mean maximum temperature during incubation to be 37.7°C while the mean minimum temperature during periods off was 31.8°C. The lowest and highest egg temperatures recorded were 15.7 and 41.3°C, respectively. The temperature below which no embryonic development takes place at all is believed to be about 25–27°C, and in the domestic fowl no embryos survived continuous incubation above 40.5°C or below 35°C (see Haftorn, 1988 and references therein). In relation to ambient temperature, the Norwegian study by Haftorn and Ytreberg found that periods on the nest decreased with increasing air temperature, the average decrease being 0.8 min for each degree rise in air temperature; mean length of periods on was 24 min at 6°C but only 9 min at 26°C. Increasing air temperatures, however, had a much smaller effect on periods off the nest: an increase in temperature of 20 degrees only increased the length of periods off from 4.3 min to 5.9 min, i.e. by about 0.1 min for each degree increase. These findings are in accordance with what von Haartman (1956b) found when he regulated the temperature inside a nest box with a thermostat. In that experiment periods on became shorter while periods off showed no change as nest temperature increased. As with periods on the nest, the proportion of the active day spent on incubation decreased in the Norwegian study with increasing air temperature, from an average of 80% at 6–7°C to 65% at 20–22°C. Nest attentiveness was lowest at noon, in both cold and warm weather (Haftorn and Ytreberg, 1988). Similar results were obtained by Haftorn and Reinertsen (1990) in a study in Norway. They manipulated two nest boxes so that one could be cooled and the other heated. They found that if the box was heated during the female's absence, she departed again after only a few minutes of incubation, while if the box was cooled she clearly lengthened the periods on the nest. Thus, most variation in incubation attentiveness was due to the length of the periods on the nest. Likewise, during nightly incubation the female reduced her metabolic rate if the nest was warmed whereas metabolic rate was increased if nest-box temperature was lowered. Based on nest watches in Germany, Curio (1959b) came to the opposite conclusion to that found in Norway, namely that periods off increased with temperature while periods on showed no change.

During the course of the breeding season, there are clear changes in the weight of females, while male weights change little. From arrival until the start of nest-building females typically lose weight (Silverin, 1981), but during the pre-laying period they become very heavy (16–17 g), being close to or above weights recorded at resting places during autumn migration. This weight increase is mainly due to gonadal growth and egg production. From the start of laying female body weight steadily decreases until the early incubation phase when the female again puts on weight. Mass losses during incubation are related to the size of the clutch so that females incubating large clutches lose more mass than females incubating small clutches (Moreno and Carlson, 1989). After hatching

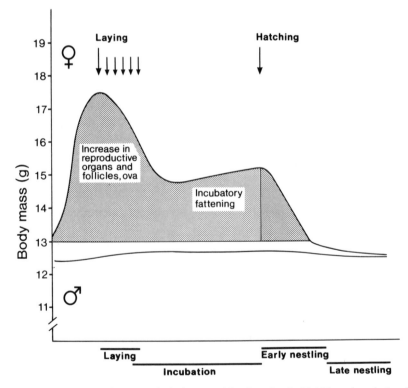

Fig. 42. *Approximate changes in the body mass of female and male Pied Flycatchers during the breeding season.*

the weight rapidly drops to the pre-breeding level, the same as that of males (Fig. 42). At the end of the incubation period the reproductive organs are almost totally atrophied, and the observed mass increase during the later part of incubation is due to storage of fat. Incubating females quite often leave the nest for foraging, and they are also sometimes fed by the male (see Chapter 5). Several hypotheses have been put forward to explain the observed weight changes in breeding females but they will not be treated here (for a detailed account, see Moreno, 1989). That incubation is indeed costly for females was demonstrated by Moreno and Carlson (1989). They injected females with doubly labelled water (D_2O^{18}), which is a method to measure the daily expenditure of energy. The mean metabolic intensity of incubating females was 3.25 times the basal metabolic rate (BMR), which is quite close to the maximum sustained working level of 4 BMR proposed by Drent and Daan (1980).

HATCHING

Hatching of the eggs occurs over a short period of time (i.e. rather synchronously; von Haartman, 1954, 1969). In general, the hatching order follows the laying sequence though there is much variation. Thus, for example, among eight clutches followed in detail by Creutz (1955), the first egg laid hatched first in only one clutch whereas in another clutch the last egg hatched first. Ylimaunu and Järvinen (1987) studied the laying order and hatching sequence of clutches for three seasons in the extreme north of Finnish Lapland. In two of the years, when temperatures were normal, the final egg hatched, on average, 14 and 19 hours after the median-hatched egg, and egg size increased with laying sequence. The authors suggested that the late hatching of the final egg was mainly due to females starting to sit on the eggs before laying was completed. In a cold year, however, they found the last egg laid to hatch 5 hours before the hatching of the median egg. In this year also egg size decreased with laying sequence, so the earlier hatching of the last egg might have been due to small eggs taking less time to incubate. By calculating the difference in weight between the heaviest and lightest nestling during the first days after hatching, Slagsvold (1986b) estimated the hatching spread in 120 nests and found it to be on average 1.25 days. Another method was used by Enemar and Arheimer (1989) who transilluminated eggs from 16 clutches in a mountain birch forest. They found considerable variation in developmental asynchrony between clutches, ranging from less than 0.5 day up to 1.5 days. A rather similar figure for hatching spread (23 hours; with a range of 12 to 36 hours) was obtained by inspecting nests ($n = 8$) every four hours from the day before estimated hatching until the last egg hatched (Karin Olsson, pers. comm.). The maximum recorded hatching spread is 5 days (Creutz, 1955). In Slagsvold's (1986b) study he further found that the eggs hatched over a longer time period in larger than in smaller clutches, over a shorter period if clutches were laid early rather than late, and over a longer period if the air temperature was high just before laying. The findings that hatching asynchrony increases with laying date and with clutch size were supported by the clutch-size manipulations performed by Moreno and Carlson (1989) near Uppsala in Sweden.

When Slagsvold (1986b) experimentally changed the hatching spread by transferring eggs or young between nests, he found that clutches that were made more asynchronous than normally found in nature produced fewer fledglings. Among surviving offspring, however, fledglings in nests with a large hatching spread were heavier than those in nests with a small hatching spread. Heavy fledglings have better chances of surviving until first reproduction than light ones (see also below), so in that respect asynchronously hatched fledglings were better off. In another similar experiment performed by Lars Hillström and Karin Olsson (pers. comm.) in Sweden, clutches were made synchronous or asynchronous, and were compared with unmanipulated control clutches. In this case all eggs were removed once they were laid and were replaced by clay dummy eggs of the same shape and colour; the real eggs were stored in a refrigerator at 12°C. When incubation of the dummy eggs started these were removed and all the original eggs were put back at the same time to form a synchronous clutch. To form asynchronous broods all but two eggs were put back in the nest when the female started to incubate. Of these two eggs, one was put back one day later and the other two days later.

The result of this experiment was, in short, that broods that were made synchronous produced offspring in significantly greater numbers and with longer tarsi than did asynchronous broods. There was also a tendency for higher weight in synchronous broods. Synchronous broods also produced more fledglings than natural control broods (significantly so in one of the two years), whereas control broods produced young with longer tarsi than asynchronous broods. Late hatched nestlings in asynchronous broods left the nest with shorter tarsi and of lower weight than their siblings. Similarly, when Ylimaunu and Järvinen (1987) studied the growth of nestlings that hatched one day behind the rest of the brood, they found that growth was retarded. These late hatched nestlings had significantly shorter wings and lower weight than their siblings throughout the whole nestling period, which probably led to reduced rates of survival. The results from the above studies suggest that asynchronous hatching in itself is not adaptive since nestling survival becomes reduced as hatching spread increases. Also, completely synchronous broods seem to do better than either natural or slightly asynchronous broods. This prompts us to ask why Pied Flycatchers do not hatch their eggs even more synchronously than they do. Perhaps the observed hatching spread is only an inevitable consequence of females sitting on the nest every morning during egg laying (and sometimes also during the night), thereby causing embryo development to start before laying is finished. However, it has also been argued that asynchronous hatching could be adaptive, allowing brood reduction, in the Pied Flycatcher, for example by Slagsvold and Lifjeld (1989a, 1989b). They suggested that Pied Flycatcher females, by increasing the length of the hatching period, could 'manipulate' the male to increase his share in parental duties.

HATCHING SUCCESS

Very few eggs in Pied Flycatcher nests fail to hatch. Among 840 clutches in our study areas around Uppsala we found that 7% of the eggs were lost due to hatching failure. In 19 clutches no eggs hatched at all, in most cases probably because of the death of the female. If these clutches are excluded hatching failure becomes 5%. We found approximately the same proportion of unhatched eggs, 4.0% ($n = 75$ clutches), among Pied Flycatchers breeding on the islands of Gotland and Öland in the Baltic (Alatalo *et al.*, 1990c).

Similar figures are also reported from other studies and other countries: 4.5% ($n = 1795$ clutches) just north of our study areas (Johansson, 1977), 5.8% ($n = 916$ eggs) at Lemsjöholm in southwest Finland (von Haartman, 1951a), 5.9% ($n = 290$ eggs) in southwest Norway (Meidell, 1961), and 5.0% ($n = 237$ clutches) at Trondheim in Norway (Slagsvold, 1986b). Lars Hillström (pers. comm.) removed eggs just after laying (at Uppsala) and kept them in a refrigerator until the start of incubation when they were returned (the real eggs having been replaced by dummies during laying); he found hatching failure to be about 7%. In yet another experiment Hillström kept Pied Flycatcher eggs refrigerated for three, six and twelve days respectively, and then put them back into the nests. He recorded hatching failure for each treatment, and found it to be 7%, 7% and 3% respectively, which could be compared with 7% hatching

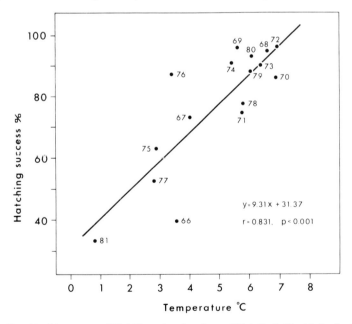

Fig. 43.   Hatching success of Pied Flycatchers breeding at Kilpisjärvi, Finnish Lapland, in 1966–81 in relation to the minimum air temperature during the 15-day period after the laying of the last egg in the population. Redrawn from Järvinen (1983).

failure for control nests. Higher proportions of unhatched eggs have been reported from a study near Berlin in Germany (21.8%, $n = 883$; Curio, 1959c). Rather high proportions of unhatched eggs have also been found in subalpine birch forest in Swedish (66°N) (Svensson, 1987) and Finnish Lapland (69°N) (Jarvinen, 1980): 12.7% and 19.1% respectively. Järvinen attributed the great losses at these high latitudes to the frequent occurrence of cold spells. That hatching failure is indeed correlated with temperature was shown by Järvinen (1983) who compared hatching success with minimum air temperature over a period of 16 years in northern Finnish Lapland (Fig. 43).

In Finnish Lapland it was further found that hatching failure was related to the laying order of the eggs, with late eggs failing more often than early. In fact, only about 35% of seventh and eighth eggs hatched, though most of them contained live embryos up to near the end of incubation (Ylimaunu and Järvinen, 1987).

NESTLING GROWTH AND TIME SPENT IN THE NEST

The young are naked and blind at hatching, and weigh only about 1.5 g. However, growth is rapid and the young add 1–1.5 g each day until they are

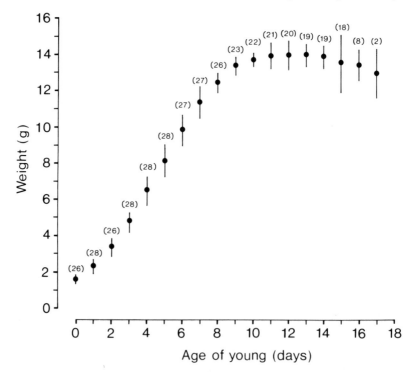

Fig. 44.   Pattern of weight increase in Pied Flycatcher broods during the nestling stage. Data from L. Hillström (pers. comm.). Figures given in parentheses show numbers of clutches weighed.

around 10 days old, when weight increase levels off. There might even be a slight weight reduction close to fledging (Fig. 44; von Haartman, 1954). At about five days after hatching the first body feathers become visible on the back, and on the following day the eyes start opening. When the nestlings are about nine days old the sheaths on the primaries and secondaries break and the vanes become visible and soon begin to grow rapidly. At fledging the total wing length is about 60 mm, compared with 75–80 mm for adults.

Von Haartman reported the mean length of the nestling period to be 16 days in southwest Finland while in northern Finland the mean nestling periods for three years were 14.5, 15.1 and 15.6 days respectively (Järvinen and Ylimaunu, 1986). In Germany, Curio (1959b) estimated the nestling period to average 14.6 days with a range of 11 to 18 days. In a literature compilation from different European study sites, Järvinen (1990) found the mean nestling period to vary between 14.7 and 16.0 days. Nestlings leave the nest rather synchronously, but during the period of nest leaving, according to Curio (1959b), the male takes care of those nestlings that have left while the female feeds those that are still in the nest. The family only stays in the vicinity of the nest for a few hours after the last nestling has left, and it splits up after 8 days or so (Curio, 1959b).

CARING FOR THE YOUNG

Both the male and the female help to feed the nestlings, but the amount of care varies with the age of the young and the pairing status of the female (Fig. 45, see also Chapter 12). When nestlings are small, up to about 3–5 days old, the female spends a considerable amount of time inside the nest-hole keeping the young warm. According to our observations females spend on average 23 min/h on the nest when the nestlings are only 2–3 days (Alatalo et al., 1982c) while Curio (1959b) found females spending as much time brooding small young (76% of daylight) as they spent on incubation (70%). However, time spent brooding is probably influenced by the ambient temperature, and the female seems to stay shorter periods on the young when the temperature is high than when it is low (Curio, 1959b). During this early nestling phase, the male Pied Flycatcher provides most of the food brought to the nest. In nests with four small young we found the female delivered food about four times an hour while the male fed at twice that rate. In broods of eight small young both parents approximately doubled their contribution as compared to broods of half that size, to 9 and 16 food deliveries per hour, respectively (Alatalo et al., 1982c). Von Haartman (1954) in Finland and Lifjeld and Slagsvold (1989a) in Norway also found positive correlations between brood size and feeding rates in nests of monogamous pairs; more food was delivered to larger broods than small.

When nestlings grow older, parents and, in particular, females increase their feeding rates, either putting the sexes on a par with respect to food delivery rates or leaving the female working slightly harder than the male. When the nestlings are 7–8 days old, the parents typically feed the nestlings about 14–19 times an

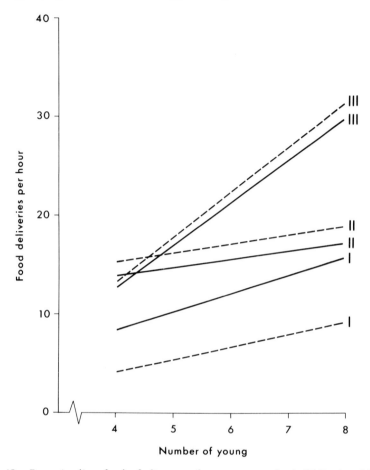

Fig. 45.   Regression lines for the feeding rate of monogamous males (solid lines) and females (broken lines) with different number of young at different nestling stages (I = 2–3 days old, II = 7–8 days old, and III = 12–13 days old). Redrawn from Alatalo et al. (1982c).

hour each. Close to fledging, in monogamous pairs, we recorded males feeding on average 19.4 times an hour ($n = 66$) and females 19.8 ($n = 67$) (Alatalo et al., 1988c). In the same study we further found that males bring slightly fewer but heavier loads. Correcting for delivery rates revealed that males and females brought almost the same food quantity per hour to the nest: 304 and 296 mg dry weight, respectively. These figures on feeding rates are similar to those found in the Norwegian study cited above, in which males and females in monogamous nests both fed the nestlings at a rate of about 14 visits per hour when nestlings were 5 days old and about 22 times an hour at 13 days of age. A similar increase in feeding rates with nestling age has been documented by von Haartman (1954).

He used both direct observations and automatic recordings, and found that the combined effort of males and females increased rather linearly from about 15 feedings an hour at a nestling age of 1 day to a peak of about 30 feedings an hour at the age of 9–11 days. After that feeding frequencies stayed rather constant. In Finnish Lapland the number of feeds to a nest in a day was around 190 when nestlings were 1–5 days old, increased to about 370 at day 6, and thereafter levelled off (Hannila and Järvinen, 1987). This maximum feeding rate approximately corresponds to an hourly feeding frequency of 19, which is about half the frequency found further south. The reasons for this lower feeding activity in the far north are unknown but can possibly be partly related to smaller brood sizes (mean = 5.3). It could also be because parents are able to collect larger prey items in the north than in the south.

Von Haartman (1954) followed the feeding of young throughout the day and showed that feeding of nestlings (at 60°30′N) started between 02.00 and 03.00 and ceased between 21.00 and 22.00. From about 04.00 the feeding rate was rather constant over the day, which agrees with our findings from Uppsala (Alatalo *et al.*, 1982c). Based on his daily observations of nestling feeding, von Haartman (1954) estimated the average length of a 'working day' for Pied Flycatchers to be around 19 hours. This estimate is supported by data collected by the Swedish explorer Sten Bergman who in 1934 recorded each feeding by the male and female Pied Flycatcher at a nest close to his home outside Stockholm. The male started feeding at 02.17 and ended at 21.16 while the female started at 02.23 and ended at 21.24, which gives a working day of almost exactly 19 hours.

The diurnal rhythm of nestling feeding has also been recorded from sites at different latitudes. In the south, in Germany, Creutz (1955), Curio (1959b) and Pfeifer and Keil (1962) found the average working day for a Pied Flycatcher pair to be about 17 hours in central Europe, i.e. two hours shorter than in von Haartman's study mentioned above. At Ammarnäs in Swedish Lapland, at 66°N, Lennerstedt (1969, 1987) in two separate studies found the night rest to be 4.0–4.5 and 5.5 hours, respectively, giving a working day of 18.5–20 hours, with no specific peak of activity during the day. In both study years the parents started feeding nestlings around 03.00, and in the first year (1965) the parents did not cease until between 23.00 and midnight while in the other study year (1984) they stopped on average at about 21.30. Going even further north, to Kilpisjärvi in Finnish Lapland (69°N), Hannila and Järvinen (1987) found the working day for females to be about 19.5 hours, and for males 18.5 hours; both parents were resting at the same time, so the nestlings were unattended for about 4.5 hours. The parents stopped feeding just after midnight and started again at about 05.00, slightly later than found in studies further south. The authors also found feeding activity to peak in the afternoon. As in other studies cited earlier in this chapter there was an increase in feeding rate as the brood grew older.★ To summarize, there seems to be little or no change towards longer working days with increasing

★ Local times at the date of the studies are used throughout. Daylight savings time was introduced in Scandinavia in 1980.

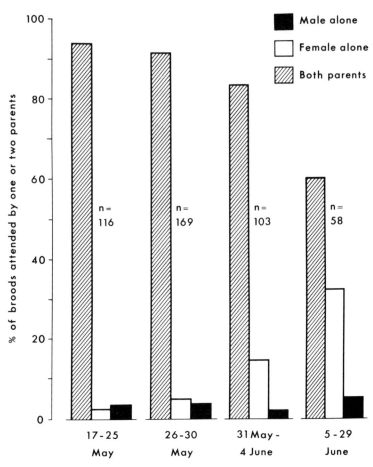

Fig. 46.   Percentages of Pied Flycatcher broods attended by males and females or both over the breeding season. Based on von Haartman (1969).

day-length from about 60°N northwards. In Germany, however, the parents seem to be active about two hours less than in Scandinavia.

Not all broods are attended by two parents, and this is especially the case among late broods. Von Haartman (1969) found that among early clutches, most had two parents feeding the young and very few were fed by only one parent. However, as the season progressed, more and more broods were raised by single parents, in most cases by the female. Only between 2% and 5% of the nests were attended by single males (Fig. 46). It was suggested by von Haartman that most of these late clutches fed by a lone female were secondary nests of males mated with more than one female (see also Chapter 12), because polygynous males seem to give priority to the first (primary) female. Indeed, secondary nests of

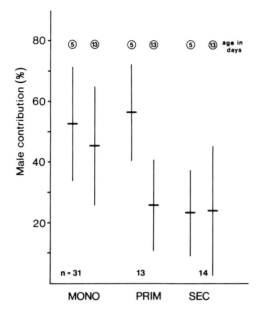

Fig. 47.   *Male contribution to the feeding rate of Pied Flycatcher nestlings in monogamous, primary and secondary nests when nestlings are 5 and 13 days old. Only males whose status was identified from colour rings are included. Horizontal lines indicate means and vertical bars standard deviations. Data from Uppsala, Sweden, 1980 and 1983, and Konnevesi, Finland, 1988. From Alatalo and Lundberg (1990).*

polygynous males are mainly found among clutches laid late (Chapter 12), and the male contribution to feeding young is clearly reduced in secondary nests (Fig. 47). This division of labour between nests among polygynous males was examined in more detail in a study by Lifjeld and Slagsvold (1989a). They found that primary females received more male assistance than did secondary females. They further found that male assistance at secondary nests was less in a year with unfavourable weather conditions than in a year with better weather, that male assistance at secondary nests increased when the hatching interval between the primary and secondary broods was short, and that males tended to give less aid to secondary nests that were located far from the nest of the primary female. This study was followed up by an experimental one (Lifjeld and Slagsvold, 1990) where they reversed the hatching order of primary and secondary broods; later they swapped the broods to change the age of the young in each nest. In a third experiment they made primary and secondary clutches hatch on the same day. It was then found that males mainly allocated their feeding efforts to the brood that hatched first, but if the young later became exchanged they reallocated their efforts and gave priority to the clutch with the oldest nestlings. When primary and secondary clutches were made to hatch at the same time, males only showed a slight preference for the brood of the primary female though this preference became more pronounced with increasing distance between the two nests. Probably travel costs for the male increase with inter-nest distance, leading males to allocate their efforts mainly to one nest, which seems to be the nest of the primary female.

The reduced male assistance in secondary nests can partly be compensated for by the female. That females are capable of compensating for the absence of the male was shown by experiments in which we removed males or either parent (Alatalo *et al.*, 1982c, 1988c). In the first experiment males were removed when the female started laying, and the female was therefore unassisted during the whole chick-feeding period. In that case, when nestlings were small or half-grown, unassisted females fed their young at about twice the rate of assisted monogamously mated females. Close to fledging, however, feeding rates of unassisted and assisted females became more similar, though females without male help still fed their young more often than assisted females. Summed over the whole nestling period, we found that single females increased food delivery rates by about 50% compared to monogamously mated females. Unassisted females, however, often fail to raise a full brood (see below). By analysing the feeding data, but correcting for brood size, we found feeding frequencies per live nestling to be doubled among unassisted females, and almost equal to the total feeding rates of monogamous pairs (Alatalo *et al.*, 1982c). In a second experiment we removed either the male or the female when nestlings were 5 days old, and found that both single males and single females increased their feeding rates by about 90% 2–3 days after removal as compared with the respective sex in monogamous pairs (Alatalo *et al.*, 1988c); in the long run, however, they might be unable to uphold this high feeding rate.

Substantial increases in feeding effort must have some costs. To cast some light on this we, in the first experiment mentioned above, weighed females of all categories (monogamous, primary, secondary and widowed) during early incubation and close to fledging of the young. In the second experiment we weighed single parents and pairs when nestlings were 5 and 13 days old. In no case did we find any statistically significant differences in initial or final weights, nor in mean weight loss. However, if we combine single and secondary females in the first experiment, and compare them with monogamous plus primary females we found that the first category was 0.3 g lighter when nestlings were about to fledge. Likewise, in the second experiment we found single parents to lose more weight than pair members, but the changes in weight loss were not statistically significant. However, these findings indicate that increased feeding efforts may lead to weight losses, which in turn might lead to increased mortality risks.

The cost of increased reproductive effort in Pied Flycatchers was looked at in more detail by Askenmo (1977b, 1979) near Gothenburg in southwest Sweden. Instead of removing one parent, he manipulated the size of the clutch and obtained clutches with between two and nine young. These manipulations showed that there was a positive correlation between initial brood size and female weight loss, i.e. females raising large clutches lost more weight from the start of incubation to the fledging of the young than did females raising small clutches. Askenmo further looked at return rates of males from enlarged and normal broods (females more seldom return to their previous breeding site, see Appendix 4). The average return rate for males raising their own broods was 38% while only 18% of the males raising enlarged broods came back the next year. This difference could of course be due to males avoiding their former breeding area if they had had to work unusually hard there, but Askenmo (1979) thought it more likely that the difference in return rates reflected increased mortality of the hard-working group of males. All in all, the available data rather uniformly indicate that increased parental efforts lead to weight reduction and thereby increased mortality. It is therefore likely that secondary Pied Flycatcher females of polygynous males suffer some costs as compared with monogamously mated females.

Unlike the females in the male–removal experiments mentioned above, many secondary females do receive some male assistance (Fig. 47), and they therefore do not have to compensate as much as completely single parents. So, for example, Lifjeld and Slagsvold (1989a) found that when nestlings were 5 days old, 51% of secondary females received male assistance while at 13 days of nestling age 69% of the females were helped by the male; the corresponding figures for primary females were 95% and 80%, respectively. Thus, secondary females do not have to double their food delivery rate to keep it on the same level as in monogamous pairs. In accordance with this we found secondary females on average to increase their feeding rates by about 60% compared to monogamously mated females, for all nestling stages combined (Fig. 48; Alatalo *et al.*, 1982c). Lifjeld and Slagsvold (1989a) found secondary females increased their feeding rates by only 25% when nestlings were 5 days old, and when nestlings were close

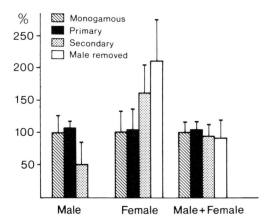

Fig. 48.   Feeding rates of males, females and the pair, for different nest categories in relation to monogamous nests (= 100%) with the same number of young combining all nestling stages (SD indicated by bars). From Alatalo et al. (1982c).

to fledging secondary females fed with the same frequency as females in monogamous pairs. Lifjeld and Slagsvold also had six cases of a male having three females; in those cases the male contribution to tertiary nests was very low (<1 feeding/hour). Tertiary females feeding 5-day-old chicks increased their feeding rate by almost 50%, but again, at 13 days of nestling age, they did not feed more often than monogamously mated females. It seems unlikely that a female with little or no male assistance can maintain a highly increased feeding rate through the whole nestling period without putting her own life at risk.

Primary females (i.e. first mated females of polygynous males) also suffer from reduced male assistance as the males spend some time at secondary nests. However, neither our own data nor the data provided by Lifjeld and Slagsvold (1989a) demonstrate any significant increases in feeding rates of primary compared to monogamous females (Fig. 48).

FLEDGING SUCCESS

In our total data set we found that among all eggs laid in clutches that hatched, on average, 82.0% resulted in fledged young. Similar figures have been obtained from other areas in Europe, and they are reproduced in Appendix 3. Low success is mainly reported from rather extreme localities such as subalpine forest in northern Finland (64%) and an exposed coastal spruce forest in southern Sweden (60%).

A few young in the nests may die of starvation, especially in secondary nests (see below), and other nestlings may succumb through predation or disease. In

Table 8. *Fledgling numbers of Pied Flycatchers breeding in deciduous and conifer-ous forest at Uppsala, Sweden in different years. The data are split into 'All pairs' and 'Monogamous pairs' since polygyny frequency is higher in coniferous forest. Differences are statistically significant (All pairs: t = 5.32, P = 0.006; Monoga-mous pairs: t = 3.99, P = 0.016, paired t-test, d.f. = 4).*

Year	Deciduous			Coniferous		
	Mean	SD	n	Mean	SD	n
			All pairs			
1979	4.98	1.74	54	4.35	2.12	26
1981	4.64	2.40	115	3.25	2.30	53
1982	5.18	2.04	128	3.96	2.51	26
1983	6.10	1.62	135	5.54	2.02	26
1984	4.99	2.40	147	3.96	2.39	34
			Monogamous pairs			
1979	5.40	1.46	40	5.20	1.66	15
1981	5.47	1.73	83	5.16	0.94	25
1982	5.59	1.66	108	5.38	1.71	16
1983	6.28	1.42	116	5.59	1.94	17
1984	5.45	2.06	119	4.85	1.96	20

our study areas such reductions led to a mean (±SD) production of 5.40 ± 1.49 fledglings in nests fledging at least one young and 4.78 ± 2.23 young for all nests. Corresponding figures from other parts of Europe are shown in Appendix 3. Again, low figures mainly come from extreme localities. Comparing habitats, birch forest seems to be among the worst, but the birch forest sites are in the far north or at high altitudes. In two cases, in central and south Sweden, we can make comparisons between deciduous forest (mainly oak) and coniferous forest (mainly pine). In southernmost Sweden, in three years combined, pairs in pine forest produced significantly fewer young (4.79, $n = 29$) than pairs breeding in oak forest (5.79, $n = 170$, $P < 0.01$; Källander, 1975). The same pattern emerges from our data from central Sweden. Nestings in deciduous woodlands (data from five years) produced on average 5.22 fledglings while those in coniferous forest, over the same years, produced 4.04 young. There were great variations between years, and in Table 8 we show the total data separated into different years. From these yearly variations in fledging success one can see that good years in deciduous forest are also good in coniferous forest ($r_s = 0.80$, $P \approx 0.10$). However, the relationship is such that if breeding success becomes reduced in deciduous forest it becomes even worse in coniferous (Fig. 49). One confounding variable when comparing fledging success between coniferous and deciduous forest is the frequency of polygyny, which is much higher in the former than in the latter habitat (see Chapter 12). If we therefore control for pairing status and restrict our comparison to monogamous pairs, the difference in fledging success between habitats becomes reduced: 5.69 fledged young in deciduous compared with 5.22 in coniferous. However, the difference is significant ($P = 0.016$, paired

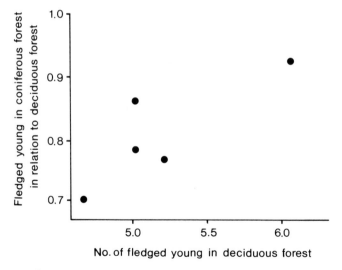

Fig. 49. Breeding success in coniferous forest in relation to that in deciduous forest at Uppsala. The relationship is such that if breeding success becomes reduced in deciduous forest it becomes even worse in coniferous.

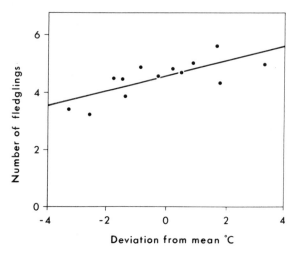

Fig. 50.   Correlation between number of fledglings and the temperature expressed as the difference between the yearly and the long-term mean. Regression equation: Number of fledglings = 0.26 × Deviation + 4.55, n = 13 years, P < 0.01. Data from southern Finland (Virolainen, 1984).

t-test, n = 5 years). The yearly differences in fledging success among monogamous pairs are also given in Table 8.

'Another factor influencing reproductive success is the weather during the breeding season. So, for example, it has been found in Finland that there is a statistically significant correlation between the number of young produced in a year and the mean ambient temperature during the main period of raising the young (Fig. 50). An even more important factor than either habitat or temperature in influencing fledging success is the mating status of the female. As mentioned earlier in this chapter male assistance is much reduced in secondary nests, and slightly so in primary nests (Fig. 47), and this can only partly be compensated for by the female. Thus there is reduced fledging success for both primary and secondary females compared with concurrently breeding monogamous females. This factor will be treated in greater detail in Chapter 12.

PROSPECTS FOR RECRUITMENT TO THE BREEDING POPULATION

The number of Pied Flycatcher nestlings that need to be recruited to the breeding season will be dealt with in Chapter 8. In this section we instead focus on how nestling condition at fledging influences the probability of surviving the first year. In the sibling species, the Collared Flycatcher, survival is greatly influenced by the weight of the offspring at fledging (Lars Gustafsson, pers. comm.). Unfortunately very few Pied Flycatcher offspring return to their natal area where

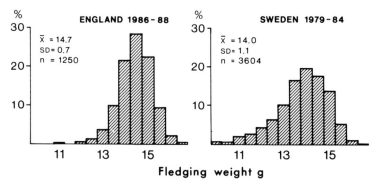

Fig. 51. Fledging weights of Pied Flycatcher young in central Sweden and northwest England.

we have worked in Sweden (Appendix 4). However, using our few recoveries ($n = 18$) we found a difference in mean ($\pm$SD) fledging weight between those that had survived at least two months compared to all the offspring at fledging (14.2 g $\pm$ 0.8, $n = 18$ versus 14.0 g $\pm$ 1.1, $n = 3604$). Mean values do not differ significantly ($t = 1.3$, $P = 0.28$) though the variance is smaller for recaptured birds ($F = 2.08$, $P = 0.04$). This means that there is a 'tail' towards light birds in the fledgling weight distribution (Fig. 51) and these birds most likely will not survive. If we compare the fledging weight of nestlings in our study areas in

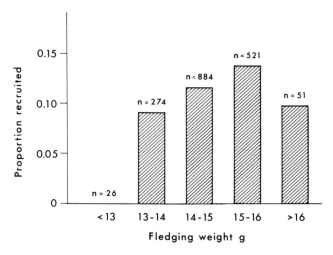

Fig. 52. Return rate in relation to fledging weight among Pied Flycatcher nestlings born in Cumbria, northwest England. Recruited fledglings were significantly heavier when leaving the nest (14.74 g $\pm$ 0.64, n = 205) than were fledglings that were never found again (14.59 g $\pm$ 0.75, n = 1555, t = 3.08, P < 0.01). Numbers above columns show number of nestlings weighed within each weight class.

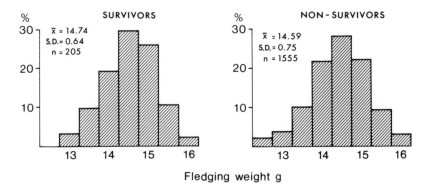

Fig. 53.   *Weight distribution of recruited nestlings compared with those that did not return to their natal area. Data from Cumbria, England.*

Sweden with those in our study areas in Cumbria, England we found Cumbrian fledglings to be significantly heavier (14.7 g) than central Swedish ones (14.0 g) (Fig. 51). There is also a significant difference in fledging weight variance, with a much less pronounced tail towards light birds in the English sample. This probably reflects foraging conditions, our English site having richer and more stable prey populations. For the English birds, which show high natal site fidelity, we have also calculated return rate in relation to fledging weight. No offspring lighter than 13.0 g returned, but for each weight class (in 1.0 g units) above that, return rate varied between 9% and 13%, rather independently of weight (Fig. 52). Comparing all recruited fledglings with those that did not come back to their natal area we found a difference both in mean weight (14.74 g and 14.59 g, respectively; $t = 3.08$, $P < 0.01$) and in variance, the latter being smaller among returning fledglings ($F = 1.39$, $P < 0.01$; Fig. 53).

In summary, the Pied Flycatcher data suggest that prospects of future survival for nestlings are weight dependent. However, rather than survival being linearly related to fledging weight the data suggest that there is a threshold value necessary for survival (e.g. Fig. 52). Fledglings lighter than 13 g seem very seldom to survive, while among those heavier than 13 g the proportion surviving is quite independent of fledging weight. A similar pattern was also found for tarsus length (Alatalo and Lundberg, 1986a), where nestlings with shorter tarsi than 18.5 mm seldom seemed to survive.

LIFETIME REPRODUCTIVE SUCCESS

In several studies of passerine birds it has been shown that a sizeable proportion of breeding pairs never contribute with any surviving offspring to future generations while a few pairs may contribute many. For example, in the Collared

Flycatcher, about 50% of all breeding birds failed to produce any local recruits while the rest produced from one to seven (Gustafsson, 1989).

Fortunately there is one study of lifetime reproductive success in the Pied Flycatcher. Helmut Sternberg has studied Pied Flycatchers near Wolfsburg in eastern Lower Saxony, Germany since 1964, and in 1989 he reported on the results to date. He was able to calculate the total number of fledglings raised during the lifetime of 953 males and 1298 females, on the assumption that all breeding attempts occurred within the areas studied. Some 2% of males and 8% of females that attempted to breed never produced any fledglings while the remaining part produced between one and 37 fledged young in their lifetime. About 9% of the fledglings were later recruited to the study areas (thus at least equally many must have bred elsewhere, see Chapter 8). Just above 50% of males and females did not produce any local recruits (calculated from Sternberg's Fig. 4.2), including one female that produced 36 offspring in her lifetime but no recruits. The most successful male produced eight local recruits (from 21 fledglings), and the most successful female seven (from 26 fledglings). One male actually produced four recruits from the four fledglings produced in his lifetime. Overall, Sternberg found a significant positive correlation between number of fledglings raised in the lifetime and the total number of offspring recruited to the local population in future generations. Thus, the most important factor enhancing lifetime reproductive success should be a long life, with other important characteristics being early laying, large clutch and brood size, and production of heavy fledglings. According to Sternberg's data, polygyny should also allow males to increase their lifetime reproductive success, though in this case paternity in any instance is unknown (see Chapter 12).

SUMMARY

The female Pied Flycatcher lays one light blue egg per day early in the morning and she takes sole responsibility for incubation, which commences at the laying of the last egg and normally takes two weeks. The female regulates the egg temperature by spending a variable time each day outside the nest or by changing her metabolic rate. There are clear changes in the weight of females during the course of the breeding season; they become very heavy during the pre-laying period, but from the start of laying weight decreases to reach the pre-breeding level – equal to that of males – in the early nestling stage. Hatching of eggs occurs rather synchronously, normally within 1.5 days. Hatching failure is low, about 5%. Nestlings grow fast until they are around 10 days old, and then stay another four to six days in the nest. Both males and females feed the nestlings. However, when the young are small, the females spend a considerable amount of time inside the nest-hole to keep them warm, and the males collect most of the food during that time. Later on, the two parents deliver food to the nest at the same rate, which is normally about 20 times an hour when the nestlings are close to fledging. Parents often start feeding the nestlings between 2 and 3 a.m. and do not cease until 9 or 10 p.m., giving a working day of 18–20 hours.

Not all nests are fully attended by two parents, usually because the male is polygynous. Polygynous males give priority to the first female's nest and tend to give less aid to secondary nests that are located far from the nest of the primary female, and also less when the hatching interval between primary and secondary broods is long. The reduced male assistance in secondary nests can only be partly compensated for by the female.

About 70–80% of all eggs laid normally result in fledged young, and the mean number of fledglings for all our nests was 4.8 young. Nestings in deciduous woodlands produce more offspring than nestings in coniferous forest, and monogamous females produce more offspring than secondary females. Another factor influencing reproductive success is the weather during the breeding season. Among offspring leaving the nest only those heavier than 13 g at fledging seem to have any chance of surviving to the following year.

CHAPTER 8

Longevity, Age at First Breeding, and Dispersal

In many species of birds males, females and fledglings all show fidelity to the breeding or natal area in successive seasons. This is also true for the Pied Flycatcher where individuals often – though not always – return to their former breeding area or the area of birth, and this after a migratory journey of several thousands of kilometres. A general explanation for breeding area fidelity among adults is that birds may gain by returning to their former breeding area because familiarity with local food resources and/or potential breeding sites could increase reproductive success. The short movements which occur have often been interpreted as a means of acquiring a better territory than the previous one. However, movements can also become necessary as, for example, when former territory was already occupied at the time of arrival.

Similarly, young birds may either show a high natal philopatry or they may disperse from their place of birth; and at the same time the sexes often show different degrees of propensity to disperse. These patterns of movements may have important ecological and evolutionary consequences since they may affect population dynamics, genetic structure and rate of evolutionary change. Dispersal patterns have also been shown to influence social behaviour, which under some conditions may lead to the whole family staying together for several years; in other cases dispersal may instead lead to avoidance of relatives, and may for example function to reduce the risks of inbreeding. With this outline as a background we will in this chapter review and try to interpret published data on life span and mortality rates of Pied Flycatchers of different age and sex classes, and on dispersal distances between sites of birth and first breeding and from the first to the next breeding attempt. We will also briefly comment on the sex ratio during breeding, which is important for understanding the evolution of polygyny in this species (see also Chapter 12).

LONGEVITY

Pied Flycatchers are relatively short-lived birds. The highest mortality occurs between the time of leaving the nest and the first breeding, with deaths probably concentrated in the first days or weeks out of the nest and during autumn migration. From a long-term study in Lower Saxony in northern Germany, Sternberg (1989) estimated that of all young produced in a year 22.0% of all male and 21.6% of all female fledglings must enter the breeding population in some subsequent year for the breeding population to remain stable. This estimate coincides with von Haartman's (1949) and Curio's (1959c) computations which suggest that, with an adult yearly survival rate of 40–50%, the overwinter survival of young birds must be between 23% and 29% for the population not to decrease in size. Of male offspring surviving to the first year, Sternberg further calculated that on average 53.8% survive to the second, 25.3% to the third, and 11.6% to the fourth year; the corresponding figures for females are 53.1%, 27.7% and 13.1%, respectively. Then, how old can a Pied Flycatcher become? In his total sample of more than 2000 breeding adults ringed as nestlings, Sternberg found 7 males and 11 females breeding at the age of 7, and 1 male and 2 females breeding at the age of 8 years. Similar maximum ages are reported from ringing recoveries in other countries: the oldest known British bird was recorded at the age of 8 years (Mead and Clark, 1987), the oldest known Finnish bird was 7 years and 2 months (Saurola, 1988), and in Sweden two birds have been recovered at

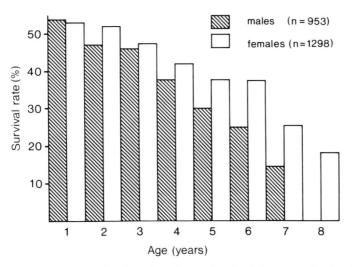

Fig. 54. Survival rates of male and female Pied Flycatchers in relation to age. Based on data from Lower Saxony, Germany (Sternberg, 1989).

the age of 8. However, the world record is held by a bird ringed in Norway which was still alive at 9 years and 3 months (Staav, 1989).

It has earlier been suggested (e.g. Nice, 1957; Lack, 1966; von Haartman, 1971) that the annual survival rate for birds is independent of age. In contrast to this, Sternberg (1989) found that in the Pied Flycatcher mortality rates steadily increased throughout life in a similar way in both sexes, though the increase seems slightly more gradual in females (Fig. 54). However, an increased probability of breeding failure with increasing age could produce similar results if birds that fail are not caught and identified. It has also been suggested that male mortality might be affected by plumage coloration (males are variable in plumage), but this topic will be dealt with in Chapter 10 and not here.

SEX RATIO AND AGE AT FIRST BREEDING

The sex ratio of Pied Flycatchers at birth seems to be about even; in 20 broods examined by Silverin (1975) 52% of the nestlings were males and 48% females, which is not significantly different from a 50–50 sex ratio. However, judging from catches at bird observatories it seems that more females than males migrate through during spring. So for example, at Heligoland, off the coast of northwest Germany, it was found that among 463 sexed individuals 46% were males and 54% were females (Bub *et al.*, 1981, cited in von Haartman, 1985). Among 1125 birds trapped in spring at Finnish bird observatories (Lågskär and Rönnskär) in the southwestern part of the country, 45% were males and 55% were females (von Haartman, 1985). A sex ratio skewed in the opposite direction, however, was found by Curio (1959c) who studied birds breeding near Berlin in Germany; males in that case outnumbered females, 58% as against 42% ($n = 406$). The difference in the proportion of males to females, compared to a 50–50 sex ratio, was not statistically significant at Heligoland ($P = 0.10$), but was highly so at Lågskär and Rönnskär ($P \approx 0.001$) as well as in Curio's study ($P < 0.01$; binomial test).

In our study areas we always notice unmated males, the proportion of which varies between years and areas but, on average, amounts to some 10–15%. The discrepancies between all these studies may occur because the samples are not randomly collected; for example, males could be more difficult to catch during spring migration or they could be easier to observe on the breeding grounds than are females. Taking all information on sex ratios together, there is no conclusive evidence that one sex significantly outnumbers the other at the start of the breeding season. During the breeding season, however, it is possible that female mortality exceeds male mortality, creating a slightly male-biased sex ratio. From our study areas we have very few certain records of males dying. Males may occasionally be found dead inside nest boxes, probably having been killed by Great Tits during fights over sole rights to the nest-hole. Some other males may be taken by predators such as Sparrowhawks. There is probably a heavier mortality among breeding females. In natural cavities (see Chapter 14) the predation rate on nests was 40%, and in nine cases of predation during incubation, the female was killed in six (67%).

Male Pied Flycatchers on average seem to start breeding at a greater age than females. Sternberg (1989) calculated that 38% of males bred for their first time at the age of one year while the corresponding figure for females was estimated as 51%. Another 43% of males start to breed in their second year of life while among females this proportion was 36%. A few males and females do not start breeding until they are 3–5 years old, giving a mean age at first breeding of 1.9 years for males and 1.5 years for females. The figures given by Sternberg on the proportion of individuals starting to breed at age one seem low for a short-lived species like the Pied Flycatcher, and might be underestimated because of a higher frequency of breeding failures among one-year-old birds, i.e. these birds might have started breeding but were not caught. The difference between males and females in the proportion starting breeding in their first year of life could also be explained by the efficiency in catching them: males are more difficult to catch than females, especially if the breeding attempt fails at an early stage.

By using observations of the age at which males and females start breeding, Sternberg (1989) estimated the proportion of non-breeders, and found that in any one year, about 60% of males and 40% of females in his population were probably not breeding. In his calculations he assumed that the survival rate was the same for breeding and non-breeding birds, and that both groups of birds had the same degree of breeding-site fidelity (but see below). These calculated figures are much higher than those observed by Curio (1959c) near Berlin in Germany. He found that about 30% of males were unmated compared with only 3% of females. This discrepancy between estimated and observed figures may be due to many unmated birds, especially females, escaping detection (many unmated males do hold territories and sing).

Sternberg further calculated that among one-year-old birds as many as 83% of males and 62% of females were non-breeding. The possibility that many individuals do not attempt to breed in their first season is supported by other field studies; e.g. Harvey *et al.* (1985) found that 40% of both first-year males and females probably did not breed in the Forest of Dean in southwest England. Von Haartman (1985) used several methods to calculate the proportion of unmated birds among one-year-old males and found, depending on the method used, figures that ranged between 41% and 59%. He further stated that probably a considerable fraction of one-year-old females also do not breed. Thus, all studies cited so far support the idea that many Pied Flycatchers do not breed in their first year of life.

Among recruited nestlings, Curio (1959c) found, near Berlin, that 46% of males started to breed in their first year of life while 54% did not start until the second; the corresponding figures for females were 64% and 36%, respectively. A somewhat higher proportion of recruited nestlings breeding in their first year was found at our study site in Cumbria, England. Of 102 recruited males ringed as nestlings in 1986 to 1988, and later recovered, 69% turned up as breeding birds in their first year of life, 26% in the second year, and about 5% were not found until the third year (Fig. 55). The corresponding figures for 99 females ringed as nestlings were 76%, 20% and 4%, respectively (Fig. 55). Of the birds not caught until their second year of life, twice as many must have been alive the previous year (if mortality is about 50%), which means that over half of the recruited individuals passed unnoticed in their first year of life. Some of these birds might have started breeding but failed, some might have bred in natural

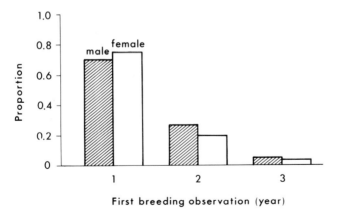

Fig. 55. Proportion of Pied Flycatcher males (n = 102) and females (n = 99) ringed as nestlings and first found by us as breeding birds in their 1st, 2nd or 3rd year of life. Data from Cumbria, England 1986–90.

cavities or in boxes in nearby gardens, and some might not have mated at all, perhaps because they arrived so late that they became excluded from breeding. That this might be the case is supported by our finding that some males (11.5%, $n = 26$) could not be found in the second year after their first appearance but were found again in their third year. Thus, they must have been alive in the 'missing year' but could not be found by us and, in the same way, some males must have been overlooked in their first year.

The reason why more males than females passed unnoticed in their first year of life could be due to early hatching failures, in which cases only the female could be caught and thereby identified. Yet, all these reasons do not explain why so many birds pass unnoticed in their first year of life; our guess, based on data from Cumbria, is that about half of the individuals do not breed in their first year of life. But why is this?

The reason why so many one-year-old birds do not breed is as yet unknown, though Sternberg (1989) suggested that a major reason could be that these birds are excluded from reproduction by scarcity of nest-sites. This, however, cannot be the full answer since in most studies on Pied Flycatchers nest boxes have been provided in excess (see, e.g. Harvey et al., 1985). It may be that one-year-olds hang around breeding areas unnoticed, or it could even be that some birds do not leave their wintering grounds in their first year of life. Clearly, the estimated proportion of one-year-old non-breeding birds is much higher than we find through direct observations in the field.

RETURN RATE AND BREEDING DISPERSAL OF MALES

Male Pied Flycatchers generally show a higher breeding-site fidelity than females (see below); on average slightly less than half of the breeding males in any one year return to their former breeding grounds the next year. In Cumbria, in England, where site fidelity is high we found that on average 44% ($n = 288$; Fig. 56) of breeding males later returned, with the maximum of 56.2% for males breeding in 1987. In a five-year study in Germany, Curio (1959c) found the return rate of breeding males to vary between 30.5% and 52.5%, while Slagsvold and Lifjeld (1990), when removing or adding females to study plots near Oslo in Norway, found male return rate to vary between 17% and 55%. Our figure from

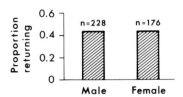

Fig. 56.   *Survival rate measured as proportion of males and females that returned from one year to the next. Data from Cumbria, England.*

England in 1987 together with that cited from Norway are probably the highest return rates found among Pied Flycatcher males. Among males breeding for the first time, in subalpine birch forest in Swedish Lapland, Nyholm and Myhrberg (1983) found return rates to subsequent years to vary from 8.8% to 30.3% during a 10-year period. In Appendix 4 we present a compilation of male return rates found in the literature together with some of our own unpublished data. From this appendix one can see that average return rate varies considerably (20–49%) between study sites, but there does not seem to be any trend in breeding-site fidelity with latitude. Factors which, however, could explain some of the differences in return rate are size (see Barrowclough, 1978) and isolation of study sites, though we have no data on this. If woodlands under study are isolated and few nest-sites are available in between, as in our study area in Cumbria, many males will be found returning, while if many potential nest-sites are available between study sites, as at Uppsala, fewer males seem to be found in the next year. It is also likely that a higher proportion of returning males will be found if the study is performed in one large area than if study areas are small and scattered but of the same total size; in the latter case a higher proportion of birds may breed outside the area under observation. We do not have information on size and degree of isolation for all the study sites listed in Appendix 4.

In our Cumbrian data set we further found 23.4% of the males breeding in 1986 and 19.2% of the males breeding in 1987 to return two years later, and 9.8% and 9.6%, respectively, to return three years later. In the much larger data set collected by Sternberg (1989), of all males breeding for the first time in their first year of life, he found 43.5% to return in the following year, 22.9% to return in the third year and 12.4%, 5.4% and 1.4% to come back in their fourth, fifth and sixth year of life, respectively. Again, these figures could be underestimates if older birds more often fail in their breeding attempts, and hence cannot be caught.

Many studies on Pied Flycatchers have focused on breeding dispersal (the distance between successive breeding sites). The main message from most of these studies is that if a male has started to breed at a certain site he, if having survived, is very likely to return to the same area, or somewhere in the close neighbourhood, in the next year. Most studies have found dispersal distances, from one year to the next, to range between 100 m and 300 m (Table 9). A few males may breed in the same nest-hole in two successive years; in the closely related Collared Flycatcher it was found that 8% of males reoccupied their previous nest box (Pärt and Gustafsson, 1989). Pied Flycatchers have to compete for nest-holes with tits, Nuthatches and sometimes also Redstarts (see Chapter 4), all of which normally start breeding earlier than them. Therefore nest-sites used in the previous year may already be occupied by another species upon arrival, and the Pied Flycatcher male has to find another nest-hole in the vicinity (see also Harvey *et al.*, 1984). This is probably more likely to occur if the males arrive late because more sites are then occupied. However, many males move to a new nest-site even if the former site remains available on arrival, as shown from the studies on the Collared Flycatcher cited above. This can also be seen in data

Table 9.   Dispersal distance between successive breedings of male Pied Flycatchers.

Country	Latitude °N	Distance (m) median	Source
Sweden	66	100–200	A
UK	52	c. 90	B
UK	52	c. 75	C
Germany	52	100–200	D
Germany	52	200–300	E
Germany	50	c. 150	F

Sources: (A) Nyholm and Myhrberg (1983); (B) Campbell (1959); (C) Harvey et al. (1984); (D) Berndt and Sternberg (1969); (E) Winkel (1982); (F) Creutz (1955).

from the Forest of Dean, where it was found that among nest boxes used by Pied Flycatchers in one year, 23% were used by other species the following year, 42% remained unoccupied, while 35% were reoccupied by Pied Flycatchers (Campbell, 1959).

RETURN RATE AND BREEDING DISPERSAL OF FEMALES

In England and central Europe as high a proportion of females as males return to their previous breeding grounds; on average 31.8% ($n = 8$ studies) and 33.1% ($n = 9$), respectively (Appendix 4). In our study areas in England it was 44% for both males and females (Fig. 56). In Scandinavia, however, it seems as if far fewer females than males return to their former breeding areas (11.6%, $n = 5$ and 32.1%, $n = 10$, respectively). This difference is not likely to be caused by a higher mortality among females breeding in the north compared to those breeding in the south, but is more likely due to higher propensity for dispersal among northerly breeding females. However, there is also great variation in return rates between years at the same site. Near Berlin, Curio (1959c) during a five-year study found female return rates to vary between 18% and 49%. Likewise, among females breeding for the first time in Swedish Lapland, Nyholm and Myhrberg (1983) found a yearly variation in subsequent recovery rate ranging from 2.7% to 16%. Return rates to successive years from first breeding are given by Sternberg (1989), who found 50.2% of females breeding in their first year of life to return in the following year, 26.3% to return in the third year and 12.9%, 5.4% and 2.4% to come back in their fourth, fifth and sixth years of life, respectively.

So why do fewer females return to their former breeding grounds in the north than in the south? A possible explanation is as follows. Since males take up the territories, it is probably most often of selective advantage for them to return to the same area for breeding again since it is likely that potential breeding sites are

Table 10. Dispersal distance between successive breedings of female Pied Flycatchers.

Country	Latitude °N	Distance (m) median	Source
Sweden	66	200–300	A
UK	52	*c.* 115	B
UK	52	*c.* 130	C
Germany	52	100–200	D
Germany	52	400–500	E
Germany	50	*c.* 150	F

Sources: (A) Nyholm and Myhrberg (1983); (B) Campbell (1959); (C) Harvey *et al.* (1984); (D) Berndt and Sternberg (1969); (E) Winkel (1982); (F) Creutz (1955).

known. For females it should be less costly to find and evaluate the quality of a nest-site than for males since they can use the song of males as a guide to finding a nest-hole, while males have no such easy cues (apart from the song of other males, see Chapter 4). If, however, patches of suitable habitat are few and dispersed it might also be of high selective advantage for females to return to the same area for breeding once again. If habitat is more continuous, as in northern Scandinavia, females probably can, more easily than males, find good quality nest-sites before having reached the previous breeding area. We have, however, no data supporting (or contradicting) this scenario.

Among individuals that have returned to their former breeding area, the distance between successive breeding sites appears to be slightly longer for females than for males, the median distance in different studies ranging from about 100 m to 500 m for females (Table 10). That female flycatchers disperse further than males is also supported by the study of Pärt and Gustafsson (1989) on Collared Flycatchers breeding on the island of Gotland in the Baltic. These authors made their comparisons within and between cohorts of one-year-old and older birds that successfully fledged at least one young or that failed to fledge any young. In all four comparisons females dispersed further (median 147–241 m) than did males (median 89–126 m).

CAUSES AND CONSEQUENCES OF BREEDING DISPERSAL

There are very few studies of the factors causing breeding dispersal in flycatchers and of what the reproductive consequences might be. We are aware of only one such study on the Pied Flycatcher (Harvey *et al.*, 1984) in the Forest of Dean in England and one on the closely related Collared Flycatcher on the Swedish island of Gotland (Pärt and Gustafsson, 1989). The results from these two studies will be briefly reviewed in this section. Studies on other bird species have revealed that after a poor or unsuccessful breeding individuals often move, which may lead to improved breeding performance in the next year. Movements have also been interpreted as an attempt to acquire better territories. It has been noted that males commonly move shorter distances than females, as do older individuals compared to younger (e.g. Harvey *et al.*, 1979).

In the Forest of Dean study it was shown that in the Pied Flycatcher also, older birds of both sexes moved shorter distances between years than did young birds, and that females dispersed further than males. The shortest median dispersal distance (52 m) was recorded for birds that re-established the pair bond from the previous year. This is also what is to be expected from chance effects: if the pair members of the previous year both disperse a short distance the probability for them to remate must be much higher than if one or both disperse further. Among Pied Flycatchers very few pairs reunite in the next breeding season; in the Forest of Dean 14 cases of mate fidelity were observed. In the Collared Flycatcher it was found that of all pairs where both parents survived about 6% of the bonds were re-established. Pied Flycatcher males that mated with a new female (old female still alive) or with a new female (previous female dead) moved slightly further (Md = 82 m in both cases) than pairs that reunited, and no difference was found in breeding dispersal between monogamous and polygynous males. Females in the Forest of Dean that did not remate (old mate alive) or had lost their mate after a (presumed) death dispersed further (Md = 127 and 133 m, respectively) than did males of the same categories. Unsuccessful females of the previous year moved a distance (Md = 124 m) similar to that of females that changed mates. After a change of mate there was no difference between the sexes in the age of their new mate, and no tendency for the male with a new partner to have higher reproductive success than his previous female with her new partner.

The pattern of breeding dispersal was similar in the Collared Flycatcher to that found in the Pied Flycatcher. From the Collared Flycatcher study it could, however, further be added that body size or condition was not related to dispersal distance, and that unpaired males moved further the following year than did mated males. Young females with poor or no breeding success dispersed further than young successful females, while there was no such difference between unsuccessful and successful old females. Because of these movements, previously unsuccessful females tended to do better the following year if dispersing further while successful females did worse after a longer move. One can conclude from this study that if an individual bird has been reproductively unsuccessful in one year, it tends to be more careful in its choice of a territory the following year compared to previously successful birds. As a consequence, unsuccessful individuals end up further away from their previous breeding site than do successful birds.

The study on Collared Flycatchers was done in an area with several rather small woodlands separated from each other, so the workers could compare dispersal distances within and between woodlands. Pärt and Gustafsson then found that males breeding in their natal wood subsequently made shorter between-year moves than males that had immigrated from nearby woods (all were ringed as nestlings); this was especially pronounced for yearling males. However, no difference was found between 'resident' and immigrant females. Pärt and Gustafsson argued that locally born individuals probably made a better choice of nesting site in their first year of life and therefore moved less in subsequent years.

RETURN RATE AND DISPERSAL OF OFFSPRING

Natal dispersal (the distance between place of birth and first breeding site) in the Pied Flycatcher is greater than is breeding dispersal. Somewhat more than 20% of the fledglings have to enter the breeding population for it to remain stable (see the section on longevity at the beginning of this chapter) but the highest return rate we know of is about 14% (Appendix 4), as found by us in Cumbria, England (nestlings born 1986–8). This means that many birds must breed away from their natal area, and be compensated for by immigration. High return rates of nestlings have also been recorded in northern Germany, while rates in Scandinavia have been very low. They also seem to be rather low in southern Germany and southwest England (Appendix 4). Again, as in breeding dispersal of females, we believe that differences in natal dispersal between sites can be influenced by habitat fragmentation and isolation. In the study site in the Cumbrian mountains, areas of suitable breeding habitat are restricted and very isolated, and natal philopatry is high. At Uppsala in central Sweden, sites with potential nesting places are common over a much larger area than in Cumbria, and natal philopatry is very low. Some additional support for this hypothesis comes from the study by Berndt (1960) in Germany. He had about 5200 nest boxes in 21 different woodlands (total area about 1000 ha) within a study area of more than 2000 km². The return rate of offspring was only 3.5%, and the median distance from birthplace to site of first breeding was 1–2 km. In this situation 18% of the returning offspring established territories more than 10 km away from the place of birth, and the most distant bird found was breeding 235 km away.

Among nestlings returning to their natal area, the distance from birthplace to site of first breeding is on average longer than the dispersal distances recorded for consecutive breedings of adult birds (Table 11), but there seems to be no difference in dispersal distance between male and female offspring (Table 11). Moreover, the data on recruited fledglings in England shows that young that returned as males (nestlings cannot be sexed) were significantly heavier (14.9 g) as fledglings than were recruited females (14.6 g; $t = 2.75$, $P < 0.01$; Fig. 57).

The causes and consequences of natal dispersal in the Pied Flycatcher are at the moment almost completely unknown. There is, however, one study dealing with this topic on the Collared Flycatcher (Pärt, 1990, 1991). Pärt found, first, that natal dispersal is significantly greater in females (Md = 840 m) than in males (Md = 518 m), as it is for breeding dispersal. Second, he found no significant influence of breeding density, date of egg-laying, fledging weight, tarsus length, or condition on subsequent dispersal distance. The only relationship found was that females born in small broods moved further than females born in large

Table 11.   *Dispersal distance between natal and first breeding sites. (Md = median, M = mean.)*

Country	Latitude °N	Distance (m) males	females		Source
Sweden	66	500–1000	2000–3000	Md	A
UK	52	*c.* 320	*c.* 295	Md	B
Germany	52	1000–2000	1000–2000	Md	C
Germany[1]	52	975	2000	Md	D
Germany	52	883	798	M	E
Germany	50	250	300	Md	F

Sources: (A) Nyholm (1986); (B) Campbell (1959); (C) Berndt and Sternberg (1969); (D) Berndt and Winkel (1979); (E) Winkel (1982); (F) Creutz (1955).
(1) Eggs, nestlings and caged fledglings exchanged between two areas 250 km apart. Distances are from place of fledging or release. For further details see text, p. 123.

broods, possibly implying that young born in poor territories disperse further. In looking at the subsequent performance of birds, Pärt found that females hatched at the middle or end of the breeding season produced fewer young with increasing natal dispersal distance, and that males dispersing long distances had reduced survival. Males that bred in the neighbourhood of the natal site also had a mating advantage. One possible reason why birds dispersing short distances seem to have better reproductive performance could be that they have better prior knowledge of the breeding area, and hence choose better breeding sites than those with longer natal dispersal and probably poorer local knowledge.

So when is knowledge about the breeding area acquired? Or is it in fact innate? To answer parts of these questions, Berndt and Winkel (1979) both exchanged

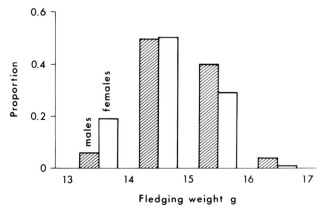

Fig. 57.   *Weights of Pied Flycatcher males and females as fledglings. Recruited males were significantly heavier at fledging than females (14.86 g ± 0.60, n = 102 against 14.61 g ± 0.66, n = 99, t = 2.75, P < 0.01). Data from Cumbria, England.*

Pied Flycatcher eggs and nestlings between two areas in northern Germany, and transported away and released caged fledglings (about 36 days old; from one area to the other only). All returning birds came back to the area of fledging or, in the case of transfer, to the area of release, and the authors concluded that knowledge of birthplace must be learned. Moreover, knowledge about the 'home area' can be acquired after 36 days of age, i.e. about three weeks after fledging. In a similar experiment on the Collared Flycatcher, Löhrl (1959) found that after a release at 40–50 days of age many birds returned to the release area in the following year, while after a release at about 60 days of age only one bird came back. Löhrl suggested 60 days of age to be about the end of the sensitive period for learning the 'home area'. He also found that about two weeks of experience of an area was enough for fledglings to be able to return.

By mist-netting juvenile and adult Pied Flycatchers throughout the summer in a forest in the Hoge Veluwe region in The Netherlands, van Balen (1979) was able to demonstrate that the initial dispersal seems to occur within two weeks of fledging, and that juvenile birds stay in their natal area for about 45 days. Van Balen also caught more fledglings than expected from a random distribution within 600 m of the hatching site. During the period when most catches were made, i.e. up to 35 days after fledging, the median distance to the nest for juveniles trapped was 400–600 m. These data suggest that many juveniles stay in their natal area, and for a period long enough for imprinting to be possible, and probably they could also acquire information on potential nest-sites and favourable feeding areas.

SUMMARY

Pied Flycatchers are relatively short-lived birds, with an adult mortality rate of 50–60%. This means that for the population to remain stable, at least 20–25% of

the fledglings have to enter the breeding population. The sex ratio at birth seems to be about even, and is not markedly skewed during the breeding season. At any time about 70–75% of the birds to be found breeding will have started breeding at one year of age and the rest will not have started until they were two or even three years old, which means that about half of the birds do not breed in their first year of life. There is also a tendency for males to start breeding at a greater age than females. In general males show a higher breeding-site fidelity than females, and females breeding in the north show an especially low propensity to return. The dispersal between birthplace and first breeding site is much greater than is breeding dispersal. High local return rates of nestlings (up to 14%) have been recorded in England and Germany, while return rates in Scandinavia have been low (about 1%). Differences in dispersal rate between study sites are probably influenced by habitat fragmentation and isolation.

CHAPTER 9

Song

Some bird species produce rather simple calls while others have very elaborate and beautiful songs. In some species songs are often repeated in bouts while in others songs are built up from a repertoire of figures that can be combined in different ways. These between-species differences in singing behaviour also partly apply within species, and become obvious if details of the song can be analysed in detail. As Darwin noted, males are the predominant singers among birds. Also, bird song is mainly produced during the pairing season which suggests that acoustic signals are produced mainly in the context of sexual selection, either for attracting mates or as a keep-out signal towards other males, or both. In this chapter we describe the vocalizations of Pied Flycatchers and the contexts in which they are used. Possible mating benefits of singing a lot and of having complex songs will be discussed in Chapter 11. After pairing the singing activity of male Pied Flycatchers is dramatically reduced, though many males resume singing at about the time of egg-laying, but in another territory (for reasons that will be treated in Chapter 12). In the present chapter, we also comment on the form and context of vocalizations other than male song.

STRUCTURE, INTENSITY AND TIME OF SONG

STRUCTURE AND LEARNING OF SONG

The smallest unit that we recognize in the song of a male Pied Flycatcher is the 'figure', defined as a continuous unit of sound, recognized on the sonogram as an unbroken trace (see Fig. 58). The male sings a series of figures together; such a series, separated by a pause from the next series, is termed a 'strophe'. Typically some of the figures in the beginning of each strophe are repeated a couple of times, after which there follows a mixture of new figures. Individual males do not sing set song types, like for example the Great Tit and the Song Sparrow, but instead recombine figures in novel ways, so that successive song strophes are very seldom identical. Thus, the repertoire of song types is almost infinite. Each song strophe lasts on average for 1.7 s ($n = 48$ males) though some are short while some are very long, lasting for over 4 s. The frequency of the song ranges between approximately 3 and 6 kHz (Fig. 58).

We have counted the number of unique figures used in each song strophe to calculate different measures of song complexity. Thus, we define 'repertoire' as the total number of unique figures used per 20 strophes, while 'versatility' is defined as the mean number of different figures per song strophe in 20 strophes.

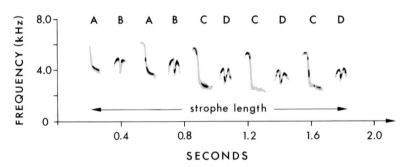

Fig. 58.   Song strophe of a male Pied Flycatcher. Letters denote similar figures within the strophe.

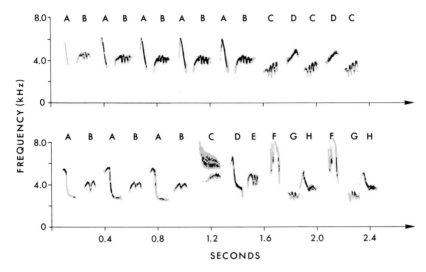

Fig. 59.   Examples of a simple (top) and a complex Pied Flycatcher song strophe. The simple song is made up of four different figures while the complex strophe contains eight figures.

The mean number of unique figures per 20 songs in our Swedish sample is 24 (range 6–71), and the total number used in a season by many males probably exceeds one hundred. The mean total number of figures used in each strophe averages ten and the versatility averages 4.4 (range 2–6). Thus, some males sing complex song strophes while others sing simple strophes, and we give an example of each in Figure 59. The complex song in this figure includes eight different figures compared to four in the simple example. In complex songs the figures are also repeated less often than in simple ones.

Pied Flycatchers probably have to learn their songs, though we do not know from whom nor when. Dag Eriksson at the Zoology Department in Uppsala hand-raised a brood of nestlings up to the age of two years. One bird was certainly a male because it later started singing. To the human ear there was no resemblance between the stereotyped song this male used and the normal song in the wild. This observation suggests that song indeed has to be learned, but when? The normal pattern in songbirds is that males are most sensitive to song learning from the time of fledging up to about 50 days of age. For example, laboratory experiments have indicated that song learning is mainly restricted to the first 60–80 days of life in Long-billed Marsh Wrens (Kroodsma and Pickert, 1980). Similarly, in the White-crowned Sparrow, birds exposed to tape-recorded conspecific songs learned them mainly between the ages of 10 and 50 days. However, if exposed to live tutors this period of song learning could be increased beyond 50 days of age (Baptista and Petrinovich, 1986).

Adult Pied Flycatcher males seem to sing very little after their young have hatched. Curio (1959b) observed a breeding male for a total of 26 hours while his young were nestlings and only heard him sing a total of six strophes, indicating that song learning from the father is less likely to take place during this period. Moreover, the male sings even less frequently after the nestlings have fledged, and the family stays together for only a rather short time. Thus, it seems that the possibility of learning the songs from the father between hatching and independence is limited. Alternatively nestling or recently fledged males may learn to sing by listening to other adult males singing during this period, during autumn migration, or in the wintering quarters. A few adult males might still be singing to attract females when the earliest broods have young in the nest, but this probably does not apply to late clutches. In the North American Long-billed Marsh Wren, Kroodsma and Pickert (1980) (see also above) put some nestlings into isolated chambers with a photoperiod simulating a 'late' (August) hatching and some with an 'early' (June) hatching. The late hatchlings in this experiment seemed to learn fewer songs and at an earlier stage than the early hatchlings. However, the late hatchlings also imitated songs from training tapes played back in the spring, whereas early hatchlings did not. The results from this experiment suggest that song can probably be learned as late as just before the first breeding season. The frequency of singing by Pied Flycatcher males during autumn migration and in the wintering areas is, to our knowledge, unknown. What is clear, however, is that one-year-old males can sing a typical Pied Flycatcher song upon arrival on the breeding grounds.

An increase in song repertoire size might occur with increasing age of the male. Thus, for example, we found that the mean ($\pm$SD) song repertoire size of one-year-old males was significantly smaller than that of older birds in 'random territories' (19.7 ± 8.0, $n = 31$ as against 28.8 ± 11.9, $n = 44$, respectively; $t = 3.66$, $P < 0.01$, d.f. $= 73$; see Chapter 11 for how 'random territories' were identified). Thus, older males might have a larger vocabulary than one-year-old males or, alternatively, they might be better at learning other males' song figures. An alternative explanation is that males with small repertoires more often become evicted from their territories, thereby causing mean repertoire size to increase with age even though individuals do not add song figures to their repertoires between years. However, Pied Flycatcher males almost never become evicted after establishment of their territory. Lars Wallin (pers. comm.) tape-recorded individual males in successive years outside Uppsala and found no significant increase in repertoire size between seasons. Some individuals increased the number of unique figures that they used while others decreased their repertoire size or stayed at the same level compared with the previous year (Fig. 60). This pattern of minimal change in repertoire size between years has also been shown to occur in Song Sparrows (Hiebert et al., 1989). The possible mating advantages of having complex songs as compared with simple ones will be discussed in Chapter 11.

Pied Flycatcher males may pick up song figures from singing neighbours. Some support for this view comes from the fact that Pied Flycatcher males incorporate song figures from other species occurring close by. We have for example heard and recorded Pied Flycatcher songs that sounded very much like

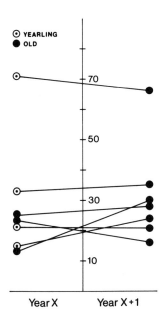

Fig. 60.   Mean number of unique figures per 20 song strophes (= repertoire) used by individual males in two successive years. Data from Lars Wallin (pers. comm.).

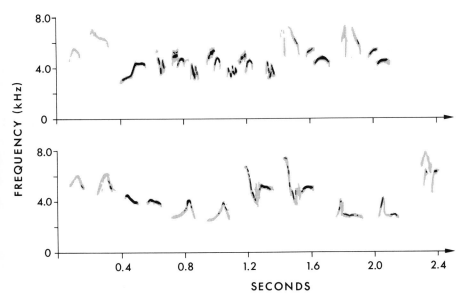

Fig. 61.   Sonograms of the song of a male Pied Flycatcher singing like a Dunnock (top) and another like a Willow Warbler (bottom).

those of the Willow Warbler, Dunnock, Chaffinch, Reed Bunting and Ortolan Bunting. In Figure 61 we give an example from tape recordings of a Pied Flycatcher male singing like a Willow Warbler and another male singing like a Dunnock. Some further evidence comes from comparisons between woodlands holding different numbers of males. In ten areas studied the number of males varied between 4 and 17, and a Spearman rank correlation between repertoire size (i.e. number of unique figures) and number of singing males revealed a highly significant relationship ($r_s = 0.31$, $P < 0.01$, $n = 82$ males). This result also holds if controlling for the effect of other variables such as age, arrival order and colour (multiple regression analysis, $F = 12.7$, $P < 0.01$). Thus, the more males that were present the more figures were used; the analyses are based on tape recordings of males in what we call 'random territories' (see Chapter 11). Alternatively, however, the increase in repertoire size with the number of males present could also be due to the fact that large repertoires are more important in dense or large populations, for example for territory acquisition. When analysing songs from 'pairs' of close male neighbours, Dag Eriksson (pers. comm.) found no evidence that males incorporate song figures from the neighbouring male into their own song. Instead, however, he found some resemblance between a male's song and the song of last year's neighbour.

Intensity of Song

In a study of the causes of variation in song rate in male Pied Flycatchers performed outside Uppsala, Gottlander (1987) found that singing activity was influenced by weather conditions, time of day and season. Air temperature is intercorrelated with time of day and date in the season and therefore Gottlander used multiple regression methods to try to sort out which of the three factors had most influence on song rate. It turned out that all three variables, independently of each other, had a significant effect on song rate. Under good conditions, and when in full song, males sing about forty strophes ($\bar{x} = 37.9$) per five minutes, and von Haartman and Löhrl (1950) estimated the total number of strophes sung per day to be about 7000. However, song rate varies with the three variables mentioned above and singing also often becomes interrupted, e.g. by feeding or by the intrusion of other males. In the following we will look in more detail on the factors causing changes in singing activity.

At temperatures just above freezing point ($<4°C$) the mean song rate in Gottlander's study was about 9 songs per 5 min while it increased to about 25 at 20–23°C. However, she also found that in late May males sang more than early in May at comparable temperatures, and that males increased their song rates from arrival until pairing, even after having corrected for the effects of temperature, time and date. Early in the season, and at low temperatures, males probably spend their time foraging instead of singing. She further found that supplementary feeding influenced singing activity (Fig. 62), especially at low temperatures. This finding was corroborated in an experiment by Alatalo et al. (1990c). We fed

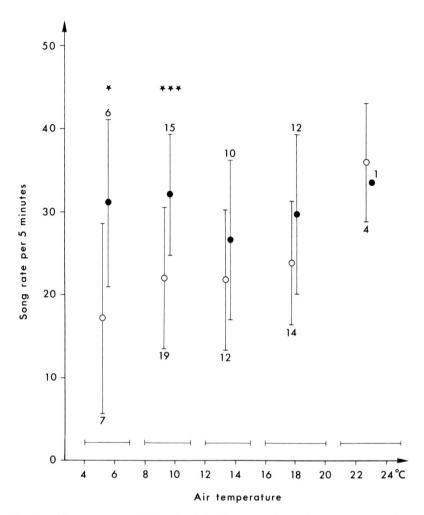

Fig. 62.   Mean song rate of fed males (solid dots) and of control males (open) at different temperatures in 1985 at Uppsala. SD is indicated by bars and the significance between the two groups by ★ = P < 0.05 and ★★★ = P < 0.001. Number of males are given for each 4–5 degrees temperature interval. Redrawn from Gottlander (1987).

half of the males in several woodlands with mealworms during cold (<7°C) and rainy periods. We found that males provided with extra food on average sang at a rate of 34 strophes per 5 min (n = 13 males) while unfed control males only sang 16 strophes per 5 min (n = 13; Fig. 63). When not singing these unfed males foraged, and in 21% of the five-minute periods we recorded them they did not sing at all.

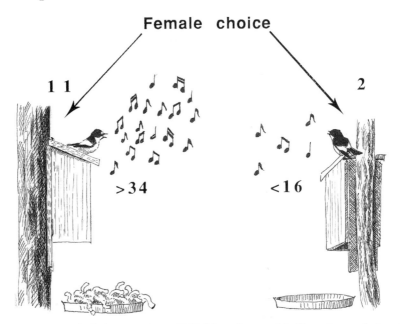

Fig. 63.   Design of a feeding experiment. Half of the males were fed with mealworms during cold and rainy weather. The result of this was that fed males sang more than unfed males, and the former also attracted females sooner in 11 of 13 cases.

TIMING OF SINGING

The most intense singing occurs in the early morning, after which singing decreases. Thus, Gottlander (1987) found that males sang about half as much at 14.00 hours as at 06.00 hours. In the afternoon another, but smaller, singing activity peak has been recorded (Curio, 1959b). Many hypotheses have been suggested for the dawn chorus peak of unmated males, which has been observed in most songbirds. All the hypotheses assume that males sing to attract mates or repel intruders, and that birds cannot sing and eat simultaneously. In brief, the hypotheses are as follows: dawn provides the best conditions for sound trans-mission (Henwood and Fabrick, 1979); dawn is the worst time for foraging and therefore the relative profitability of singing is higher (Kacelnik and Krebs, 1982); if migrant females arrive overnight the probability of attracting a female should be highest in the morning (see Mace, 1987). It has also been suggested that dawn is the best time for non-territorial males to seek vacant territories, and males should therefore announce their presence in a territory most intensively in the morning (Kacelnik and Krebs, 1982). A very different hypothesis was proposed by Montgomerie (1985), who argued that morning is the worst time to sing because at that time, after their overnight sleep, the birds have the lowest reserves of energy. If males want to show their quality to females they should do so at the most difficult time, i.e. at dawn. Hence, song becomes an uncheatable signal, and by choosing a male singing a lot early in the morning the female can mate with a high quality male. A general discussion on support for the various hypotheses is given by Mace (1987), who concluded that no single hypothesis could explain the patterns of dawn chorus found in the numerous species that have been studied.

On the basis of our observations on the singing behaviour of the Pied Flycatcher we can neither refute nor give full support to any single hypothesis, but we have found that a male's singing ability does influence his mating success (for further details see Chapter 11). Clearly, however, singing and foraging compete for time, as shown in the experiment with fed and unfed birds on cold mornings. Also, female Pied Flycatchers arrive at night or in the morning, and almost all pairings we have observed have occurred between dawn and midday (more than a hundred seen).

THE FUNCTION OF SONG

Bird song is generally assumed to have two main functions: attraction of a mate and defence of the territory against other males. In the Pied Flycatcher song seems primarily to serve the first function. There are two pieces of evidence pointing in favour of that view.

First, after having attracted a female to the territory the male's singing activity dramatically drops, as in many other songbirds, implying that an important function of the song is indeed mate attraction. Thus when we presented caged females in front of the nest boxes of unmated males their song rates dropped, on average, from 40 songs per 5 minutes to 3 ($n = 15$ males). We have no quantitative data showing the reduction in song rate after pairing, but in our experience it is possible to tell within a few minutes of observation whether a male has become mated or not by the intensity of his singing. Mated males may resume singing for short periods of time if the female is out of sight (males follow females during the pre-laying period, see Chapter 12). Males occasionally sing even if the female is close, but these songs are often short and incomplete as compared with full song. If the female is removed from the male, he normally starts singing full songs again within 10 minutes, and after about an hour he sings as much as unmated males do. Likewise, females often inspect several males before mating. If a nest-site is rejected by a prospecting female, the male will immediately start singing again after her departure. After the start of egg-laying males may resume their singing activity in a separate distant territory (for further details see below and Chapter 12).

The second piece of evidence favouring the view that males sing to attract females comes from an experiment performed by Eriksson and Wallin (1986) on Pied and Collared Flycatchers. They used special traps in the shape of a nest box which automatically trapped birds that perched on the entrance (Fig. 64; we use the same type of trap to catch unmated males). These nest-box traps were arranged in groups of four, with one in each corner of a square about 30 m per

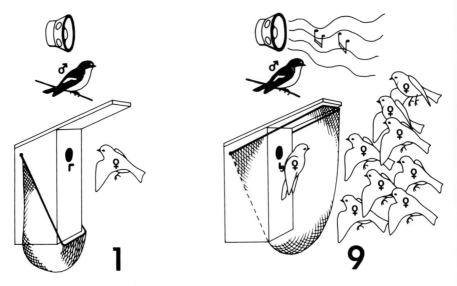

Fig. 64.   Experimental design of a song attraction experiment with boxes in which females became caught when perching at the 'nest box trap'. Figures denote the number of females caught at boxes with song broadcasted and boxes without male song. Figure based on the results of Eriksson and Wallin (1986).

side. Each trap was fitted with a dummy male about one metre away from it. At two of the traps song was broadcast from a tape recorder with a cassette containing a continuous loop of flycatcher song. The two other positions were silent, and the silent and singing positions were switched each day. In total seven groups of traps were used. The result of the experiment was that significantly more females were trapped in 'singing traps' than in 'silent traps', nine compared with one (Fig. 64). One objection might be that the study involved two species, though they are closely related. However, the result holds even if testing only for the Pied Flycatcher (six against one). The result of the experiment, thus, corroborates the idea that male song is a mate-attraction signal.

The second function of bird song is to keep other males out of the territory, and Pied Flycatcher song may well be used for this purpose too, though we do not have supporting data. The observation reported above regarding higher repertoire size in dense populations may, however, be an example of song serving a function in male–male interactions. Clearly, intrusions by males into other males' territories are frequent, and we have estimated the rate of territory intrusions to be about six per 100 min before female arrival (Alatalo *et al.*, 1987). Intruding males may be either neighbours with established territories or recently arrived males seeking a territory. Apart from possibly having a repellent function, song also attracts other males. In the song play-back experiment reported above many males were caught in the 'singing traps'. Likewise, in another experiment, nest-box groups with play-back song became occupied by males earlier than 'silent groups' (for details see Chapter 4), indicating that males are attracted by the song of other males. This might help prospecting males to find suitable breeding areas or nest-holes.

SINGING IN SECONDARY TERRITORIES

At about the time the female starts laying the male may move away into another separate territory and start singing again, most likely in an attempt to attract a second female (see Chapter 12 for details). The song of already-mated males in secondary territories closely resembles in structure and intensity that of unmated males in their primary territories. An example of the song strophes of a polygynous male in his first and second territories is shown in Figure 65. We have also made observations on already-mated males in secondary territories and on unmated males in the same area at the same time to look for differences in singing intensity. In this situation unmated males, on average, sang 26 strophes per 5 min while already-mated males in secondary territories sang at a rate of 21 strophes per 5 min (data mainly collected at Konnevesi, Finland; see also Fig. 85). This difference is statistically significant (Mann–Whitney U-test, $z = 2.03$, $P < 0.05$), but the difference is caused solely by the fact that already-mated males sometimes leave the secondary territory to visit the female in the first territory, while unmated males are present most of the time in their single territory. When present in secondary territories, already-mated males sing as much as unmated

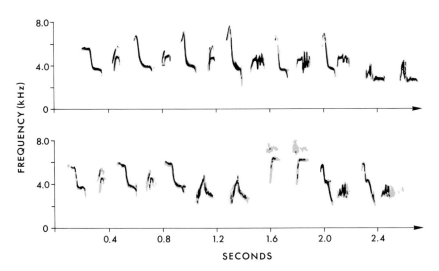

Fig. 65.   Sonograms of a male Pied Flycatcher singing at his primary territory (top) and the same bird singing at his secondary territory (bottom).

males, and hence males of different mating status are difficult to separate on song features. This statement is supported by a recent study at Uppsala, Sweden (Searcy *et al.*, 1991) which showed that the song rate of unmated males was about 40 strophes/5 min when present in the territory while the corresponding figure for already-mated males in secondary territories was 38 strophes (Mann–Whitney *U*-test, $P > 0.10$). The implications of this similarity in song rates will be discussed further in Chapter 12.

OTHER VOCALIZATIONS

Detailed descriptions of calls other than song have been given by von Haartman and Löhrl (1950), Creutz (1955) and Curio (1959b). The former authors identified 12 different male vocalizations (including song) and 9 different female vocalizations. Seven of these are used by both sexes. Among the most commonly heard are three types of alarm calls, of differing intensities: low (*'bit'*; *Warnlaut*), medium (*'tk'*; *Schmatzen*) and high (*'tzi'*; *Rivalenlaut*). The first two are mainly used against potential predators, and can especially be heard if we approach the nest; ringers of Pied Flycatcher nestlings must be very familiar with these sounds. The high-intensity alarm call is mainly associated with territorial combat between males. A third category of sounds are those used at the time of female arrival, and these probably have the function of persuading a female to inspect the nest-hole. When a female has been detected by the male he starts a high-pitched song (*Gepresster Gesang*) and, if she approaches, he will enter the nest-hole while switching to a different call (*Einschlüpfflaute*) before again turning to the high-pitched song inside the nest cavity. This behavioural sequence is further described in Chapter 11 and in photographs on pp. 158–159. These nest-presentation sounds can be heard from a distance of more than 100 m, and an experienced observer can immediately tell if a prospecting female is close by. However, as males are very excited when females are around they may some-times utter these nest-presentation calls to individuals of a completely different species; thus many nest-presentation calls are only false alarms. For description and interpretation of other, more rarely heard, vocalizations we refer the reader to the above cited authors since we have not made sufficient study of these calls and are, therefore, uncertain of their contexts.

SUMMARY

The song of the male Pied Flycatcher is built up of a repertoire of figures which can be combined in different ways into a strophe. Typically some of the figures in the beginning of each strophe are repeated a couple of times, after which there follows a medley of new figures. Each song lasts for about 2 s and contains on average a total of ten figures, four or five of which are usually different. The mean number of unique figures per 20 strophes is about 25, and the total number used in a season probably exceeds one hundred. Repertoire size, here defined as the total number of different figures used per 20 strophes, is smaller for one-year-old males than for older, though on an individual level we could not detect any significant increase in repertoire size between years. Singing intensity is influenced by air temperature, time of day and season. In full song under good conditions, males sing about forty strophes per five minutes. The main function of Pied Flycatcher song seems to be for the purpose of mate attraction, though we cannot exclude the possibility that it also serves to keep other males out of the territory. Apart from male song another 11 male and 9 female vocalizations (7 being shared) have been described, of which the most commonly heard are three types of alarm calls.

CHAPTER 10

Male Plumage Colour and its Variation

In most bird species males are more colourful than females, and it is generally assumed that elaborate male characters have evolved by sexual selection (e.g. Darwin, 1871; Hingston, 1933; Krebs, 1979), because females prefer males with such characters, or because these characters are employed as intrasexual aggressive signals, or both. Not only are Pied Flycatchers sexually dimorphic in colour, but males are very variable in their breeding plumage, and the species is one of the most variable of European birds. The head and back of males varies from jet black to brown or greyish-brown. Males of the latter category are sometimes almost indistinguishable from females. In this chapter we describe age differences in male colour as well as variation in colour within and between populations. We also speculate about how this plumage variation may have evolved, and what the adaptive advantages may be of having different colours. The importance of male colour for female choice, however, will be treated in Chapter 11.

COLOUR CLASSIFICATION AND VARIATION WITH AGE

Pied Flycatcher males moult into their breeding plumage on the wintering grounds in Africa (see Chapter 3). However, not all males become completely black on the back after their winter moult, so some of them will have a variable amount of brown feathering in their breeding plumage, and may therefore even look like females. The occurrence of brown-coloured Pied Flycatcher males has been known since the end of the 18th century. The German zoologist J. M. Bechstein (1757–1822) described brown Pied Flycatchers from Hessen in Germany, and considered them a separate species which he named *Muscicapa muscipeta* (In Lathams allgem. Übers. d. Vögel II, p. 319, 1794– ; as cited in Hartert, 1910). In a later handbook, this time about the breeding birds of Sweden, Nilsson (1835) adds a note to the description of the Pied Flycatcher where he mentions the occurrence in Sweden of breeding males in brown or female-like plumage. He examined some of these brown specimens but could not find them in any way different from dark males, apart from their colour. He suggested that brown males might be a form of 'normal' Pied Flycatchers in which the development of colour had stopped at too early a stage. In the next edition of his book (1858), he more correctly suggested that brown males were one-year-old individuals. Later studies have revealed that the pattern of colour variation is indeed age dependent, though in a more complex way than Nilsson thought.

It has long been known that in central European populations of the Pied Flycatcher, males are lighter in plumage than they are in northern Europe (e.g. Hartert, 1910). The first to examine the colour variation in detail was Rudolf Drost who in 1936 published a work on the breeding plumage of male Pied Flycatchers. From observations and trapping of Pied Flycatchers at the Heligoland Bird Observatory, off the northwest coast of Germany, he found migrants heading for the north to be darker than those breeding at lower latitudes. He therefore examined skins of males from museum collections in Germany, Austria and the Scandinavian countries, in total 237 individuals, and compared the amounts of black and brown feathers on head, back and rump. This allowed him to categorize males into seven colour groups (I–VII), from jet black to fully brown. In group I a male has black head, back and rump, and in group II a male is black but with a lightish rump. From III to VII males, according to this classification, become increasingly more brownish on the head and on the back. This categorization has been used in many later studies on male colour variation and is referred to as Drost's score. Males of score I, i.e. with a black rump, are very rare and, in fact, we have never seen a type I male. In addition to Drost's score we have also used a system of classifying males by estimating the surface area on the back and head (but not the rump) covered by non-black feathers (from 0 to 100%). An attempt to translate Drost's scores to our percentage estimates is as follows: I = 0%, II = 0–10%, III = 15–35%, IV = 40–60%, V = 65–85%, VI = 90–99% and VII = 100 %. Apart from very dark and very brown individuals, it is not possible to estimate exactly the percentage area that is black or brown, so we have used 5% intervals for birds of types III to V.

From his examination of skins, Drost (1936) found one-year-old Scandinavian males (including migrants collected on Heligoland) to be of mean colour type 4.2 (range: score II–VI) while those from Germany (probably also including some migrants) were browner (mean: 5.2, range: II–VII). Corresponding figures for older males were 3.0 (range I–V) and 4.6 (range: II–VII). Thus, Drost's study showed that older males were darker than one-year-old males, although there was a great overlap between the two age groups, and further that Scandinavian males were darker than German males. Drost's scores for Scandinavian birds coincide almost exactly with the figures we have obtained from Uppsala in central Sweden; we found older males to be of mean colour type 3.0 (range: II–VI, $n = 222$; Fig. 67) while the average colour type for one-year-old males was 4.2 (range: II–VII, $n = 186$; see also Appendix 5).

Since Drost's pioneer work many studies of the Pied Flycatcher have focused on male colour and its variation, though in many cases with the aim of studying

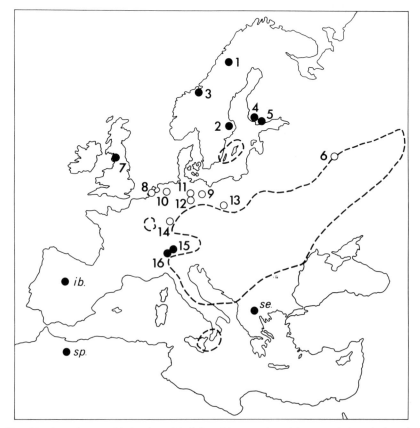

Fig. 66.   Distribution of dark-coloured (solid) and brown-coloured (open circles) Pied Flycatcher populations. The range of the Collared Flycatcher is indicated by the broken line. Numbers refer to sites listed in Appendix 5. ib., F. h. iberiae; sp., F. h. speculigera; se., F. h. semitorquata.

female choice (see Chapter 11) or avoidance of hybridization with the Collared Flycatcher (see Chapter 13). The general pattern that emerges from these studies confirms Drost's findings, namely that in central European populations of the Pied Flycatcher, males are indeed duller in breeding plumage than in more northerly or southerly populations (Appendix 5 and Fig. 66), but before going into the geographical variation we will explore colour variation between age classes.

As suggested in Nilsson's (1858) handbook and confirmed by Drost (1936), older males have a darker breeding plumage than do one-year-old males. This is the case for all examples listed in Appendix 5. However, in the Spanish subspecies (*iberiae*) there seems to be no change in the colour of males between the ages of one and two years (both are dark), while they become browner after that (Potti and Montalvo, 1991a). In Figures 67 and 68 we illustrate the distribution of colour types for one-year-old and older males from Uppsala, Sweden and Cumbria, England. The figures show that there is a marked skew towards dark plumage among older males (70–80% being of score II–III) while young birds show a more normal distribution over colour types. Separating males into more age classes (Table 12) shows that the main colour change occurs from the age of one to the age of two, while later they stay the same colour as when two years old. In our small sample of very old males we have no indications of males becoming light again, as was suggested from studies in Germany by Winkel *et al.* (1970) and in Spain by Potti and Montalvo (1991a), and might be expected if senescence occurs. In Table 12 we show the mean colour type, according to Drost's score, for males of different ages in our study area in Cumbria and from a site in Germany (Winkel *et al.*, 1970). The same pattern of males mainly becoming darker between the ages of one and two (as shown in Table 12) emerges if we follow the changes in the same individual males throughout their lives. By looking at changes between years we found that individual males from Cumbria

SWEDEN, 1982-86

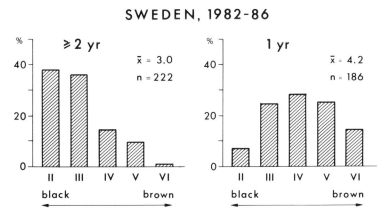

Fig. 67.   Distribution of male plumage colour of one-year-old and older Pied Flycatcher males according to Drost's (1936) score at Uppsala, central Sweden.

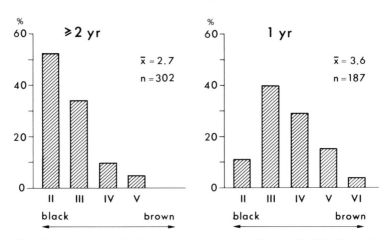

Fig. 68.   *Distribution of male plumage colour of one-year-old and older Pied Flycatcher males according to Drost's (1936) score in Cumbria, England.*

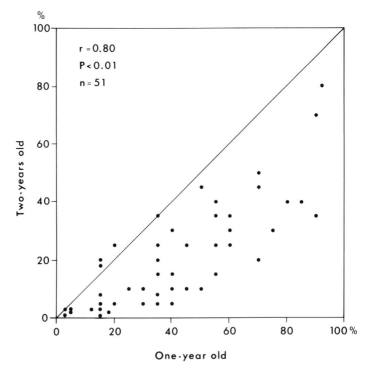

Fig. 69.   *Change in colour of individual Pied Flycatcher males from one year of age to the age of two. The colour is classified by estimating the area on the back and head covered by non-black feathers; thus 100% means a brown, female-like male. Data from Cumbria, England.*

*Table 12.   Male plumage colour at different ages according to Drost's
(1936) score. Data from Cumbria, England are from our own studies and
those from Germany from Winkel et al. (1970). Only birds of known age
are included.*

Age (years)	England Colour	n	Germany Colour	n
1	3.6	187	6.8	95
2	2.6	121	6.1	75
3	2.7	53	6.1	46
4	2.7	16	5.7	22
5	3.0	2	5.2	10
6	–	–	6.2	4

became on average 20% units darker from one year of age to the age of two
(paired t-test, $t = 9.6$, $P < 0.01$, $n = 51$, Fig. 69). In the next year there was no
significant change in plumage colour ($P = 0.26$, $n = 31$, Fig. 70) though two-
year-old individuals were more variable in plumage than were the same individuals as three years old ($F = 1.90$, $P < 0.05$). Again from three to four years of

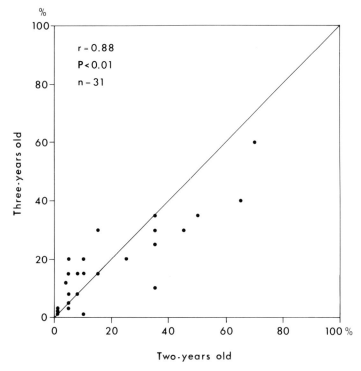

*Fig. 70.   Change in colour of individual Pied Flycatcher males from two years of age to the age of
three. Colour is classified as in Fig. 69. Data from Cumbria, England.*

age there was no significant change in plumage coloration, though in this case the sample was very small ($n = 11$). In conclusion, plumage colour is clearly age dependent with most of the colour change occurring between the ages of one and two years although there is also a great deal of variation within age classes (Figs 67 and 68). Possible costs and benefits of being black or brown in terms of mating success within populations will be discussed in Chapter 11, while in the present chapter we focus mainly on describing the differences in male coloration to be found within and between populations.

COLOUR VARIATION WITHIN AND BETWEEN POPULATIONS

Both black and brown colours in bird feathers are caused by melanin pigments, which are produced by special cells. Melanin is known to be formed by oxidation of the amino acid tyrosine; while the mechanism for regulation of the amount of melanin and hence of the colour of the feather is not fully known, it has been suggested that it depends on the stage at which oxidation of tyrosine ends (Ralph, 1969). While the synthesis and deposition of melanin are known to be affected by hormones, light intensity, day-length, temperature and the bird's general condition (Francis, 1986), the relative importance of each factor for the colour differences arising after the winter moult in the Pied Flycatcher is almost completely unknown. However, since old males are blacker than one-year-old males, older and more experienced individuals and/or birds in better condition may be able to produce darker feathers at moult as compared with young and inexperienced birds. Alternatively, the number of feathers moulted may vary between different males such that some males only moult a few body feathers while others moult most of them, implying that the brown feathers seen on males during the breeding season need not have been renewed in Africa.

Indeed, brown body feathers carried by newly arriving males are much more worn than are the dark feathers (Klas Allander, pers. comm.), which suggests that the brown feathers have not been moulted in Africa (moulted feathers should not be older than about 3 months). Alternatively, all body feathers could be moulted on the wintering grounds but brown ones are less resistant to wear than are black feathers and have therefore become more worn. It has been demonstrated in other species that the abrasion on feathers without melanin is much higher than on feathers with melanin (Burtt, 1979; Barrowclough and Sibley, 1980). However, if age, experience, or nutritional status when moulting are the main factors determining breeding plumage coloration, it becomes difficult to understand why Collared Flycatcher males almost invariably become fully black on the back after the winter moult while not all Pied Flycatcher males achieve this. Moreover, it seems unlikely that males in the brown German populations should be less able than males from other populations to grow dark feathers, or to moult at all. However, if the benefits of being black are small, the costs may easily exceed the benefits in some populations (e.g. those in Germany; see below for examples of such costs), and males should then stay brown the whole year. The easiest way to achieve a brown breeding coloration would be not to moult the body feathers in Africa. In this context it would be interesting to know whether females, which stay the same colour throughout the year, really moult their body feathers in winter as stated in the literature.

In our Cumbrian study population offspring largely return to their natal woodlands to breed, and we have therefore been able to study the resemblance between fathers and sons with respect to colour variation. In that analysis we controlled for the change in male colour by age by assigning a 'relative' plumage rank to each male in relation to the total distribution of colour scores within age classes (one-year-old or older). Thus, for example, a male with about 20% brown feathers on his head and back became classified as a 'median coloured bird' if he was old, but was given a rank to the darker end of the plumage range if he was a one-year-old. After these transformations we regressed the plumage rank of sons on their fathers and thus obtained an estimate of the heritability of male colour (Fig. 71), i.e. the extent to which the genes of the father influence the colour of the son. Our estimate, based on 92 father–son comparisons, is 50%. This would mean that about half of the observed phenotypic variation in

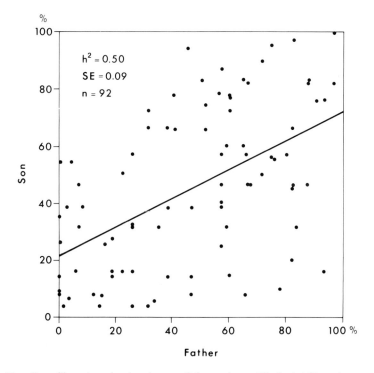

Fig. 71.   *Resemblance in male colour between fathers and sons. The heritability estimate amounts to 50%, as described by the regression line. See text for how we controlled for the change in male colour by age. Data from Cumbria, England.*

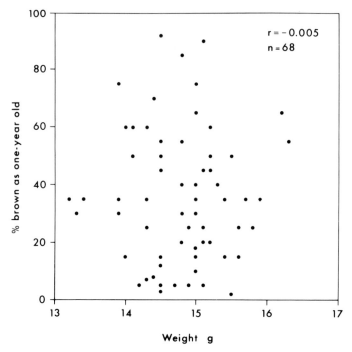

Fig. 72.   Relationship between weight at fledging and plumage colour as a one-year-old. Data from Cumbria, England.

plumage colour can be attributed to the additive effects of genes while the rest of the variation must be explained by some other factors, most likely environmental ones. However, we found no relationship between the weight of the bird as a fledgling and its colour as a breeding male the next year ($r = -0.005$, $n = 68$; Fig. 72), which may indicate that conditions outside the breeding area and season are more important for the determination of male breeding coloration than are conditions during the nestling stage, if the bird's condition is at all important for subsequent colour development. In this context it is worth pointing out that most nestlings recruited into the breeding population in Cumbria were rather heavy as fledglings, and thus probably were in good condition when leaving the nest (Figs 52 and 72).

Dark-coloured Pied Flycatcher populations are mainly found in Scandinavia, England and Switzerland while brown-coloured populations occur in Germany, Poland and the USSR (Fig. 66). The subspecies in Spain (*iberiae*), in northwest Africa (*speculigera*) and in the Balkans (*semitorquata*) are dark in plumage, in fact even darker than *hypoleuca* from Scandinavia. Also males of the closely related Collared Flycatcher have a very black and white breeding plumage (see Appendix 1). So why this geographic variation in breeding plumage in the Pied Flycatcher?

Røskaft *et al.* (1986) proposed several explanations: (1) following Baker and Parker (1979), predation pressure might vary geographically, and in populations exposed to heavier predation males should be more brightly coloured because conspicuous individuals might be avoided by predators; (2) in Pied Flycatcher populations sympatric with the Collared Flycatcher, males should benefit by being browner because brown males should be avoided by Collared Flycatcher females and therefore risks of interspecific matings should be reduced; or (3) because of competition between Pied and Collared Flycatcher males for nest-holes and territories, brown Pied Flycatcher males might be favoured by selection because they resemble females and as a result may avoid harassment from the dominant Collared Flycatcher males.

With respect to predation risks and coloration, von Haartman (1985) took the completely opposite view to that of Baker and Parker. He argued that by being conspicuously coloured a bird is more easily discovered by a predator and therefore runs a greater risk of being taken; one important predator of the Pied Flycatcher, according to von Haartman, is the Sparrowhawk. The view that brightness might enhance predation risks is supported by the facts that males moult into a cryptic plumage outside the breeding season and that females are inconspicuous throughout the year. Von Haartman suggested that Sparrow-hawks are more common in central Europe than elsewhere, and that they might be the selective force behind the occurrence of brown-coloured Pied Flycatcher populations in Germany.

With regard to colour variation within populations, Slagsvold and Lifjeld (1988a) proposed that a black colour might better signal presence in the territory which should be more important for early than for late arriving males. To explain the geographical variation in male blackness they argued that if males and females arrive simultaneously, rather than males arriving in advance of females, there are reduced benefits in being dark. We will now examine these explanations for colour variation between and within populations at greater length. In doing so we will group them under such new headings that they will fall into more mutually exclusive groups.

PREDATION IN RELATION TO MALE COLOUR

The hypothesis that bright coloration should have evolved in response to predation was originally suggested as an explanation of sexual dichromatism in birds (Baker and Parker, 1979). This hypothesis, named the 'unprofitable prey hypothesis', states that, by being conspicuous, an individual informs a potential predator that it is in good condition and therefore difficult to catch. So far, however, there is little empirical evidence favouring this idea. Indeed, Røskaft *et al.* (1986) argued that the unprofitable prey hypothesis was unlikely to explain the geographic colour variation in male Pied Flycatchers. Their main argument was that brown males do not suffer higher mortality rates than black ones as predicted from the hypothesis. Instead they found dark males in their study area in Norway to suffer a higher mortality than brown males, although the sample size was not very large. Moreover, if the unprofitable prey argument was to work, it is difficult to understand why males should moult into a cryptic plumage during the winter stay in Africa, where predation pressure may well be higher than on the breeding grounds. Whether predation, such as that by Sparrowhawks, is higher in areas with brown Pied Flycatchers than in areas with black populations, as suggested by von Haartman (1985), also remains to be determined.

As mentioned above, Røskaft *et al.* (1986) found a higher mortality, measured by return rate to the breeding area of the previous year, among dark (with plumage score <IV on Drost's scale) than among brown males in their sample from Trondheim in central Norway. However, in none of the three other data sets, namely one from Finland and two from Germany, presented in the same publication, was any significant differences found in return rate between black and brown males. Contrary to these findings, and in accordance with the derived prediction of the unprofitable prey hypothesis, Slagsvold and Lifjeld (1988a) found a lower return rate among brown males than among dark males. Surprisingly, this study was carried out in the same area as that of Røskaft *et al.* Slagsvold and Lifjeld, however, did not interpret their data as support for the unprofitable prey hypothesis since only a few males disappeared during the breeding season, and these disappearing males were not particularly brownish. Instead, Slagsvold and Lifjeld interpreted their results in terms of age and experience: dark males are often old and because they are experienced they survive better between years. In none of the studies referred to above was the effect of age fully controlled for; but it was accomplished in a Spanish study where it was found that, among older birds, brown males returned at a significantly lower rate than black ones (Potti and Montalvo, 1991a).

We have data on return rate in relation to the colour of male breeding plumage and to male age, from both Uppsala, Sweden and Cumbria, England. In Figs 73 and 74 these data are shown for one-year-old and older males separately, but in none of the four comparisons was there any difference in return rate in relation to male colour, and we therefore conclude that breeding plumage coloration is unlikely to affect overwinter survival chances very much. This conclusion is based on data sets large enough to reduce the risk of obtaining significant differences by chance. As mentioned earlier (Chapter 8), some males breed when they are one year old while others do not turn up until their second year of life, and one can ask whether some might delay their breeding for a year in order to develop a more conspicuous breeding coloration. However, when we looked at plumage darkness of males starting breeding at the ages of one and two years, respectively, we found no significant difference in colour between these two groups in their second year of life. Similarly, von Haartman (1985) found no significant difference in the colour of second-year males starting breeding at the ages of one and two years old, respectively. These observations imply that colour is unrelated to survival though, of course, we do not know the colour of males

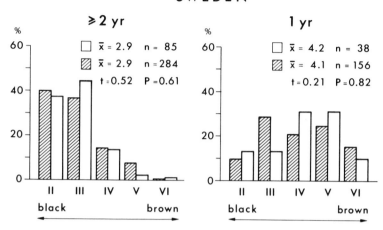

Fig. 73. *Return rates of one-year-old and older Pied Flycatcher males in relation to their plumage colour according to Drost's (1936) score at Uppsala, central Sweden. Hatched columns show males that did not return the following year and open columns those that did return.*

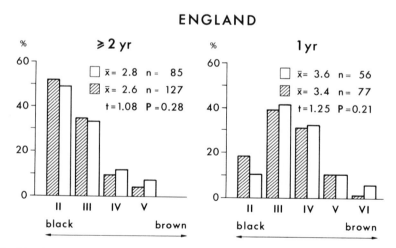

Fig. 74. *Return rate of one-year-old and older Pied Flycatcher males in relation to their plumage colour according to Drost's (1936) score in Cumbria, England. Column symbols as in Fig. 73.*

not found as one-year-olds and which died before they reached the age of two, or the colour of two-year-old first breeders when they were one year old.

AVOIDANCE OF COLLARED FLYCATCHER FEMALES

This hypothesis assumes that a brown breeding plumage confers a mating advantage in areas of sympatry with the Collared Flycatcher. Male Pied Flycatchers can be of any colour between brown and black, while almost all male Collared Flycatchers are jet black on the back. Thus, if both species are present in the same area, brown Pied Flycatcher males may more efficiently avoid mating with Collared Flycatcher females as compared to black (for costs of mating with the wrong species, see Chapter 13). Røskaft *et al.* (1986) found reason to support this explanation because, on the whole, brown Pied Flycatcher populations occur in the zones of contact or overlap with the Collared Flycatcher (see also Fig. 66). We have analysed how male colour influences the probability of obtaining a partner of the wrong species in an overlap area on the island of Gotland in the Baltic Sea. We compared the colour of males which did and did not mate with Collared Flycatcher females. The mean plumage coloration of Pied Flycatcher males on this island did not differ from that of males in allopatric populations on the mainland. If Collared Flycatcher females avoid brown males, we would expect dark Pied Flycatcher males on the island of Gotland to form mixed pairs more often than brown males. An obvious complication is that colour seems not to be a character used by Pied Flycatcher females as a cue in their mate choice (see also Chapter 11), and this might also be true in the Collared Flycatcher. Anyway, the mean colour of Pied Flycatcher males that mated with females of their own species did not differ significantly from that of males mating heterospecifically (mean colour score ($\pm$SD): 3.29 ± 1.47, $n = 87$ versus 3.52 ± 0.98, $n = 27$; Alatalo *et al.*, 1990b). Thus, the mean values do not suggest that brown Pied Flycatcher males are less likely to mate with the wrong species than are dark males.

However, a closer examination of the colour distribution of males mating with the correct and the wrong species, respectively, revealed that the variances differed significantly ($F = 2.27$, $P = 0.01$) with few black or brown but many intermediate males (scores III and IV) having heterospecific mates (Table 18). The colour distribution of males mated with a conspecific, on the other hand, more closely fitted the 'normal' colour score distribution. This may mean that brown males are indeed avoided by Collared Flycatcher females, but the same would also apply to dark males. An explanation of this seemingly contradictory result will be offered in the next section. None the less, without being able to demonstrate convincingly that brown male coloration in the Pied Flycatcher actually confers a mating advantage in areas where both flycatcher species occur together, we find it plausible that brown male Pied Flycatchers may be less likely to mate with a heterospecific female.

AVOIDANCE OF COLLARED FLYCATCHER MALES

Kral *et al.* (1988) advanced the idea that interspecific male–male interactions may play an important role in the evolution of brown coloration in the
male Pied Flycatcher. They presented black- and brown-coloured Pied Flycatcher dummies on top of nest boxes inhabited by Collared Flycatchers,
together with a song play-back, and measured male aggressiveness towards the
dummy. From the results of their experiment, the authors concluded that
brown-coloured males were less frequently attacked than were dark males. Lars
Gustafsson (pers. comm.) made a more realistic experiment using live Collared
and Pied Flycatchers on the island of Gotland. He moved nest boxes occupied
by Pied Flycatcher males, in small steps, towards Collared Flycatcher nest-
sites, and measured the distance at which the Pied Flycatcher became evicted
from its box. Gustafsson found that brown Pied Flycatcher males could be
moved closer to a Collared Flycatcher nest-site than could dark ones (Fig. 75),
which supports the idea that a brown plumage does confer an advantage in
avoiding interspecific aggression (see also Røskaft *et al.*, 1986; Kral *et al.*, 1988).

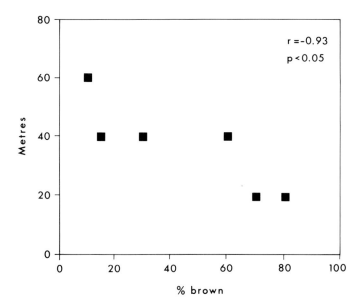

Fig. 75. *On the island of Gotland where both Collared and Pied Flycatchers occur together, nest
boxes defended by Pied Flycatcher males were moved towards a box defended by a Collared Flycatcher
male. The figure shows at what distance from the Collared Flycatcher box the Pied Flycatcher male
was evicted in relation to the latter's plumage colour. Browner males could be moved closer to a
Collared Flycatcher than could dark males.*

In sympatric populations the Pied Flycatcher seems to be subordinate in re-lation to the Collared Flycatcher and is often relegated to less preferred habitats (Löhrl, 1955; Alatalo *et al.*, 1982a). Thus, by being brown, Pied Flycatcher males might reduce competition from the socially dominant Collared Fly-catcher and as a result be able to take up territories of better quality than can dark males.

In this context we will recall the results reported in the previous section, namely that we found fewer black and brown as compared to intermediately coloured mating with the wrong species (Table 18). This pattern may arise because Pied Flycatcher males of different colours tend to occupy different parts of the breeding habitat when living in the same area as the Collared Flycatcher. A closer analysis of the data from Gotland shows that males breeding in coniferous forest were significantly darker than those in deciduous forest (mean colour score ($\pm$SD): 3.02 ± 1.32, $n = 53$ versus 3.61 ± 1.35, $n = 62$; $t = 2.38$, $P = 0.02$). Within the deciduous habitat (preferred by both species), Pied Flycatcher males breeding in the periphery of woodlands were significantly darker than were males breeding in more central parts (colour score ($\pm$SD): 3.19 ± 1.22, $n = 31$ versus 4.00 ± 1.03, $n = 18$; $t = 2.35$, $P \approx 0.02$). Colour is known to be age dependent, but there were no significant differences in the age of Pied Flycatcher males breeding in coniferous as compared to deciduous forest, nor between those in interior and exterior parts of deciduous woodlands (Lars Gustafsson, pers. comm.). Alternatively, and as seems more likely, this pattern of Pied Flycatcher males of different colours occupying different forest types or parts of a woodland may arise because dark Pied Flycatcher males are prevented from taking up territories in the habitats most highly preferred by Collared Flycatcher males. As a result they are forced to breed in less preferred places, such as coniferous forest or forest edges. Collared Flycatcher females might search less intensively for mates in coniferous forest, since Collared Flycatcher breeding density is much lower in coniferous (0.6 pairs/ha) than in deciduous forest (3.2 pairs/ha; Tomas Pärt, pers. comm.). Likewise, a much smaller proportion (18%) of all Pied Flycatchers become engaged in mixed matings in coniferous forest than in deciduous forest (36%). Therefore, by being forced into less preferred areas, black Pied Flycatcher males become less likely to mate with the wrong species.

Brown males, on the other hand, may be able to take up territories in the centre of deciduous woodlands because Collared Flycatcher males do not recognize them as potential competitors, while Collared Flycatcher females may avoid them because they do not look like potential mates. Consequently, Pied Fly-catcher males of intermediate colour may suffer most because some of them might be able to take up territories in the most preferred habitat and also be chosen by Collared Flycatcher females. As a consequence, brown Pied Flycatcher males might be favoured in sympatric populations if interspecific male–male competition is a strong selective force.

'SIGNALLING OF PRESENCE'

This hypothesis mainly concerns colour variation within populations and suggests that by having a conspicuous plumage coloration a male can more efficiently advertise his ownership of a territory to potential intruders (Slagsvold and Lifjeld, 1988a). These rivals can thus more easily discover if a territory is occupied or not; territory owners are usually victorious over intruders, but fights might last longer if an intruder has spent a long time in the territory without having detected its owner. Thus, conspicuous coloration might reduce the cost of holding a territory. The cost of being conspicuous was thought to be a greater danger from predators. Slagsvold and Lifjeld further argued that early males should benefit more by being conspicuous than should late males because early in the season visible cues should be more important than late in the season, when deciduous trees have developed a dense canopy. Also, rates of intrusion into territories are higher early than late in the season, and early males have to wait longer before mating than do late arriving individuals. Slagsvold and Lifjeld also proposed that if the arrival time of males and females to the breeding grounds overlap to a high degree this will make the benefits of conspicuous colour less important because then males will not have to wait so long to mate. In accordance with this prediction Slagsvold and Lifjeld found that the sexes of a brown-coloured population in Germany arrived more synchronously than was the case for their study population in Norway. The more synchronous arrival of Pied Flycatcher males and females in Germany than in Norway could be that the presence of Collared Flycatchers delays the establishment of territories by Pied Flycatcher males in Germany.

In order to test these predictions one would wish to obtain information on the arrival times of the two sexes from more parts of the distribution range – e.g. from the black populations in Spain and North Africa – even though that would still not be enough to prove the validity of the 'signalling of presence' hypothesis. Recently some data on arrival time from one year in central Spain has been published by Potti and Montalvo (1991b). Their data suggest that the difference in arrival time between the sexes is about the same in Spain as in Scandinavia, i.e. males are about a week ahead of females (as predicted by Slagsvold and Lifjeld for dark populations; median arrival dates were 9 and 17 May).

Despite the logic of the 'signalling of presence' hypothesis, we do not feel convinced that it is a selective force strong enough to explain the large colour variation within and between Pied Flycatcher populations. One objection is that it does not explain why Collared Flycatcher males do not exhibit colour variation, for they also arrive in early May and inhabit the same types of deciduous forest. Another is that it must be important for late Pied Flycatcher males too, to signal their presence; moreover, song may serve this function much more efficiently than visual stimuli, and indeed all unmated males sing vigorously.

WHY DOES THE PLUMAGE OF THE PIED FLYCATCHER MALE VARY?

In our view, no single one of the hypotheses so far presented can explain all the patterns of male colour variation within and between Pied Flycatcher populations. Yet, we agree with Røskaft *et al.* that interspecific competition with the Collared Flycatcher must in some way be involved. Both species compete for resources in areas of sympatry: for example, both are hole-nesters, both prefer deciduous woodland, and they have greatly overlapping foraging niches (e.g. Alerstam *et al.*, 1978). Collared Flycatcher males are probably socially dominant over Pied Flycatcher males (Löhrl, 1955) because of their slightly larger size (Alatalo *et al.*, 1982a). This explains why Pied Flycatchers, in areas of sympatry, are more often found in less preferred habitats and along woodland edges than would be expected from the species' habitat distribution where Collared Flycatchers do not occur. By being brown rather than black, Pied Flycatcher males might be sufficiently different from Collared Flycatcher males to escape aggression from them (see Fig. 75). This does not necessarily imply that Pied Flycatcher males have to mimic the plumage of Collared Flycatcher females to avoid aggression, as has been suggested. The most important thing might simply be to differ in plumage. However, female choice might also be involved in the process selecting for brown male plumage. Brown Pied Flycatcher males seem to be less often involved in heterospecific matings, which adds another benefit to wearing a brown coloration in sympatric regions. One problem with this 'avoidance of Collared Flycatchers' explanation, however, is that many of the brown-coloured Pied Flycatcher populations in central Europe live far from any areas inhabited by the Collared Flycatcher (Fig. 66), and therefore the selection pressure for avoiding hybridization cannot be very strong. A fuller treatment of hybridization risks in relation to morphology and age will be given in Chapter 13.

The presence of brown-coloured individuals in areas far outside the Collared Flycatcher's distribution range might be a result of gene flow between populations. As shown in Appendix 4, natal fidelity is quite weak in most Pied Flycatcher populations and therefore exchange of individuals between brown and black populations might occur. But why then are not all male Pied Flycatchers brown? We assume that there must exist some selective advantages of black as opposed to brown coloration in areas of allopatry, and in our view these advantages are most likely to be related to male–male interactions, mating advantages, or mating system. These possible benefits of blackness in populations far from the Collared Flycatcher's range will be discussed in the following two chapters.

SUMMARY

No bird species breeding in Europe, with the possible exception of the Ruff and maybe also the Common Buzzard and the Honey Buzzard, shows so much variation in breeding plumage coloration as does the male Pied Flycatcher. This variation ranges continuously from fully black on the back to fully brown, in which case males become very similar to females. The coloration also varies geographically. Within populations, one-year-old males, on average, are browner than older males, though there is a great deal of overlap. In a comparison between populations central European birds stand out as exceptionally brown, and are surrounded by blacker populations. This colour variation has been the subject of many studies, but so far there has been no generally accepted explanation for the within-population nor for the between-population variation. However, there is some evidence to suggest that in zones of contact between the Pied and the Collared Flycatcher, males of the former species obtain a greater benefit from wearing a brown plumage than they do elsewhere, because they can attain better territories and also avoid mating with the wrong species.

CHAPTER 11

Pair Formation and Female Choice

The cues used in choosing a mate have been the subject of many studies on bird behaviour, not least in the Pied Flycatcher. There are many reasons to believe that choice of mate should be an active process, as opposed to a random one, because individuals differ in quality, as do the resources in their possession. Thus, many kinds of benefits may accrue to a bird choosing one mate rather than another. In most bird species, including the Pied Flycatcher, females are the choosing sex at pair formation. Inevitably, this choice process has costs. For example, if a female for some reason rejects a male but then cannot find a better breeding situation after a further search, the first option may no longer be free. The degree of female discrimination will depend on the cost of this mate sampling procedure. If importance is attached to immediate benefits such as paternal care or quality of territory, then female choice should be based mainly on these factors rather than on others that might only give some future benefits.

Pair formation in the Pied Flycatcher takes place on the breeding grounds and soon after female arrival. In this chapter we will describe male and female behaviours during the period of female settlement, and discuss what cues may possibly be used by females when choosing a male and a nest-site. Variations in male singing performance, plumage coloration and territory quality are likely cues for female choice in the Pied Flycatcher.

MALE AND FEMALE BEHAVIOURS AT PAIR FORMATION

Males arrive on the breeding grounds ahead of the females (Table 3 and Fig. 14), and start to sing as soon as they have occupied a nest-hole. Females usually arrive during the night and most pairings seem to occur between early morning and midday. Very little is known about female behaviour before pair formation; for example, the usual time lapse between arrival and pair formation, the number of males inspected, and the cues used to find and evaluate males are almost unknown components of female pre-mating behaviour.

If a prospecting female approaches a singing male, he will vigorously demonstrate the nest-hole by repeatedly flying to and from the entrance, while emitting a characteristic high-pitched song (equivalent to the *Einschlüpflaute* described in Chapter 9, and in von Haartman and Löhrl (1950), and Curio (1959b)). If the female approaches more closely, the male often jumps into the nest cavity, more or less continuously emitting a low-amplitude vocalization, which might entice the female to perch at the entrance and enter the hole. The male then leaves the nest-hole and perches outside it (see also the photographs on pages 158–159). After the female has left the hole, the behaviour described above might be repeated several times. After these nest inspections the female either departs, and the male resumes singing, or she remains in the vicinity of the site, having accepted the breeding situation offered. The fact that females sometimes leave a male suggests that they do indeed inspect and compare several males and nest-sites before making their choice. The nest-site presentation phase is often followed by a chase in the neighbourhood of the nest-site. It looks as if the male was attacking the female which flies away with the male following close behind. This pursuit can last for more than a minute and looks rather violent. It may take the birds in all directions from the ground to the tree-tops, often with abrupt turns, and ends by both members of the newly formed pair perching near the nest-site. We have no interpretation for this chase, although it looks more or less

A female has been attracted to a male's territory and he shows the entrance of the nesting cavity. (Photo: M. W. Pettersson.)

The male enters the nest site. (Photo: M. W. Pettersson.)

The male tries to persuade the female to inspect the nest site, and is calling from inside. (Photo: M. W. Pettersson.)

The female starts inspecting the potential breeding site. (Photo: M. W. Pettersson.)

like an attempt by the male to force a copulation. Von Haartman (in von Haartman *et al.*, 1963–72) called the chase 'sexual flight' and actually saw males trying to force copulation with the female during the chase. Alternatively, the chase may be some kind of test of the quality of the other partner. For example, males should avoid females if they have been already inseminated by other males, and such females, if carrying developing eggs, might have reduced manoeuvrability and endurance which could be shown up in a flight pursuit. On the other hand, we have never seen a male reject a prospecting female. The flight-chase could also be interpreted the other way around, the female trying to test the quality of the male; or the chase could simply be some form of initial aggression before pair-bonds are formed.

The singing male is very watchful of the goings-on around the nest-site, and approaching females are often quickly discovered. However, males sometimes make mistakes, and react with their special female attraction call to other birds in the neighbourhood. This particular call is very conspicuous, and to a practised observer it is easy to hear, even at some distance, when a male is visited by a female. The call is probably just as noticeable to other male flycatchers and we have several times seen unmated males, sometimes with their own territories several hundred metres away, trying to enter a nest box prior to the male that has attracted the female.

CUES FOR THE FEMALE'S CHOICE OF MATE

There are several possible benefits for females in being particular in their choice of a mate. These include male quality, for example good genes or superior paternal ability, the quality of the resources held by the male or, of course, some combination of these factors. Another possibility is that choice of a mate is completely random. If female choice is not random, the criterion used might depend on whether she expects future or immediate rewards. We try to deal with both these possibilities in the following account.

From observational studies alone it is often difficult to tell which factor is the most important for female choice. Let us take an example. Older Pied Flycatcher males arrive at the breeding grounds earlier than do one-year-old males (Chapter 3). Older males on average are also darker than yearling males (Chapter 10) and have longer wings (Table 4). Early males, which are old and dark, can take the best territories, leaving poorer breeding situations for later-arriving young and brown individuals. Thus, if we find that older males mate first, this may be due to a female preference for old males, or for black males, or the preference may be for certain territories regardless of male age and plumage colour. This issue is further complicated by the fact that early arriving females can of course only choose between the males that are already present at that time. Thus, we do not know which male they would have chosen if all males that later might take up territories in the area had been present at the arrival of the first female. To be able to study these problems and to distinguish between the importance of male arrival time, male characteristics and territory quality for female choice one has to conduct field experiments. In the following we will describe the results from one such experiment we carried out in 1985 and 1986 outside Uppsala.

To separate the effects of male arrival time, male age, plumage colour and territory quality we (Alatalo *et al.*, 1986b) put up nest boxes in such a way as to prevent males from choosing a particular territory; they therefore occupied what we shall hereafter call 'random territories'. The procedure to achieve this was as follows. We picked several deciduous woodlands without existing nest boxes, numbered suitable trees on which boxes could be put up, and then drew the random order in which to use these sites. Before the arrival of the first Pied Flycatcher male we erected two nest boxes close to each other (5–10 m) at the first, randomly drawn, site within a wood. We consistently used new boxes with an entrance diameter of 28 mm to ensure high-quality nest-sites and to reduce the variance in quality between sites. Thus, the first male to arrive at each woodland found only a single site to occupy (note that Pied Flycatchers prefer nest boxes over natural cavities). As soon as this male had occupied this site and had begun to sing, another pair of nest boxes were put up at the next randomly chosen site in each woodland. Arriving males thus had no choice of territory because only a single vacant site existed at any given time, and also they were not allowed to change sites. If a male tried to take over the new site provided for the next arriving male the second site was removed; then the male always returned to defend his original site, and the next site in the random order was prepared for the next male. In this way we distributed 87 males at random sites relative to territory quality in six different woodlands over two years.

All the males were ringed for individual recognition, weighed, measured and aged, and their plumage coloration was determined. Their song was recorded before they attracted females, and we made sonograms for samples of 20 songs from each male. For each box we also measured variables of habitat quality such as nest height, angle of box, nest-tree circumference, and the number of trees of different species around the nest-site. When the last male arrived many females had already settled in the study areas. On a given day all these females were trapped and released about 20 km away, so they were unlikely to return. Beginning on the following day we recorded the new pairing order of males until all were mated. In one study area, in 1985, we repeated this removal and gave a second set of females an opportunity to settle. The two settling orders of females in that particular area were significantly correlated (Spearman rank correlation $r_s = 0.78$, $P < 0.01$, $n = 15$), which shows that males were chosen in a similar way by both sets of females. This supports the idea that females make an active choice and select males and nest sites according to some standard, and not just randomly. Likely cues then are male traits or territory features. We therefore correlated female mating order with male arrival order, song performance, male characteristics and nest-box and habitat measurements. Each male within each area was given a rank value for pairing order, thus the first male to pair got rank 1, the second 2, and so forth. To be able to combine areas and years into one data set we transformed these ranks according to the formula $(2 \times \text{rank} - 1)/(2 \times n)$

which gives standardized ranks so that the first male gets rank 0 and the last rank 1 (n = total number of males in an area; for further details see Alatalo *et al.*, 1986b).

IMPORTANCE OF MALE CHARACTERISTICS FOR FEMALE CHOICE

Under natural conditions there is usually a positive correlation between male arrival order and female mating order, that is, the first Pied Flycatcher male to arrive at an area is also the first to be mated while the last to arrive is the last to be mated. Thus, by only observing the natural pattern of female settlement, one gets the impression that males that arrive early are preferred by females (Alatalo *et al.*, 1984d). However, in the experiment described above, in which males were not allowed to choose between territories, this correlation between male arrival order and female mating order was removed ($r_s = 0.07$, $P = 0.53$; Table 13, Fig. 76), implying that arrival time *per se* had no significant influence on pairing order.

What about male morphology and song performance? The results of the random territories experiment showed that no significant correlations existed between male traits, including song characteristics, and the pairing order of females (Table 13), which means that male traits are probably of little importance in female choice. Thus, for example, everything else being equal, dark males did not attract females sooner than brown males, nor older males than younger males, nor heavier males than lighter males. However, males singing complex songs seemed to have a slight mating advantage over males singing simple songs. In the following pages we will look at the importance of song performance and male morphology in more detail.

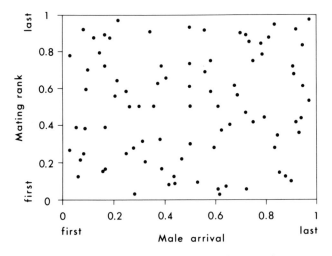

Fig. 76.   *Correlation between male arrival and mating order in random territories.* $r_s = 0.07$, $P = 0.53$, n = 87.

Table 13. Spearman rank correlations between male characteristics, male singing performance and female mating order in the experiment with random territories (see p. 161 for details).

Male characteristic	Range	r_s	n	P
Arrival order		0.07	87	0.53
Age (years)	1–4	−0.02	80	0.81
Plumage darkness (%)	1–95	0.08	87	0.44
Tarsus length (mm)	18.0–20.5	−0.06	85	0.57
Wing length (mm)	75.0–84.0	0.04	85	0.70
Weight (g)	11.0–14.0	0.05	84	0.68
Song repertoire[1]	6–71	0.17	82	0.13
Song versatility[2]	2.4–6.0	0.16	46	0.27
Mean strophe length (s)[3]	1.4–2.4	0.01	48	0.93
Song rate[4]	17.0–56.5	0.03	48	0.86

(1) Total number of unique figures per 20 songs. (2) Mean number of different figures per 20 songs. (3) Mean strophe length of all songs sung in 5 min. (4) Mean number of songs in 5 min.

Male song

In the random territories experiment there was a tendency for males with large song repertoires (see Chapter 9 for how repertoire is defined) to attract females more quickly than males with small repertoires (Table 13). Laboratory studies on Song Sparrows, Red-winged Blackbirds, Great Tits and *Acrocephalus* warblers have shown that hormone-implanted females (see below) respond more to complex than to simple play-back songs, suggesting that repertoire size is indeed important for female attraction (see review by Catchpole, 1987). We have performed laboratory experiments on the Pied Flycatcher with hormone-implanted females. By implanting females subcutaneously with oestradiol (a female sexual hormone), packed in silastic tubing which permits a slow release of the hormone into the bloodstream, it is possible to induce copulation invitations or other displays by certain external stimuli. In 1987 and 1988 we trapped females in nest box areas around Uppsala just after pairing and brought them to the laboratory. They were kept in individual cages and fed on a mixture of live mealworms and dried insects. A few days after capture a subcutaneous hormone implantation was made in the pectoral region, with oestradiol packed into 10 mm long silastic tubings, by making a small incision in the skin and inserting the implant. The incision was closed with a detergent plaster spray. The implantation clearly caused very little harm to the birds, and they were very calm throughout the operation, which took 1–2 minutes. Some 10 days after implantation the tests took place with the birds in a larger cage. After the experiment the implants were removed and the birds released.

Each female was tested only once, and for a period of 30 minutes she was confronted with a nest box behind which, in random order, we broadcast a complex and a simple Pied Flycatcher song as well as a Willow Warbler song. All trials started with 5 min of silence, and the bouts of song were each separated by 5 min of silence. Complex and simple songs were fabricated by broadcasting sequences of seven different strophes or repeating the same strophe seven times. The total broadcast time per minute was the same in all cases. Of 17 females tested in this experiment, 15 responded and visited the nest box. Nine females made a larger number of visits when complex Pied Flycatcher song was broadcast and three when simple song was played back, while in two cases it was a draw. In total, 77 nest-box visits were made when complex Pied Flycatcher song was played, 33 during simple song, and 11 when Willow Warbler song was broadcast. The mean ($\pm$ SD) number of nest-box visits was significantly higher for the large-repertoire stimulus (5.07 ± 4.51) than for the small (2.20 ± 2.91, Wilcoxon matched-pairs signed-ranks test, $T = 11$, $n = 12$, $P = 0.028$; for further details on this experiment see Eriksson, 1991). Thus, this experiment indicates that complex songs might be more attractive for females than are simple songs. Eriksson (1991) further found that song repertoire size significantly correlated with male arrival time, such that early arriving males had larger repertoires. His interpretation of this was that since early males, in the natural situation, can take the best territories, repertoire becomes an indicator of territory quality. Therefore, by listening to repertoire size, females would quickly be able to sort out the worst breeding situations. Thus, by using repertoire size as a cue when choosing a mate females may reduce the costs of sampling, and be able to find the best territory more quickly.

In the random territories experiment we found no correlation between the males' song rates and the females' order of choice (Table 13), though such a pattern has been found in several studies, including some of our own. Thus, for example, in the experiment with fed and unfed males (Chapter 9; Alatalo *et al.*, 1990c), we provided additional food to half the males (randomly chosen) in some of the woodlands on cold and rainy days. As a result, fed males approximately doubled their song output. We also found that these fed males, which sang more, were more successful in attracting females than were unfed males. Among the 13 duos of males (one fed, the other unfed) included in the study, in 11 cases the fed male paired before its control (Fig. 63; binomial test, $P = 0.011$, one-tailed). We then removed all the females and tested the males again, but this time no food was given to any of the males. With no supplementary food, in only 6 of the 13 cases did a previously fed male pair before its control, which is a significant change from the previous experiment (Fisher's exact test, $P = 0.048$, one-tailed). Thus, the most likely factor making fed males more successful in mate attraction was their increased song rate. Reasons why females should prefer males with high song rates may be that a high song rate may indicate that food is plentiful in the territory (Gottlander, 1987; Radesäter *et al.*, 1987), or that a low song rate might indicate that the male is already mated with another female elsewhere (see Stenmark *et al.*, 1988), and should therefore be avoided. The preference for high song rates might, however, be illusory and only due to passive attraction: these males are more easily noticed, and females visit and pair with them first.

Why was song rate unimportant as a choice criterion for the females in the random territories experiment (Table 13), in contrast to other data that suggest it is quite important? The reason for this discrepancy may be that the song rate in the random territories experiment was measured in normal mid-May weather when conditions often stay fine, and consequently many insects are available. Thus, favourable environmental conditions may have allowed a high song rate in many males, without a great deal of variation between them. It is also possible that females might use some threshold method in their response to song, such that song rate variation above a certain level has very little influence on their decision whether or not to mate with a particular male, and in our random territories experiment most males could have been above this threshold.

Male colour

The importance of male plumage coloration for female choice in the Pied Flycatcher has been a highly controversial issue. Undeniably, the fact that males moult into their conspicuous breeding plumage just before the start of the breeding season and lose it again after breeding, suggests that the plumage has evolved primarily in response to selection pressures during the breeding season, because females prefer colourful males, or because such characters are favoured as signals in male–male competition, or both. What then is the message from studies on the Pied Flycatcher with respect to a sexual selection explanation for the conspicuous male breeding coloration?

Curio (1959b) suggested that the behaviour of the courting male was more important for the choice made by females than was the colour of the male. Creutz (1955) also called attention to the white underparts, the white patch on the wings, and the white parts on the outer tail feathers, which the male contrasts with darker feathers during the nest-hole presentation. Both these studies, however, were performed in Germany where males are rather brown and much less variable in coloration than further north (Chapter 10).

On the basis of observations in central Norway, Røskaft and Järvi (1983) suggested that black males were the primary choice of Pied Flycatcher females although, according to these authors, the actual cue for the choice made could equally well have been some character correlated with blackness, such as quality of the territory (see below). After adding data from two more years the same authors (Järvi *et al.*, 1987) became strengthened in their view that colour is indeed a character used by females in their choice of mates. Yet another study of female choice was made by Slagsvold (1986a) in the same part of Norway. He altered the attractiveness of nest boxes after male but before female settlement by changing the positions of the boxes (tilted or upright). Females were then found to base their choice of mate on the position of the box while the characteristics of the male seemed unimportant. In yet another experiment Lifjeld and Slagsvold (1988b) removed some feathers from the wing and tail of randomly chosen males, and later noted the time that elapsed before pairing in relation to male characteristics.

The results from this study were analysed with multiple correlation analyses since many variables were being looked at simultaneously, and it was found that, in one year out of two, darker males mated earlier than did browner males (unmated males were also included in the analysis). The authors concluded from this experiment that choice of mate cannot be based exclusively on male plumage colour, but is more likely to be based on one or more traits that are correlated with it.

'After a lifetime of research' on Pied Flycatchers in southwest Finland, Lars von Haartman (1988) was still not able to conclude unambiguously that male plumage coloration has evolved as a response to female preference. Our interpretation of von Haartman's paper is that he favours the view that a black breeding plumage in some way improves a male's chances of attracting a mate, although he also holds the possibility open for male–male competition being the main selective force. He offered a suite of seven possible criteria for female choice, of which one was male colour. However, von Haartman then added that, unless male colour 'brings some compensating advantage', females should avoid conspicuous males because they are more likely to be killed by predators before the brood is raised to independence than are more cryptically coloured males. Clearly, breeding success becomes reduced if only one parent survives to feed the nestlings (see Chapter 7).

All in all, then, the general message from the studies reviewed above seems to be that male coloration may be important for choice of a mate, but that female choice could also be based, partly or entirely, on some other character correlated with colour; the most obvious of such factors are male age and territory quality. However, before going into correlated characters we must report on our own findings with respect to male coloration and female choice.

In the random territories experiment we described earlier in this chapter we found no correlation between female mating order and male blackness (Fig. 77; Table 13), which suggests that male colour has little influence upon female choice. This finding has been supported by some other experiments of ours, both in the field and in the laboratory. In 1986 and 1987 we performed a field experiment in which some Pied Flycatcher males were painted black (Alatalo *et al.*, 1990e). All males in several woodlands were checked for day of arrival and plumage colour. Among these males we randomly picked duos of males, up to a few hundred metres apart, with the same arrival date (±1 day), and among duos of males we made two kinds of treatments. We know that early arriving males can take better territories than later arriving males, but in this experiment we could control for arrival time and probably also for territory quality by comparing males that arrived on the same day. Any differences in territory quality – which must still have existed – would have been randomized in this experiment such that no group of males on average had better territories than the other. The first treatment was: among duos of males with more than 40% black dorsal feathers (i.e. dark males), one randomly chosen male per duo was painted on the black feathers only with a solution of Nyanzol (a black dyestuff). This dye is indelible and remains on the feathers until they are moulted in autumn. After

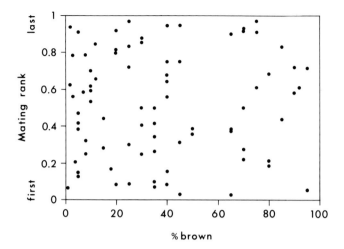

Fig. 77. Correlation between male plumage blackness and mating order in random territories.
$r_s = 0.08$, P = 0.44, n = 87.

painting, these males looked the same as before since only black feathers had been painted. The other male of each duo was handled in a similar way but only painted with water. These duos of males served as our treatment control group, to check whether the Nyanzol dye, irrespective of colour change, affected male attractiveness.

The second treatment was as follows: among duos of males with less than 40% black dorsal feathers (i.e. brown males), one randomly drawn bird was painted entirely black on the back, while his 'partner' was painted with water. Then we checked for whether dark males became mated before brown males. The results of the experiment was that among the 12 male duos of the first treatment (no colour change), 5 water-painted males and 7 males painted on the black feathers became mated first, which is not a significant difference (binomial test, P > 0.70). Nor, if we also take into account the time span between painting and pairing date, is there any significant difference (Table 14, Wilcoxon matched-pairs signed-ranks test, $T = 40.5$, $n = 12$, $P > 0.10$). Thus, the painting of males *per se* did not lead to a disadvantage in attracting females. Among the 15 male duos in the second treatment (one brown male per duo painted black on the back), 7 water-painted males and 5 black-painted males became mated first; in one case it was a draw, and in two cases one male from each category remained unmated. Again no significant difference could be found (Table 14, Wilcoxon test, $n = 15$, $P > 0.10$). The conclusion is that black males do not attract females more quickly than do brown males arriving simultaneously.

We also performed another experiment in order to examine the influence of male plumage colour on female choice, this time in the laboratory, using hormone-implanted females (see p. 163 for methods). Here we gave females a

Table 14.   Time in days to attract females in a field experiment with painted Pied Flycatcher males. In the first treatment male colour was unchanged, while in the second treatment one male per duo was painted jet black on the back (see pp. 166–167 for further details; from Alatalo et al., 1990e). ∞ indicates an unmated male. Observe that the males in the two treatments are not the same individuals. See p. 167 for statistics.

Male duo no.	1st treatment		2nd treatment	
	Male painted on black feathers	Control	Male painted fully black	Control
1	14	5	∞	4
2	14	16	13	5
3	13	12	10	6
4	11	10	9	7
5	7	5	8	3
6	4	2	8	8
7	4	6	8	10
8	3	7	7	6
9	3	6	6	4
10	3	5	5	3
11	2	5	5	6
12	2	3	4	7
13			2	9
14			1	∞
15			0	1

choice between two nest boxes with two stuffed male dummies (Fig. 78), one being dark (Drost's colour score II = 90% black feathers on back) and the other brown (score VI = 10% black feathers). The positions of the dummies and the nest boxes was randomly switched during the experiment. Behind each nest box we played a tape recording of the same male's song. The female was offered a stick in the centre of the cage to perch on (Fig. 78), but when she was introduced she could not see the nest boxes or the dummies because of two curtains. After the female had settled and rested on the central perch, we removed the curtains and started the play-back song, and for 15 min we recorded the number and duration of female visits to the two nest boxes. Females typically sat for a few minutes on the perch, watching the two boxes and stuffed males, before approaching them.

As a control, to see whether females react to dummies, we presented 10 Pied Flycatcher females with a choice between a stuffed male Brambling and either a black or a brown stuffed Pied Flycatcher male. Also in this case a Pied Flycatcher song was broadcast behind both boxes.

Eight out of the ten females used as controls responded to the treatment, and in all cases they only visited the Pied Flycatcher male and his nest box (on average 2.8 times per 15 min), but never the Brambling. Thus, implanted Pied Flycatcher females clearly make choices between the potential breeding situations offered,

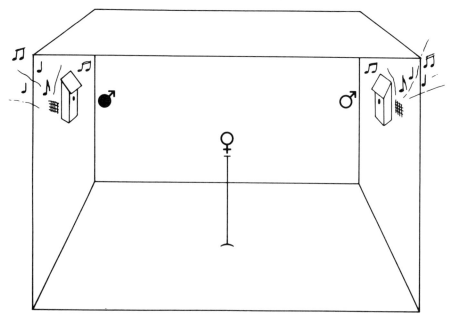

Fig. 78. Experimental design in which we presented hormone implanted Pied Flycatcher females with stuffed males and play-back song. On opposite sides of the cage we fitted two nest boxes which broadcast the same song. Black and brown males were put outside each box, in a random order. Single females were released into the cage for 15 minutes and we scored how many visits they made to each box. Trials started when the female perched on the central stick.

and they can at least distinguish visually between stuffed Bramblings and Pied Flycatchers. When presented with a choice between a black and a brown Pied Flycatcher male, females showed no preference. Of the 12 females showing any response, half first visited the black male and the other half first visited the brown male. In total, black males were visited 23 times and brown males 17 times, which is a non-significant difference (Wilcoxon matched-pairs signed-ranks test, $T = 42$, $n = 12$, $P > 0.10$; for further details see Alatalo *et al.*, 1990e). The conclusion from this experiment is that females have no preference between black and brown males, which supports the findings from our field experiments.

Bringing all this together, we cannot explain the black plumage of males as being due to female choice, unless sexual selection by female choice is so weak that we could not measure the benefits and costs by the methods we used. Another piece of evidence favouring the view that male plumage colour does not influence female choice comes from comparisons between males that attracted one or more females. An early arrival improves a male's chances of mating polygynously (see next chapter), and because early males are old and dark most males mated to more than one female will accordingly be darker than monogamously mated males. One way around this problem would be to compare polygynous and monogamous males that are more than two years old, since colour does not change noticeably after the second year (Table 12). Thus, if females prefer black males one would expect older polygynous males to be darker than older monogamous males. This possibility was checked by von Haartman (1985), who failed to find any significant difference in plumage colour between these two groups of males (Mann–Whitney U-test, $P \approx 0.13$; test made by us). We found the same result in central Sweden where older polygynous males were of colour type 2.92 while older monogamous males were of type 2.89 ($P > 0.50$). Thus, among older males, darker birds do not seem to be more attractive to females.

Other male characteristics

One of the most likely male characteristics, apart from song performance and coloration, that might influence the female's choice of mate in the Pied Flycatcher is age; selecting an older male rather than a younger one might increase future reproductive output because older males may be of higher genetic quality. In theories of sexual selection and mate choice it has been suggested, by Trivers (1972) and Halliday (1978) among others, that by surviving longer, older males prove that they carry good genes for survival.

To judge from natural pairing data on the Pied Flycatcher it would seem as though females actually prefer to mate with older males. This pattern occurs because older males arrive on the breeding grounds first (Table 2), allowing them to take the best territories and also giving them time to attract secondary females. Hence, the correlation between male age and mating success could result from the females choosing the best territories without regard to male age. And, indeed, the results from the random territories experiment described earlier indicated that there was no effect of male age on female preference.

We then examined (Alatalo *et al.*, 1986a) the potential benefits that females might derive from preferentially mating with older males. To analyse this question one has to take into account and standardize for the decrease in clutch size with time of the season (see Chapter 6). To do this we calculated the regression line for reproductive parameters against date of egg–laying for females mated with older males. Then, for each nest attended by a one–year–old or older male, respectively, the actual reproductive value was divided by that expected from the regression line for older males on that date; for number of fledglings this was done for all pairs and for monogamous pairs separately. From these analyses we were able to conclude that no measurable benefits will be gained by females from choosing older males (Table 15); and in fact they obviously do not exhibit any such preference. The same applies for female choice of male tarsus length, wing length and weight, all of which are measurements of size (Table 13). Thus, everything else being equal, females do not seem to prefer larger or heavier males.

In a study of Pied Flycatchers in Spain (subspecies *iberiae*), where males are

Table 15. *Standardized number of fledglings, their tarsus lengths and weights at fledging for female Pied Flycatchers mated with one-year-old and older males, among monogamous pairs in deciduous forest, and among all pairs irrespective of mating status and habitat. The standardized value for females mated with an older male is one. From Alatalo et al., 1986a.*

	Monogamous pairs	All pairs		
	Number of fledglings	Number of fledglings	Tarsus length at 13 days of age	Weight at 13 days of age
Females mated with one-year-old males				
$\bar{x} =$	0.97	0.99	1.000	1.000
SD =	0.38	0.33	0.022	0.072
$n =$	107	149	112	112
Females mated with older males				
$\bar{x} =$	1.00	1.00	1.000	1.000
SD =	0.30	0.29	0.023	0.066
$n =$	82	245	179	179
Test	$z = 0.955$	$z = 0.084$	$t = 0.167$	$t = 0.030$
P	>0.30	>0.90	>0.80	>0.95

rather dark (Appendix 1), Potti and Montalvi (1991b) searched for possible cues for female choice. The only sexual character they found to be important was the size of the white forehead patch, which in this subspecies is always rectangular whereas it is variable in shape in *hypoleuca*. The authors argued that a large forehead patch might be important in the male displays during presentation of the nest-hole.

QUALITY OF PATERNAL CARE

As mentioned above, one possible cue in the female's choice of mate could be his ability to provide paternal care, though it is difficult to imagine how this could be assessable unless it is correlated with male age or morphology. Since males do not incubate, their main contribution to the breeding success of the pair consists of feeding the nestlings. As shown earlier (Chapter 7), males contribute approximately half of the food delivered to the nestlings. But how does their competence in this respect relate to the phenotype of individual males? To study this we recorded feeding rates of monogamous males, and analysed the data in relation to whether the males were old or young, or darker or larger than the average male in the population under examination. It turned out that no single male character was significantly related to his share in the parental care (Table 16). Thus, male age and morphology do not seem to influence the paternal care quality of particular males to any great extent, and it must therefore be difficult for prospecting

Table 16.   Male feeding intensity in relation to age and morphology. Feeding frequency is expressed as number of food deliveries per young and hour when nestlings are about 7–8 days old.

	Mean	SD	n	P
Older	2.91	1.06	38	NS
One-year-old	2.66	0.82	28	
Darker than median	2.88	1.06	44	NS
Browner than median	2.62	0.79	26	
Heavier than median	2.94	0.98	33	NS
Lighter than median	2.75	0.98	38	
Longer wing than median	2.83	1.02	31	NS
Shorter wing than median	2.82	0.97	41	
Longer tarsus than median	2.70	0.83	31	NS
Shorter tarsus than median	2.91	1.08	41	

NS, not significant.

females to tell how much a male will later help in feeding the nestlings on the basis of his morphological or other traits. (However, already-mated males should be avoided; how to tell them from unmated males is discussed in Chapters 7 and 12.) In conclusion we cannot imagine any male characteristics that might serve as reliable cues to Pied Flycatcher females with respect to the probable future investment of the male.

TERRITORY QUALITY

So far we have been unable to demonstrate any obvious benefits accruing to females choosing a male of a particular type. In one sense this finding is unsurprising because, in a hole-nesting species, females can probably gain more by choosing a good quality nest-site defended by a below-average male than choosing a bad site held by a better male. With a superior male defending an inferior nest-site, the probability of breeding success may be less than if choosing a poor quality (or already-mated) male with a safe nesting site. If this scenario is true, we would expect females to pay greater attention to nest-site quality than to male quality. Moreover, there are probably more reliable cues available for female choice of territory quality than there are for choice of male or paternal care quality. Therefore, we expect that the first criterion for the choice made by Pied Flycatcher females when selecting a breeding situation should be territory/nest-site quality, the second the male's mating status (see also Chapters 7 and 12), and only the third the male's coloration and age. These deliberations lead us to the question: what is a Pied Flycatcher territory and what affects its quality?

According to von Haartman (1956a) the territory of the male Pied Flycatcher mainly consists of the nest-hole. He found that most songs were sung from the nesting tree or the trees nearest to it. Also, half of all encounters with intruders occurred within 10 m of the nest. However, the area from which nesting material and food are collected is much larger and overlaps with that of other pairs. What then is a good territory for the Pied Flycatcher? Since the defended area is so small, the most important part of the territory is probably the nest-site itself, but favourable feeding areas in the surroundings may also influence the bird's evaluation of the quality of a given territory.

In an attempt to measure territory quality, Askenmo (1984) kept records on which nest boxes were used in seven successive years in a woodland in south-western Sweden. He found that over these years some boxes were used more frequently than expected from a random choice and concluded that Pied Fly-catcher females probably 'can foresee some consequences of their mate choice, and prefer to mate with males defending nest sites that secure high breeding success'. In an experiment with nest boxes, Slagsvold (1986a) provided both normal upright and tilted boxes for arriving Pied Flycatcher males. After male settlement some of the upright boxes, randomly chosen, were tilted and some of the tilted ones were raised to an upright position (see also p. 165). Later he compared the mating success of males defending upright as against tilted boxes, with the assumption that tilted boxes were intrinsically of a poorer quality than upright ones. In accordance with this prediction, Slagsvold found that males defending upright boxes throughout the season became mated earlier, and that mean clutch size was greater for females nesting in upright than in tilted boxes. His general conclusion from this experiment was that nest-site quality was of greater importance than male quality for female choice.

In our random territories experiment, made in oak-dominated forests, we found that the properties of the nest-site and its nearest surroundings affected female choice order. By using measurements of the nest-site and the habitat around it, we found that a (multiple regression) habitat model which included the three variables nest height (the higher the better), nest-tree circumference (the thicker the better), and density of birches (the fewer the better) significantly correlated with female choice order ($F = 4.02$, $P = 0.02$, $r^2 = 0.274$). This probably means that females prefer nest-sites that are safe from predators and are located in good feeding areas. This finding is partly corroborated by the results obtained from a habitat model of flycatchers breeding in natural cavities. In that case we found nests in high (but also thin) trees, with the entrance hole not visible from the ground, to be safer in terms of predation risk than other types of holes (for data see Chapter 14). However, we do not know for certain if nest-sites categorized as safe by our models are also preferred by Pied Flycatcher females. One contradiction in our results is that female Pied Flycatchers seem to prefer nest boxes hung on thick trees but natural cavities situated in thin ones; a more detailed consideration of this issue will be given in Chapter 14.

In another experiment on nest-hole quality (Alatalo *et al.*, 1986b) we mixed new and old nest boxes (entrance size ≈ 32 mm; age up to two years) in five deciduous woodlands. When half the males in each woodland were paired, we removed the females and released them far enough away to ensure that they did not return. Immediately after the removal of the females, we also removed the boxes from the males that had attracted females and replaced each by an older one (4–5 years old) with a larger entrance hole (35 mm). The boxes of this previously successful group of males were given to the group of males that earlier failed to attract females and whose original boxes were also removed. When new females arrived, previously unsuccessful males became mated significantly earlier (median rank 0.38, $n = 18$) than previously successful males (rank 0.63, $n = 17$, Mann–Whitney U-test, $U = 73.5$, $P < 0.01$), indicating that the quality of the nest-site was the main cue for female choice.

Other experiments on nest-site quality include manipulations of entrance-hole size and nesting height, both of which should be related to safety from predation – nesting holes with smaller entrance size and sites higher up in trees should each be safer than the opposite. Further details about these experiments were reported in Chapter 4, and it suffices here to repeat the result that Pied Flycatcher females indeed prefer both narrow entrance holes and nesting sites high up in trees.

Now, what about the importance of good feeding areas around the intended nest-site? Our random territories experiment, which was performed in mainly broad-leaved forests, indicated that areas with birches were avoided – maybe birches contain fewer prey insects early in spring than do other deciduous trees. A more thorough study was performed outsite Uppsala by a student of ours, Carolyn Glynn. She set up 22 sites with identical new nest boxes for Pied Flycatchers, randomly drawn from 100 numbered potential sites, in an oak-dominated woodland. Each site consisted of three nest boxes situated less than 5 m apart. The purpose of this design was to reduce variation in nest-site quality; it lowered the risk of putting up a single nest box in an unfavourable position. All boxes were put up at a height of 1.5 m in a vertical position on trees of about the same circumference, and all were facing in the same direction (north). Since many Pied Flycatcher females arrived and mated before all males had yet settled, Glynn removed all these females at the time when each site had a male defending it, thus allowing a new set of females to settle. At each site Glynn sampled insects by putting out pit-fall traps for ground-dwellers, window traps for flying insects, and tape strips coated with an adhesive on tree trunks and branches for insects crawling on trees. Samples were collected or counted on a rotation basis – one type of trap was checked every day from the arrival of the first males through to the settling of the last females – and a mean value was calculated for each trap type and territory. In addition she measured the proportion of leaves with insect damage on two branches from each of five tree species within a radius of 20 m of each nest-site. This was done at the time the second set of females were mating.

The result of the study was that Glynn found the order of male settlement to be significantly correlated with total catches in hanging window traps ($r_s = 0.50$,

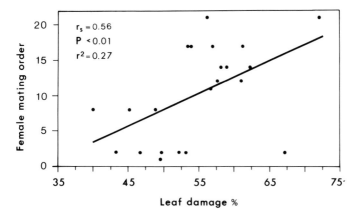

Fig. 79. Correlation between female mating order and percentage of leaf damage by insects near the nest-site. Twenty-two male territories were available to the first arriving females; territories with least leaf damage were chosen first.

$n = 22$, $P = 0.01$), i.e. the abundance of flying insects, and with the percentage of leaves damaged at pairing ($r_s = 0.37$, $P = 0.04$). The choice order of nesting sites by the second set of females was found to be only significantly related to leaf damage ($r_s = 0.56$, $n = 22$, $P = 0.005$; Fig. 79). Likewise, a multiple regression analysis that included all four insect-trapping measurements plus male arrival order revealed that only the proportion of leaves with insect damage correlated with female pairing order ($t = 2.57$, $P = 0.02$). This suggests that the abundance of caterpillars influenced female choice of nesting site. However, the correlation is such that the more leaves eaten the later a female paired in that territory – the same as for male settlement pattern. Intuitively one would expect degree of leaf damage and caterpillar abundance to be positively correlated, and females to choose the territories with most food (i.e. where there is most leaf damage). One explanation we can think of to resolve this contradiction is that a high degree of leaf damage at the time for pairing implies that larvae are at a late stage of development, which means that there will be fewer of them during the nestling stage of the Pied Flycatcher, when they are most needed. Alternatively, larvae have been more abundant at sites with more leaf damage but have already been preyed upon by other predators, so that sites with less leaf damage contain more larvae when female Pied Flycatchers arrive.

All in all, then, territory quality factors seem to be the main cues used by females in their choice of nest-site. Among such factors the quality of the nesting cavity itself, such as its safety from predators, seems to be the paramount criterion, while if nest-site quality does not differ greatly between sites, food abundance may play some role. However, how or if females trade nest-site quality against food accessibility is not known at all.

MALE–MALE COMPETITION AND MALE CHARACTERISTICS

We have, so far, been unable to find any evidence for female choice based upon male characteristics, and we cannot show that male coloration has evolved in response to a female preference for darkness. Therefore we will end this chapter by dealing with the possibility that some types of males are more successful in combat over territory ownership, especially the possibility of intrasexual selection being the main selective force in the evolution of the conspicuous male breeding plumage. One problem in studying competition between males is that prior ownership, irrespective of individual characteristics, normally gives an advantage; for example, Pied Flycatcher males that have settled in a territory are not displaced by intruders (own observations; Askenmo, 1984; Slagsvold, 1986a). To solve this problem of each individual being dominant in his own territory, in 1984 and 1985 at Uppsala we created situations where males had to compete for nest boxes over which they had no prior ownership. This was done before female arrival in the following way.

We put up pairs of nest boxes about 50 m apart, and when a box became occupied we caught, measured and colour-ringed the male for individual identification in the field. Then, when both boxes in a pair had been claimed we put up another box in between these two (Fig. 80) Then we followed the movements of the two males until we had seen that both had visited and knew about this new extra box. At that time we removed the two original boxes defended by the two males, thus forcing them to compete for the single remaining box in the middle, and we checked which male won access over it. The

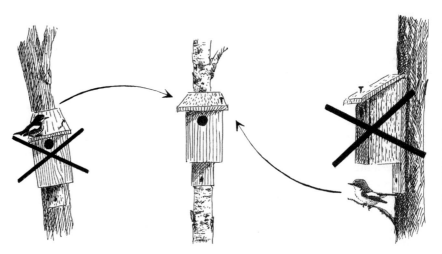

Fig. 80.   Experimental design of a male–male competition experiment. Two nest boxes were put up approximately 50 m apart. When each was occupied by a male, a third box was erected in between and the two original boxes were removed. The characteristics of the winning and losing males were compared.

Table 17.   *Outcome from male contests over a free nest box. Initially two males defended boxes 50 m apart. Later we put up a new box in between these two boxes and removed the two original boxes. Thus, males were forced to compete for a previously undefended resource. For design see also Fig. 80.*

Character	No. of wins	P
Older	11	
v.		0.21
younger	5	
Darker	28	
v.		0.59
browner	25	
Longer wing	33	
v.		0.07
shorter wing	19	
Longer tarsus	28	
v.		0.11
shorter tarsus	21	
Earlier arrival	22	
v.		0.93
later arrival	25	

result from this experiment was that no particular trait, such as colour, made a male disproportionately victorious in the conflicts over the box. Thus we found no advantage in the contests of having arrived earlier, of being darker, or older, or of having longer tarsi. However, there was a tendency for males with longer wings more often to win the competition over the single nest box ($P = 0.07$, Table 17). Wing length is probably correlated with flight speed, which might be important in male–male competition, but is also correlated with size (tarsus length, which correlates with body size, was weakly correlated with winning ability), and with age, so it is possible that size and age, either alone or in concert, affect combat capacity. However, when using all male characteristics together in a multivariate discriminant analysis to try to separate winners from losers, no single male character turned out to contribute significantly to victory in fights over a nest box which none of the males had previously defended. The same conclusion was drawn by Slagsvold and Lifjeld (1988a) who in a similar experiment could not find winning males to be of any particular type, apart from there being a tendency for the winner having been present in the area for the longest time.

Similarly, when we looked at pairing success of males of different colours in the natural situation we could not find any compelling evidence for some males being more successful than others (Alatalo *et al.*, 1990e). However, when we compared 'duos' of males with the same arrival date and holding territories

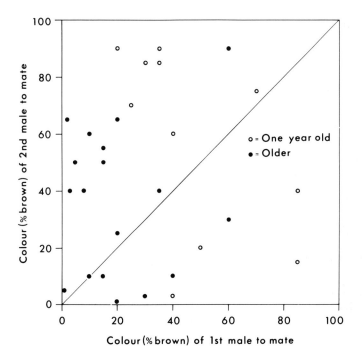

Fig. 81.   The first and second male to mate within duos of one-year-old and older males arriving to the same wood on the same day. In this case the darker male mated sooner than the browner one (T = 103, z = 2.07, P = 0.019, n = 27).

within the same wood, but being different in plumage colour, we found that blacker males mated earlier than browner males (Wilcoxon matched-pairs signed-ranks test, $T = 487.5$, $z = 2.53$, $P = 0.011$, $n = 57$). In this situation we assume that prospecting females would have been able to visit both the males of the duo before they mated. The same pattern of a preference for darker males holds if we compare the outcome within duos of older and one-year-old males ($T = 103$, $z = 2.07$, $P = 0.019$, $n = 27$; Fig. 81). However, we do not interpret these data as indicating female preference for darker males since all our other data suggest that this is not the case – instead we think that this seeming 'preference' for darker males could be a result of competition between males. Thus, if two Pied Flycatcher males of different colour arrive at the same wood at the same time, and have to compete for available territories, the darker male might possibly be able to take a better territory than the browner one. Since territory quality is important in female choice, darker males will as a result attract a female more quickly. If this interpretation is correct, it implies that dark colour confers an advantage in male–male interactions, thus having evolved through intrasexual selection. However, we have no experimental data supporting this hypothesis. In fact, recent experiments in Finland by Esa Huhta and Rauno Alatalo failed to demonstrate that colour had any significant effect on acquisition or defence of territory.

SUMMARY

Male Pied Flycatchers arrive ahead of females. Immediately he arrives a male takes up a territory and starts singing. Females mate almost immediately upon their arrival, and probably do not visit more than a few males before making their choice. Reasons for the females' hurry include the fact that a breeding situation may be occupied by someone else if it is rejected at first, and also that the expected breeding success declines with time. Females primarily base their choice of a partner on the quality of the territory defended and offered by the male; essential criteria of quality are a nesting cavity safe from predators and probably also the presence of favourable foraging areas in the neighbourhood. Male characteristics seem to be unrelated to paternal care quality and not to influence female choice, though it is possible that dark male coloration in some situations may bring a mating advantage.

CHAPTER 12

Mating Systems

Unlike the majority of mammals, most bird species are monogamous, although polygynous, polyandrous and promiscuous mating systems also occur. Natural selection favours those individuals that leave most surviving offspring to future generations. The strategies and tactics employed to maximize fitness differ not only between the sexes but also between individuals of the same sex. With regard to mating systems a conflict arises between the sexes in that males can sire more offspring by inseminating many females while females cannot increase their number of offspring by being inseminated by many males. Instead, the best method for females to increase their reproductive success is generally to increase the workforce assisting in the care of the offspring so that most or all can be raised to independence. Thus, there is a conflict between the sexes as to how to produce as many surviving offspring as possible. In birds this conflict has most often been settled by a monogamous breeding system.

Among students of bird biology the Pied Flycatcher is noted for defying this 'rule' of monogamy, and instead being facultatively polygynous. Further, Pied Flycatcher males become polygynous by attracting females into separate distant territories. This type of mating system has been termed successive or polyterritorial polygyny (von Haartman, 1949, 1951b). After the discovery of this type of mating system in the Pied Flycatcher, studies of other birds have revealed that it is not a strategy exclusive to that one species. What is still controversial, however, is the evolutionary interpretation of the advantage of being polyterritorial. In this chapter we review and evaluate hypotheses that have been proposed to explain why some males are polyterritorial; we give information of the frequency of polygyny in populations of the Pied Flycatcher, and on distances between territories of polyterritorial males. Further information about the mating system in the Pied Flycatcher can be found in Chapters 6, 7, 9 and 11.

MONOGAMY OR POLYGYNY?

When analysing the mating systems of birds David Lack (1968) found that 94% of all passerines are monogamous. Since then many studies of individually ringed birds have been made, and in a later review of European birds the proportion of monogamous passerines was estimated to be about 80% (Møller, 1986). In his analyses Møller further found that of the 46 regularly polygynous species in Europe, 63% had their females in one single territory (monoterritorial) while 37% had females in separate distant territories (polyterritorial). A list of the European polyterritorial bird species is given in Appendix 6.

Why then are so many bird species monogamous while only few are polygynous? Based on the North American avifauna, Verner and Willson (1966) showed that species inhabiting two-dimensional habitats like marshes and steppes were particularly likely to mate polygynously. They suggested that food may be more clumped in such habitats and that this in turn may lead to increased occurrence of polygyny. A similar pattern of increased rates of polygyny in marsh habitats was observed among European passerines according to Møller's review. He also analysed the importance of nest-site (hole versus open), nest dispersion (solitary versus colonial), winter quarters (tropical versus other), but failed to find any effect of these variables on mating system, if inter-correlations between variables were removed. Thus, open and simple habitats seem to favour polygyny, and one explanation might be that food or some other resources are particularly unevenly distributed in such habitats.

Given polygyny, why are some species monoterritorial while others are polyterritorial? Again relying on Møller's compilations, polyterritoriality is absent from colonial species, probably because of the strong competition for nesting sites in such species. He further found that polyterritorial species were more often long-distance migrants wintering south of the Sahara, than was the case for monoterritorial species. Whether a male is already mated or not will most often negatively affect female reproductive success, and she will therefore gain from ensuring that she mates with a bachelor. However, it should be possible for males to conceal their mating status by being polyterritorial, as postulated in the deception hypothesis (below). Long-distance migrants often arrive late and start to breed soon after arrival, and females probably cannot afford long pre-copulatory pair-bonds because of the short duration of the breeding season. Thus, among species that arrive late and where females are in a hurry to mate, one should expect males more often to be polyterritorial, as Møller also observed. With respect to sexual dimorphism in mono- and polyterritorial species, Møller found the sexes to be more dimorphic in size in monoterritorial polygynous species but more dimorphic in plumage in polyterritorial ones. He speculated that the explanation might be that, in monoterritorial systems, competition between males for territories is more intense than in polyterritorial systems, hence they favour large size rather than bright coloration.

In monoterritorial polygynous bird species, like the European Corn Bunting or the North American Red-winged Blackbird, several females share the same territory and the same male. In this situation females should be aware of each other's presence when they settle, and they thus accept paying the cost of sharing food resources and male parental assistance with other harem-mates. More than twenty years ago it was proposed (Verner, 1964; Verner and Willson, 1966; Orians, 1969) that if there are differences in quality between different male territories, it would pay a female to share a territory with another female on a good territory rather than settling with a bachelor male on a poor territory. This hypothesis has been called the 'polygyny threshold model' and is graphically illustrated in Figure 82. As originally defined, one of the predictions of this model was that secondary females of already-mated males, on average, should have at least the same reproductive success as females settling simultaneously and mating monogamously. This and other predictions of the original model, and of extended versions, have been tested on a variety of bird species. The conclusion has been that threshold models may often explain polygyny in passerine birds. However, recent work (see e.g. Davies, 1989), has partly undermined the conclusion that polygyny can be explained by the threshold model. Davies suggested that mating systems may better be viewed in terms of solutions to sexual conflict.

In polyterritorial polygyny, in contrast to monoterritorial systems, females do not share resources in a territory with other females mated to the same male, though as in monoterritorial polygyny they do have to share paternal care. When territories are separated by some distance, it is quite possible that females are unaware of each other's existence when they settle, and the polygyny threshold model is therefore probably not applicable to polyterritorial polygyny (e.g. Wittenberger, 1979). The question why the males of some species take up separate distant territories and why females mate with already-mated males will be discussed later in this chapter.

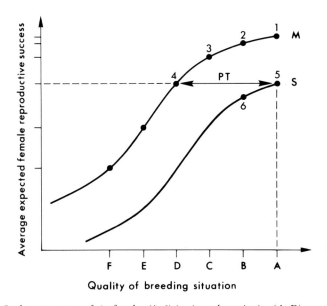

Fig. 82. Settlement pattern of six females (1–6) in six male territories (A–F) according to the Orians–Verner–Willson polygyny threshold model. The M-curve reflects the average expected reproductive success for a certain territory quality for a monogamous female. Since there is a cost of sharing a territory with another female the curve for secondary females (S) lies below that for monogamous females. In this example males A and B become polygynous, C and D monogamous, and E and F remain unmated. Females settle where their average expected reproductive success is highest. Thus, females 4 and 5 could either choose an unmated or an already-mated male and still achieve the same reproductive success while female 6 should mate with an already-mated male. This hypothetical example is based on the assumption that the first female in polygyny does not suffer by the arrival of a second female. For further elaborations of this example, see Davies (1989). PT = the polygyny threshold.

POLYGYNY IN THE PIED FLYCATCHER

HISTORICAL BACKGROUND

The earliest report on polygyny in the Pied Flycatcher of which we are aware comes from the town of Mariestad in southern Sweden, where Olofsson (1939) in his garden watched two breeding females in separate nest boxes but saw only one male. The male assisted one of the females in feeding the young while the other female had to raise her young single-handedly. Olofsson interpreted this observation as a case of bigyny in the Pied Flycatcher, and described the second female as a 'mistress'. Two early cases of polygyny were reported from Germany by Trettau and Merkel (1943). They observed males feeding young in two distant nest boxes, but interpreted these observations as accidental rather than due to polygyny. Von Haartman (1945) reported on further cases of polygyny in the Pied Flycatcher from Finland, and he considered it to be a regular, though rare, type of mating system in this species. Some years later, he (1949, 1951b) named this type of mating pattern 'polyterritorial or successive polygamy', and proposed that Pied Flycatcher males take up separate territories to be able to attract more than one female. He also put forward the adaptive explanation that selection 'may favour polygamous males, since these produce more offspring', and underpinned it by the observation that one monogamous male in his study area raised 26 fledglings during a six-year period while a polygynous male raised the same number of offspring in half the time.

Von Haartman (1945, 1951b, 1956a) also suggested that, since the two territories of polyterritorial male Pied Flycatchers are usually relatively far apart, the second female to mate might be ignorant of the fact that the male is already mated. Further studies of the mating system of the Pied Flycatcher led us to suggest (Alatalo *et al.*, 1981) that males are polyterritorial for the very purpose of hiding their true mating status. Subsequently a plethora of alternative hypotheses have been proposed as adaptive explanations for polyterritorial polygyny. We will come back to these problems later in this chapter, but, before trying to make our view convincing, we need to describe the various behaviour patterns of males and females, and also to provide information on the costs and benefits of polygyny accruing to each of the sexes.

BEHAVIOUR OF MALES

Immediately on arrival the male Pied Flycatcher starts defending a nest-hole and announces his presence by vigorous singing. The first males to arrive, however, often defend several potential nesting sites which are sometimes far apart. Thus, for example, we have observed in our nest box areas that the first male to arrive can sing at up to twenty different boxes. As more males arrive and fill up the area, the number of holes at which they sing shrinks until each male restricts himself to advertising one or two nest-holes. However, if several suitable holes are close together, a male may defend and sing at several of them.

After pair formation the male usually stays within his territory and in the close company of the female, probably for the purpose of guarding the territory against intruders and the female against copulation attempts from other males (mate guarding; for further details see pp. 195–196 and Fig. 88). At about the time of the start of egg-laying many males move away to take up a secondary territory at some distance from the first one (Fig. 83). This secondary territory is probably most often a site that the male has previously inspected and sung at. According to von Haartman (1956a) and our own observations on birds breeding in natural cavities (Alatalo and Lundberg, 1984a), about two-thirds of all males take up secondary territories. In southwestern Sweden 93% (*n* = 29) were polyterritorial (Silverin, 1980), while in northern Sweden the proportion of polyterritorial

Fig. 83. Polyterritorial polygyny in the Pied Flycatcher. After having attracted a female to his first territory the male moves away to a second distant territory where he starts singing again. A male's two territories are often several hundred metres apart, with other male territories in between.

males was only 30% ($n = 23$) (Nyholm, 1984). In this last-mentioned area many males remained unmated. There is a larger proportion taking up secondary territories among early arriving males than among late arriving males, perhaps because fewer unoccupied territories are available late in the season, or because the prospects of attracting a second female are poor at that time, or for both reasons. The number of males that will take up secondary territories might also depend on nest-hole availability, breeding density, habitat, and the timing of female arrival (further details on this topic will be given below). Under favourable conditions a few males are able to take up a third territory and even to attract a third female.

Time for leaving the first territory

The time of taking up a secondary territory is quite consistent between males. As a rule of thumb we could say that males start defending a second territory approximately when the first female starts her egg-laying. Von Haartman (1956a) found that most males left their primary territory on the day when egg-laying started or the day before. The same pattern of most males leaving their first territories at the onset of egg-laying was found by Silverin (1980). In a specifically designed study in Finland Osmo Rätti and Rauno Alatalo (pers. comm.) found that mated males began to take up secondary territories on a permanent basis between four days before the start of egg-laying by the first female and nine days after egg-laying had commenced (thus in a few cases the female was already incubating). Rätti and Alatalo were unable to find any relationship between relative time of establishing a second territory (in relation to egg-laying in the first nest) and male age, plumage coloration and morphology. Furthermore, they found no difference in high and low population densities. On average males took up secondary territories a day and a half after the start of egg-laying by their first female.

Why do males take up secondary territories at that particular time? One risk of leaving the territory earlier is that it may be taken over by another male. However, an even more immediate risk in abandoning the female, even temporarily, in order to take up a second territory too early is that the primary female might then be courted and inseminated by other males, which might lead to mixed paternity in the brood (for data see below). In general, female birds are fertile until the laying of the penultimate egg. This is because each egg is fertilized about 24 hours before laying, when one egg is laid per day, as in the Pied Flycatcher. However, female birds can store sperm in so-called 'sperm storage tubules' which means that the entire clutch can be fertilized by the female herself by using these stored sperm; thus a few inseminations before egg-laying might be sufficient to ensure fertilization of a whole clutch (Birkhead, 1988). In the Pied Flycatcher, as in many other passerine birds, copulations cease when egg-laying starts (Fig. 87). This implies that the risk of multiple paternity after the start of egg-laying is greatly reduced, and therefore a male can leave his first female without having to pay too high a cost in terms of reduced certainty of paternity. Pied Flycatcher males probably gain more by taking up a second territory, with some probability of attracting another female, than by guarding the first territory and the first female during the entire egg-laying period.

Distance between first and secondary territories

The maximum distance known between a polyterritorial male's two territories is about 3.5 km (Silverin, 1980), and the longest distance we ourselves have recorded is 1.3 km. Most males move shorter distances than that, the average reported in most studies being 200–250 m (Appendix 7); this is, however, an underestimate because long-distance movements are less likely to be discovered than short ones. Since the territory of the Pied Flycatcher is very small (von Haartman, 1956a), several territories of other males are normally situated between a male's first and second territories.

In the study referred to above, Rätti and Alatalo put up boxes at two different densities: one area with boxes 100 m apart and another with boxes about 300 m apart. After pair formation they put up extra boxes around the original ones to encourage polyterritoriality and polygynous matings. They found that the distance between a male's two territories was longer in the low-density than in the high-density situation. Rätti and Alatalo further found no relationship between distance moved by males and their age, plumage colour, tarsus length or body weight.

Polygyny frequency

Not all polyterritorial males succeed in attracting a second female, and polygyny frequencies reported in the literature vary between geographic areas (Appendix 8), and probably also between habitats, breeding densities and nest-hole availability. As seen from Appendix 8, on average 10–15% of the females end up as secondary.

In general, early arriving males are more likely to mate polygynously whereas late arriving males more often remain unmated (Fig. 84). Clearly, males that

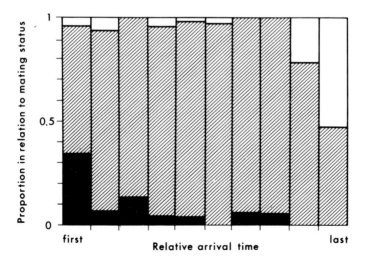

Fig. 84. Proportion of males mating polygynously (black bars), monogamously (hatched), or remaining unmated (open) in relation to arrival time. Data from Uppsala, Sweden, 1982–84; n = 214 males.

mate early also have the possibility of finding additional unoccupied nesting sites, a possibility which is much more limited for males arriving later, and thus mating later, in the season.

In the far north the frequency of polygyny seems to be low, perhaps because of the large number of unmated males in these marginal areas. No published information exists about polygyny frequencies in southwestern Europe and North Africa, although we know that polyterritoriality and polygyny occur in these areas too (Potti and Montalvo, 1991b). Thus, polyterritorial polygyny is probably a regular phenomenon over the whole distribution range of the Pied Flycatcher.

Male behaviour in secondary territories

To understand the evolution of polyterritorial polygyny and female choice of already-mated males it is of prime importance that we possess detailed knowledge of the behaviour of males in their two (or more) territories. Stenmark *et al.* (1988) suggested that the behaviour of already-mated males in secondary territories differed from that they had in their primary territory, and that therefore they are easily separated from unmated males by prospecting females, mainly on the bases of their reduced singing activity and less regular presence. However, this is not always the case.

In order to study the behaviour of already-mated males in their secondary territory and that of unmated males, while controlling for time of season and territory quality, we have performed several experiments which are summarized below. To begin with presence in the territory, it is clear that most already-mated males spend less time in their secondary territory than do unmated males in their first territory. The reason is that already-mated males sometimes visit their first territory and the primary female.

In one experiment, mainly done at Konnevesi in Finland in 1989, we created situations such that an already-mated male in a secondary territory became a close neighbour ($\approx$100 m) of an unmated male (Alatalo *et al.*, 1990d; see Fig. 93). We monitored the presence in the territory of both males simultaneously, thus standardizing for temporal variation, and found that unmated males were present for 85% of the observation time in their territory while already-mated males spent 73% of their time in the secondary territory. Both these measures are probably underestimates especially since silent males are not easy to watch. In another experiment, this time outside Uppsala, Sweden, in 1990, we provided many extra boxes after males had attracted females to the initial boxes; thus we hoped to induce a high degree of polyterritoriality (Searcy *et al.*, 1991). In this case we compared the behaviour of an already-mated male in his secondary territory with an unmated male in his first territory at approximately the same time. We presented males with an empty cage in front of the next box (for 30 minutes), followed by a period of the same length with a female in the cage. When the cage was empty we found unmated males to be present in their territories for on average 91% of the observation time compared to 73% for already-mated males (Mann–Whitney U-test, $U = 35$, $P < 0.01$). With a female in the cage the corresponding figures became 97% and 95%, respectively, which is a non-significant difference. Thus, in the presence of a female, both unmated and already-mated males were almost continuously present in their territories.

In the two experiments just described we also recorded male song rates. In the first we found unmated males to sing at a rate of 6.1 songs/min (SD = 1.2), the corresponding figure for already-mated males when present in secondary territories being virtually the same (5.8 songs/min, SD = 1.5; the difference is not statistically significant). Including periods of absence or silence, we found the song rate to be 5.2 and 4.2 songs/min, respectively. In the second experiment, the song rate when present in the territory was 8.0 strophes/min for unmated males and 7.5 strophes for already-mated males ($P > 0.10$), while a significant difference arose if we also included the periods of absence from the territory (7.2 against 4.7 strophes/min, $P < 0.001$). Singing ceases almost completely when a female appears in a male territory, and when we presented the caged females both unmated and already-mated males drastically reduced their song rates. During the half-hour presentation unmated males sang on average 0.6 songs/min while already-mated males sang 1.1 strophes ($P > 0.10$). Thus, behavioural differences between unmated and already-mated males practically disappear as soon as a female appears on the scene. (In this context the terms 'song' and 'strophe' are interchangeable.)

We have also compared the song performance and other behavioural traits of males that failed with those that later became mated, in relation to mating status. Thus, Rätti and Alatalo found the mean singing rate of unpaired males that later paired to be 5.4 strophes/min compared to 4.1 strophes for males that remained unmated. The corresponding figures for already-mated males in secondary territories were 4.4 and 3.2 strophes/min (including periods of absence; Fig. 85).

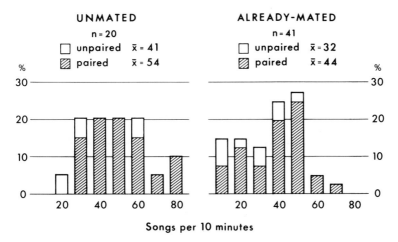

Fig. 85. Mean number of song strophes sung per 10 min by unmated males and already-mated males in their secondary territory, separated into males that later became mated and those that failed. The data include periods of absence from the territory.

Again, Rätti and Alatalo found no significant difference in song rate (corrected for periods of absence) or male morphology between polyterritorial males that later attracted a second female and those failing to do so. However, there was a relationship between song rate and distance between first and secondary territories; the greater the distance the more songs were sung in the secondary territory per observation time. What this means is that polyterritorial males with greater distances between their territories spend more time in their secondary territory than if the territories are close. These workers also found that the males most successful in attracting a second female were the ones that left their first territories early and moved a greater distance.

All in all, then, already-mated males are less often present in their secondary territories than are unmated males in their first territory, and therefore they also sing less per unit time. Consequently, by counting the number of songs over a reasonably long time it is possible with fair accuracy to classify males as to their mating status. However, when males are present in their respective territories, already-mated males sing as much as unmated males, and these two categories then become difficult to separate in the field for humans and probably also for Pied Flycatcher females. Furthermore, when a female appears in the territory, both unmated and already-mated males change their behaviour: both categories of males increase their presence in the territory, which will approach 100%, and both virtually cease singing. To distinguish an already-mated from an unmated male is therefore certainly not always easy.

Polyterritorial males normally return to the first territory during the incubation period of the first female, and Silverin (1980) found no males holding secondary territories after hatching in the first nest. However, after injecting males with long-acting testosterone (a male sex hormone), he found about 30% of the males never to return to their first territory. If mating with a secondary female, males will still return to the first female and devote most of their time to helping her raise her offspring. How males allocate their resources between broods depends, among other things, on distance between nests and nestling age. This topic, however, has already been considered in Chapter 7 (see also Fig. 40).

Behaviour of Females

The process by which Pied Flycatcher females choose a mate was dealt with in detail in Chapter 11. In the experiments referred to earlier, we were unable to find any evidence for females preferring particular types of male, for example, older, darker, or bigger; instead some aspects of territory quality seemed to be the main basis for female choice of a particular breeding situation. However, it is still not known whether they use single or multiple criteria. In this section we speculate on how many males a female may visit before mating and discuss whether females can and do discriminate between unmated and already-mated males.

How to sample males in theory

What kinds of decision rules can females use when they seek information about males and their territories, and how many male territories do they visit before making a choice? As shown in Chapter 9, the main function of the male Pied Flycatcher's song seems to be to attract females. Therefore, also, females probably mainly locate potential breeding sites by listening for singing males. The results of the experiments with random territories presented in Chapter 11 supported the idea that female choice is an active rather than a passive process, i.e. females actively reject some breeding situations in favour of others during their search for a mate.

Theoretical studies have proposed models for active female choice procedures (e.g. Janetos, 1980; Wittenberger, 1983; Real, 1990). One way could be to use a so-called threshold tactic. This means that females accept any male and/or territory if the quality is above some level set up by the female. Thus, if the first male/territory fulfils the female's threshold criterion she will pair with that male; if not, she will continue her search until she finds a male/territory that meets her minimum specifications. As an extension to this model we may add that the threshold is likely to be different for different females; for example, it may be higher for early arriving females than for late. According to Wittenberger, this threshold type of mate search tactic could be expected 'when the cost of comparing several prospective mates is relatively high and/or the benefit of choosing from among several prospects is relatively low'.

Another mate search tactic is what is called 'sequential comparison'. Here females sample males sequentially and make a choice on the basis of the last two breeding situations encountered. A female might then assess two males in sequence and accept one of them, or else defer the decision in order to visit a third male. The next assessment will be between males 2 and 3, and either she accepts one of them or continues her search, testing males pairwise until she encounters a breeding situation of high enough quality. The advantage of this tactic is that it reduces the hazard of someone else taking over the breeding situations under consideration; the disadvantage is that it diminishes the chances of making the best possible choice (Wittenberger, 1983).

A third method is what is called a 'best-of-*n*-tactic' (Janetos, 1980). In this case females sample a fixed number (n = say, 5 or 10) of males/territories, and then choose the best from this sample. The advantage of using such a pool-comparison method is that it improves the chance for a female to find a really good breeding situation; the drawback is that this may already have become occupied by another female during the first female's sampling procedure, especially if the number n is large. Janetos's theoretical work suggested that a female should ordinarily sample fewer than ten males if using this best-of-*n* tactic. In our view, this type of tactic could also be used in a variable way so that a female may pair before having sampled all n breeding opportunities, if some earlier site is of particularly high quality.

How females sample males in the wild

There have been very few studies of mate-searching behaviour by female birds in the wild. In the Pied Flycatcher search is probably restricted and also costly (Alatalo *et al.*, 1988a; Slagsvold *et al.*, 1988). To induce variation in the cost of search we made the following experiment with nest boxes. As described in previous chapters females have been found to prefer nest-holes high up in trees and to some extent also those with narrow entrances. Therefore, we provided groups of four close ($\approx$50 m) nest boxes, two at a height of 4 m and two at 1.6 m. One of the high-up boxes had an entrance diameter of 30 mm, the other 35 mm and the same was true of the low boxes. Height and entrance size were randomly assigned to the four males after all four had settled; initially all boxes were at the same height and with the same entrance diameter. The situation was compared with a set of four dispersed nest boxes (>200 m apart) placed in the same way as in the dense groups. The rationale of the experiment was the following. In dense groups males were within earshot of each other, so that females would be able to visit all four males and compare them and their territories at a low cost. Males in dispersed groups, on the other hand, were out of earshot of each other, and as a result females' search costs would be higher if they tried to visit and evaluate all four males/territories. In total we had five replicates of this experimental design. The outcome was that, in dense groups of boxes, males with boxes high up in trees attracted females earlier in comparison with males that had boxes low in trees, while entrance size did not significantly affect mating order. In groups with dispersed boxes, on the other hand, we found no preference for height or for entrance size (Fig. 86; the difference between the two treatments for height was statistically significant; Wilcoxon matched-pairs signed-ranks test, $T = 4$, $n = 10$, $P < 0.05$; for data see Alatalo *et al.*, 1988a). One conclusion from this experiment is that if choice is easy (as in our dense groups) females will discriminate between breeding situations, while if choice is more costly they will not be so choosy. Further support for a restricted search comes from a study by Slagsvold *et al.* (1988) who trapped females in certain nest box areas and released them into other areas. Subsequently they plotted the distance from the site of release to the site of settling, and found that females generally moved only short distances before mating; their conclusion was that females did not visit all advertising males in a woodland before making their choice, one probable explanation being that searching for a mate is costly.

These two studies of female search patterns indicate that females only visit and evaluate a restricted number of males, and that this number depends on the distance between the advertising males; probably, the longer the distance between males, the higher the search costs for the females. How many males then do females visit? Dale *et al.* (1990) in southern Norway released colour-ringed females into a woodland with nest boxes containing 23 unmated males, having continuously removed naturally arriving females. After the release of females, the nest boxes were watched for two days in order to identify females that visited advertising males and their boxes. Of 15 females released 14 were later seen, and 6

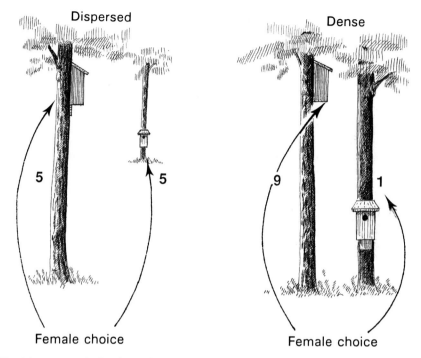

Dispersed

5   5

Dense

9   1

Female choice   Female choice

Fig. 86.   Design of a female search cost experiment. In dense groups of boxes, males with boxes higher up in trees attracted females sooner than males defending boxes low in trees. If boxes were dispersed, on the other hand, there was no preference for height, indicating that if choice is costly females will not be so choosy.

of these settled with males in the area. In total Dale *et al.* observed 131 female visits, and were able to identify the female on 41 occasions. Each male received, on average, 5.7 female visits during the two days of observation while females were found to search for mates for between 6 and 32 hours, and were seen to visit between 1 and 9 different males. Thus, Pied Flycatcher females did not seem to sample a great many males, and it was not clear what rules the females used. Dale *et al.*, however, suggested that at least some of the females in their study might have used the threshold–criterion tactic. Clearly, many more studies are needed on this subject.

COSTS AND BENEFITS OF POLYGYNY TO MALES AND TO FEMALES

Males

Males clearly benefit in terms of number of offspring produced by mating with more than one female. Sternberg (1989) followed 953 males throughout their lives and found monogamous males to produce on average ($\pm$SD) 4.9 ± 1.9

fledglings per year while polygynous males produced 10.1 ± 2.3. Likewise, over the lifetime of males, monogamous males produced 8.3 ± 5.1 fledglings compared to 18.3 ± 7.6 for males that were polygynously mated on at least one occasion during their life. Since trigyny was never observed and males were normally polygynous only once in their lifetime, it is difficult to understand how bigynous males in their life were able to produce twice as many, or even more, fledglings than could monogamous males. One reason may be that males successful in attracting secondary females also manage well in years when they stay monogamous. Another reason may be that, since males seldom succeed in becoming polygynous until they are two or three years old, the method of following males throughout their lives would bias the sample so that polygynous males seem to live longer than monogamous males, which will hence increase their lifetime reproductive success. (Further explanations why polygynous males should not raise twice as many fledglings as monogamous males are given below.) Von Haartman (e.g. 1951b, 1967a, 1985) also found polygynous males to produce more offspring as compared to monogamous males; his measure was the number of broods raised to the fledgling stage, the figures being 1.35 and 0.76, respectively. In our study areas around Uppsala, monogamous males produced on average 5.49 fledglings per year, while the corresponding figure for polygynous males was 8.05.

Von Haartman (1985) gave five reasons why polgynously mated males should not be able to raise twice as many offspring as compared to monogamous males. These were (1) late females (as secondary females often are) have poorer quality nest-holes, (2) late females lay smaller clutches, (3) late clutches have reduced success (see Chapter 6 for details on arguments 2 and 3), (4) males mated to more than one female seldom help the secondary female, which leads to reduced breeding success in the second nests (Figs 47 and 90), and (5) the difference in number of offspring produced by polygynous and monogamous males might be smaller than the number of fledged young if one takes into account the risks of extra-pair fertilization. If males leave a territory for a second one, or for some other reason abandon their female, she may become inseminated by other males. Indeed, von Haartman (1951b) saw two cases of extra-pair copulations among Pied Flycatchers, and in one case the female copulated with two neighbouring males. We studied the frequency of extra-pair copulations in the field by following males and females during two breeding seasons in an open deciduous woodland outside Uppsala in Sweden (Alatalo *et al.*, 1987). Copulations in the Pied Flycatcher are seldom seen. One reason for this is that they are very brief – only lasting a few seconds, at most. Another reason is that the birds are difficult to follow in the forest. So, for example, von Haartman (1951b) saw a total of 24 copulations in nine years of research on Pied Flycatchers, and in half of these cases he was uncertain whether they were complete. During our two-year study, when we were particularly looking out for copulations, we also saw 24. The copulations we witnessed took place between nine days before egg-laying and the day egg-laying commenced (Fig. 87). In von Haartman's study this 'time window' for copulations lasted from thirteen days before until two days after laying of the

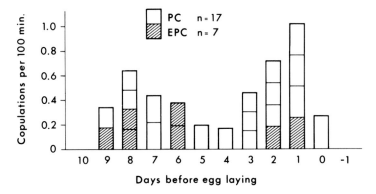

Fig. 87. Distribution of intra-pair (PC) and extra-pair (EPC) copulations in the Pied Flycatcher in relation to time of egg-laying. Redrawn from Alatalo et al. (1987).

first egg, while copulations that were certainly complete were only recorded between six days and one day before the start of egg-laying.

Of the 24 copulations we saw during our study, 17 were between pair members while 7 were between the female and another male. Thus, our study suggested that extra-pair matings are quite common in the Pied Flycatcher, at least at high breeding densities, since their proportion amounted to 29% of all the copulations we saw. We further found that the probability of extra-pair copulations was related to the distance between the members of the pair during the period of mate guarding. During the days preceding egg-laying, the male seldom moves away from the female by more than 10 m (Fig. 88), and in fact the chances of extra-pair copulations increase considerably if the distance is greater than that (Fig. 88). Björklund and Westman (1983) made an experiment to examine the

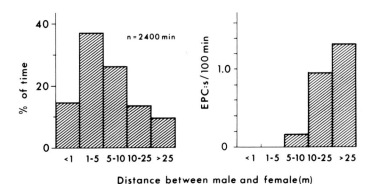

Fig. 88. Distances between male and female Pied Flycatchers one to nine days before egg-laying, and risks of extra-pair copulation (EPC) in relation to the distance between pair members. Redrawn from Alatalo et al. (1987).

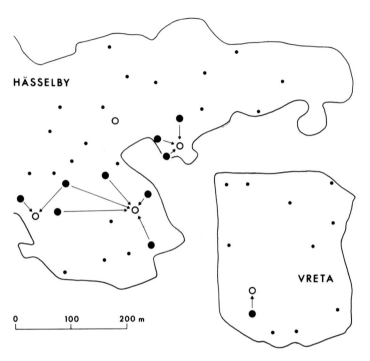

Fig. 89.   Two study areas outside Uppsala, Sweden with the distribution of Pied Flycatchers (dots). Open circles refer to nest boxes from which males were temporarily removed while solid circles show boxes from which intruder males came. Redrawn from Björklund and Westman (1983).

consequences of absence of the male from the territory. To simulate absence they captured males just before their mates started egg-laying, detained them for about 2 hours, and then released them. Meanwhile Björklund and Westman continuously watched the females and recorded all visits within the territory by other males; the behaviours were compared to what happened in a control group in which males were not removed. In four out of the five experiments other males intruded into the territories of single females, on average 10 min after the removal of the male (Fig. 89). In total seven extra-pair copulations were seen, which is a rate of 0.8 copulations per hour of observation. This rate was twice as high as that recorded within pairs (=0.42) at the same stage of the nesting cycle. These authors further found that intruding males were nearest or next-to-nearest neighbours of the experimental pairs, and that intruding males were already mated. Extra-pair copulations might result in extra-pair paternity, with the consequence that some males will feed offspring that are not their own.

To try to ascertain whether multiple paternity occurs and to estimate its frequency, we compared the tarsus length of the offspring in a nest with that of the female and the male attending the same nest. The logic behind making this kind of comparison was that morphological traits like tarsus length are known to be highly heritable (for tarsus length in the Pied Flycatcher $h^2 \approx 0.50$; h^2 is a measure of heritability i.e. the extent to which phenotypes are determined by the genes transmitted from the parents). If tarsus length of the offspring is influenced to the same degree by both of the genetic parents one would expect offspring to resemble the male at the nest as much as the female, if both are true parents. If, however, offspring should be less similar to one parent, this could indicate that this sex might not always be a true parent. Thus, one would be able to estimate the frequency of incorrect paternity or maternity assignment (females might not be true mothers to the offspring in a nest if egg dumping occurs). However, the female at a Pied Flycatcher nest is probably almost always the true mother of all the young. In one year we daily marked all the eggs in 30 nests and found no case of egg removal or of two eggs being laid on the same day, which indicates that egg dumping must be very rare.

The result of our study on resemblance in tarsus length between offspring and parents, based on studies in densely inhabited deciduous forests, was that the heritability estimate of the offspring on the male at the nest was 18% lower than on the female (Alatalo *et al.*, 1989; see also Alatalo *et al.*, 1984c). In other words, offspring more closely resembled their mother than their 'father'. The lower slope of the male regression is statistically significant and indicates that multiple paternity might occur. If paternal and maternal effects contribute to the same degree to the resemblance between parents and their offspring, our result further suggests that about 18% of all offspring have a father that is not the male feeding the young. If so, there are two further possibilities: either it could be that, on average, 18% of the offspring in all nests have another father, or it could be that all offspring in 18% of the clutches are fathered by another male than the one associated with the nest. Intuitively we regard the former explanation as more likely than the latter. Extra-pair copulations and paternity are not unique to Pied Flycatchers; our studies also suggested that they were common in the Collared Flycatcher too (Alatalo *et al.*, 1984c, 1989), and from species unrelated to flycatchers high rates of extra-pair paternity have been reported, for example, in Indigo Buntings (Westneat, 1987). Furthermore, we found that in the Pied Flycatcher offspring resembled the neighbouring males to a degree that could make up for the difference between offspring–female and offspring–male regressions, while neighbouring females had no such resemblance. Since there was no correlation in tarsus length between neighbouring males themselves we can reject the possibility of any tarsus-length–environment interaction producing the positive correlation between offspring and the neighbour male. In plain words, this suggests that the true father of some of the young in a nest is the nearest-neighbour male. This interpretation is also consistent with the results found in the study described above where males were temporarily removed from their territories and it was found that neighbouring males trespassed and tried to copulate with the females.

After we had started these studies on paternity by estimating heritabilities, there became available new and far more powerful methods for studying the degree of relatedness, such as DNA-fingerprinting. An alternative method that was available to us at the start of our study was starch–gel electrophoresis of polymorphic enzymes; we tried this, but without much success. Among the over 20 loci (a locus is a site on a chromosome occupied by a specific gene) that were examined only one (AGP) was reasonably polymorphic while another (SDH) was only weakly so. This meant that we would have needed hundreds of birds just to find a few cases of extra-pair paternity with certainty. With DNA-fingerprinting only a drop of blood is needed, and this method has recently been applied to studies on flycatchers. In one study Gelter (1989) looked at paternity in broods sired by hybrid males on the island of Gotland in the Baltic, where both Pied and Collared Flycatchers occur in sympatry and at high breeding densities (for details of the frequency of hybridization see Chapter 13). The study involved seven families with a male hybrid and a Collared Flycatcher female, and indicated that 25% of the offspring had a father other than the hybrid male. This figure is close to that we obtained by using heritability estimate regressions (see above). In another study outside Oslo in Norway, this time on pure Pied Flycatcher pairs breeding at a rather low density, Lifjeld *et al.* (1991) found a much lower frequency of extra-pair paternity. Of 135 nestlings sampled, 6 (4.4%) had a low fingerprint band sharing proportion with their putative father, and were probably sired from extra-pair copulations. Another 4 nestlings had a single band that mismatched with the male attending the nest, which was interpreted as being caused rather by mutation than by the male not being the true father. Thus, there is some variation in the data obtained so far on the frequency of extra-pair paternity. It is likely that the frequency of multiple paternity varies with the breeding conditions; for example, it may be higher in dense populations than in sparse, higher in late nests than early, higher in nests belonging to polygynous males than in monogamous nests, and higher in nests held by brown males than in nests held by black males. These interesting possibilities clearly call for further studies on shared paternity in the Pied Flycatcher using the recently developed techniques in combination with observations on the behaviour of the birds.

Females

Females paired with already-mated males suffer considerable reductions in terms of number of offspring produced as compared with primary and monogamously mated females. The main reason is that secondary females receive less male help than do females of any other mating status (Fig. 47), and single parents can usually only raise a reduced number of offspring or offspring of lower quality. However, exactly how much secondary females lose has been a debatable issue among those working on the Pied Flycatcher, especially as it influences the interpretation of the phenomenon that some females mate with already-mated males. This question will be treated later in this chapter.

In our first estimate of the relative breeding success of secondary females (hereafter denoted by x), we found them to produce 65% (i.e. $x = 0.65$) of the number of young raised by concurrently laying monogamous and primary females (Alatalo and Lundberg, 1984a; Alatalo *et al.*, 1984a). In such comparisons one has to compare females laying at the same time because clutch size decreases considerably with time (see Chapter 6), and secondary females often start laying later in the season. Also, secondary females should be compared with primary and monogamous females combined because, at the time of mating, there is no knowing whether or not their mate will attract another female. In our estimate of $x = 0.65$ for secondary females we incorporated unassisted *late*-breeding females into the secondary category. Stenmark *et al.* (1988) argued that using such a feeding criterion for classifying some late nests as secondary would be misleading. In line with this, they found x to be 0.84 for secondary females in southern Norway, which is clearly a less drastic reduction in breeding success. In their study only those nests where females could be precisely defined as to mating status, based on reading of males' colour rings, were used in the comparison. By using the same definition for classifying secondary females, in the Uppsala sample we found secondary females to produce on average $x = 0.68$ offspring compared with simultaneously laying monogamous and primary females (Fig. 90; see also Alatalo and Lundberg, 1990). Our two estimates of the relative reproductive success of secondary females ($x = 0.65$ and 0.68) are so close as to suggest that most late unassisted females are indeed secondary. But why this discrepancy between Sweden and Norway in the proportion of offspring raised by secondary females? One reason could be differences in habitat; our study was performed mainly in deciduous forest and the Norwegian one mainly in coniferous forest, which may offer more food late in the season. However, Askenmo (1977a) found a very low relative reproductive success for secondary females ($x = 0.49$) in coniferous forest in southern Sweden, though he did not

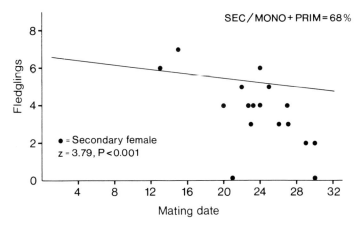

Fig. 90.   *Breeding success of secondary Pied Flycatcher females (dots) in relation to monogamous and primary females (regression line, n = 136, z = 3.79, P < 0.001). Only females mated with males whose mating status was known from colour rings are included. Data from Uppsala, Sweden, 1982–4. Modified from Alatalo and Lundberg (1990).*

correct for the seasonal decline in breeding success. In addition, females lacking males at the nest were classified as secondary. All these studies referred to above were conducted in areas supplied with nest boxes, and one could possibly argue that they do not reflect the natural situation since the effects of predation on reproductive success are greatly reduced. However, the same pattern of reduced breeding success for secondary females was found by us in a study of Pied Flycatchers breeding in natural cavities; we shall come back to this in Chapter 14.

There is a considerable variation between years in the number of offspring raised by secondary females in comparison with concurrent monogamous and primary females (range $x = 0.45$–0.96; Alatalo *et al.* 1984a), suggesting that apart from male assistance, factors such as weather and food availability are important for the number of offspring that can be raised to fledging. In good years with plenty of food many secondary females manage to raise quite large broods despite reduced male assistance, while in rainy summers many offspring die before fledging in secondary nests. Most likely because of fluctuations in food availability, monogamous and primary females do much better in some years than in others. In years when monogamous and primary females produce many offspring secondary females are also successful (Fig. 91). Again, this suggests food availability to be the main factor determining the relative reproductive success of

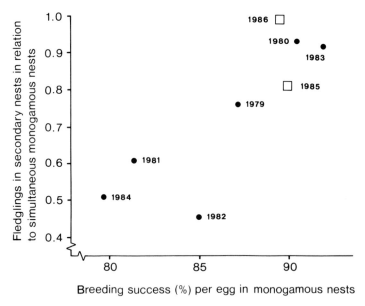

Fig. 91.   Yearly variation in the number of fledglings raised successfully by secondary females compared to simultaneous monogamous and primary females plotted against the percentage of laid eggs producing fledglings by monogamous and primary females. ●, Data from Uppsala, Sweden, 1979–84; □, data from Oslo, Norway, 1985–6 (Stenmark et al., 1988). From Alatalo and Lundberg (1990).

secondary females. If we incorporate the data from the Norwegian study cited above on reproductive success as in Figure 91 we find that they agree with the pattern found by us in Sweden. Most likely, the Norwegian study happened to be done during favourable breeding years, and many of the differences found between different studies in the relative reproductive success of secondary females might be explained by feeding conditions, which vary from year to year according to the weather.

The reduced male assistance at secondary nests leads not only to reduced fledgling numbers but also to significantly reduced fledging weight and tarsus length among offspring. Thus, their young are probably in poorer condition at fledging than are offspring from monogamous nests. Thus, for example, we found (Alatalo and Lundberg, 1986b) mean ($\pm$ SD) nestling body weight at 13 days of age in monogamous nests to be 14.00 g $\pm$ 0.98 as compared with 13.45 g $\pm$ 1.04 ($n = 45$) in secondary nests, when comparing clutches laid at the same time. Similarly, in a Norwegian study (Stenmark *et al.*, 1988), primary and monogamously mated females produced offspring of a mean fledging weight of 14.15 g $\pm$ 0.81 ($n = 117$) compared with 13.64 g $\pm$ 1.18 ($n = 41$) for secondary females. In both studies the weight differences between offspring in nests of different status were statistically significant.

The same pattern emerges for tarsus length as for weight. Both fledging weight and final tarsus length are sensitive to the amount of food given to the young in the nest. However, low fledging weight probably mainly reflects food shortage during the late nestling stage while a short tarsus is more likely to reflect undernourishment during an earlier stage. This is because weight is not a fixed character and responds quite rapidly to changes in food availability, while the tarsus is almost fully grown at about ten days of age, and would not later be affected by a deficiency (or surplus) of food. With regard to nestling tarsus length we found in our Uppsala sample that primary and monogamous females raised fledglings with a mean ($\pm$ SD) tarsus length of 19.54 mm $\pm$ 0.41 ($n = 278$ nests) while fledglings from secondary nests had significantly shorter tarsi ($\bar{x} = 19.19$ mm $\pm$ 0.56, $n = 45$; Alatalo and Lundberg, 1986a).

As shown in Chapter 7 (see also Fig. 52), nestlings with low weight or short tarsi at fledging are less likely to survive to the next breeding season, which suggests that Pied Flycatcher females paired with already-mated males not only raise a reduced number of offspring, but also that such young are less likely ever to become breeders. Thus, by pairing with an already-mated male, females seem to make a bad choice since being a secondary female leads to reduced breeding success. Moreover, since secondary females have to raise their broods with reduced male help, they have to increase their feeding efforts if they are to raise a full brood (see Chapter 7), and as a result they are likely to suffer reduced future survival. We cannot find any benefits of becoming a secondary female as compared with being a primary or monogamously mated female, though remaining unmated is certainly an even worse option. Here we want to stress that secondary females are probably not of lower quality than females mating with unmated males at the same time. As previously shown, older females arrive ahead of younger ones (Table 3), and since secondary females mate rather late in the season they are most often one-year-old birds, but then so also are late females that choose unmated males. With the purpose of looking at possible differences between females pairing with already-mated and unmated males, at the same time, we compared their morphologies and ages using a covariance analysis. The procedure is described in detail in Alatalo and Lundberg (1990). We failed to find any differences in morphology or age between monogamous and secondary females that paired at the same time, which suggests that secondary females do not differ in quality or experience from females mating with unmated males.

Not only secondary females suffer from being mated with polygynous males, but primary females too receive reduced male assistance since their mates sometimes visit and feed the nestlings at the second nest (Fig. 47). This occurs especially often when offspring are close to fledging. How polygynous males distribute their feeding efforts between nests was dealt with in Chapter 7. However, the consequences for primary females is reduced breeding success in relation to simultaneously laying monogamous females ($x = 0.90$, $n = 42$, U-test, $z = 2.24$, $P < 0.05$, data from Uppsala, Sweden). This pattern was also found in a study in southern Norway ($x = 0.93$, $n = 35$, $P < 0.02$; Stenmark *et al.*, 1988). Females clearly must have difficulties in forecasting a possible second mating by the male, and it is probably also difficult to prevent it if the male's second territory is far away.

Since there seems to be an immediate net cost of polygyny to them, why then do some Pied Flycatcher females mate with already-mated males? One possibility is that some form of delayed compensation accrues to them after the current breeding season, for example, increased mating success of their sons. This has been termed the 'sexy son hypothesis' (Weatherhead and Robertson, 1979), and implies that females will accept a reduction in breeding success to secure the genes of a sexy father, i.e. a male capable of attracting several mates. If this ability is heritable and passed to sons, secondary females could derive benefits in future generations, in terms of more grandchildren, through the increased mating success of their 'sexy' sons. One argument against this type of delayed compensation is that, as mentioned above, offspring from secondary nests are of lower phenotypic quality than other nestlings, reducing their probability of becoming polygynous in the following breeding season. Indeed, data on Collared Flycatchers breeding on the island of Gotland in the Baltic show that polygynous males were offspring procreated by monogamous pairs, and not sons of polygynous males (Gustafsson, 1985). Yet another objection to the 'sexy son' hypothesis as an evolutionary explanation of polygyny in the Pied Flycatcher is that it requires a high heritability of mating status. We have checked this by measuring what is called the repeatability, i.e. how alike individual males are from year to year with respect to number of females attracted per season. For example, are some males always monogamous while others are always polygynous? Repeatability sets the upper limit of heritability for a quantitative character. In the case of the Pied Flycatcher the repeatability of the number of females acquired by a male was as low as 0.20 (it can range from 0 to 1). From model simulations we estimated that heritability of mating status had to be about 0.80 to increase the fitness of secondary females to the level of monogamous females (a fuller treatment of the sexy son hypothesis is given in Alatalo and Lundberg, 1986b).

Our conclusion, based on data we have collected and on literature we have reviewed, is that secondary females of polygynous males do not gain any future benefits that might compensate for the immediate costs imposed on them by choosing an already-mated male as a mate. It thus seems as if some Pied Flycatcher females make unfortunate choices of mating partners, and we consider it most likely that this bad choice is a result of male polyterritoriality.

WHY ARE PIED FLYCATCHER MALES POLYTERRITORIAL?

MALE DECEPTION

We have earlier suggested (Alatalo *et al.*, 1981) that polyterritoriality may help males to conceal their true mating status. As shown above, male pairing status is important for female reproductive success, and pairing with an already-mated male means a reduced number of offspring. At the same time, Pied Flycatcher males benefit from mating with more than one female because they can then produce more offspring (for data see pp. 193–194). Thus, as so often, there is a conflict between the sexes as to how to maximize reproductive success. On one hand, females should try to avoid already-mated males while, on the other hand, males should try to become mated with as many females as possible. As shown in the previous chapter the main basis for female choice of a breeding situation is the quality of the territory, above all the safeness of the nest-hole. This makes sense because choosing an unsafe nesting place would greatly increase the risks of predation, which in turn may cause a complete failure of breeding. However, the second most important factor for female reproductive success is the extent to which the male will help in feeding the offspring. Therefore we expect females to be choosy also with respect to male mating status. Thus, females should judge the breeding situation in the following order: (1) the quality of the territory, (2) the male's pairing status, and possibly (3) other characteristics of the male. Territory features, especially nest-hole quality, can probably be quickly assessed by females, as can male song performance and coloration. If, however, a male is already mated and staying in a second territory this might reduce the speed with which prospecting females can assess his true pairing status (see pp. 188–190 for information on male behaviour in secondary territories). Following this line of argument, we believe that males are polyterritorial because it helps them to hide important information from females, namely that they are already mated. In essence, this is what we call the 'deception hypothesis'. We do not claim that polyterritoriality can completely prevent females from finding out about male pairing status, but it makes it more difficult, particularly as they are in a hurry to mate.

In this context it is of interest to point out that Pied Flycatcher males seldom manage to attract a second female close to the first nest, even if suitable nesting sites are available nearby (see also Appendix 7). This may be due to the aggression of females towards other females in the neighbourhood of their nest-site. In order to study the influence of nest-site distribution on the chances of males attracting a second female we put up groups of two to nine nest boxes very close to each other (10–50 m), and with the distance between the groups being much greater (>100 m). In such a situation males should have very good chances of monopolizing several adjacent next boxes. Among the 52 nestings in such groups we never observed a male having two females breeding within the same group of nest boxes. This is a significantly lower frequency than expected (Fisher exact test, $P < 0.01$) and implies that the two territories need to be far apart for the male Pied Flycatcher to be able to attract a second female (Alatalo and Lundberg, 1984a).

The same pattern was found by Susanne Åkesson (pers. comm.), who, for each nest box held by a monogamous pair, set up a line of eight boxes at distances of 25 m, 50 m and so on from the original box. Each line of boxes was erected on the day the nest was half-built in the original box. Later she recorded the male's singing activity at the different boxes along the line, and noted which males attracted a second female. Unfortunately the sample size for this experiment became greatly reduced because many other Pied Flycatcher males were attracted to the lines of boxes. Despite great efforts in trying to remove interlopers from the lines many succeeded in settling in the empty boxes, such that only four lines could be used. After the erection of the lines of boxes, two of the males started to sing again mainly at the box next to the one occupied by the first female, but these two males never attracted a second female. The other two males moved further away from their primary boxes, and each of them attracted a second female (Fig. 92), corroborating the fact that a relatively long distance between a male's two territories increases his chances of attracting a second female.

From Uppsala, in unmanipulated nest box situations, we have four observations of a polygynous male having his two mates within a distance of 100 m of each other. In one case a neighbouring female was taken over from a male that disappeared (died?). In two cases the first females were probably unaware of the presence of the second females until they had already settled. In the fourth case a female deserted her nest just before egg-laying after having been caught by us; she soon joined another male who already had a female, and promptly began egg-laying. Creutz (1955) and von Haartman (1969) have reported a few cases of two Pied Flycatcher females sharing the same box, and we have once observed the same phenomenon in the Collared Flycatcher. Thus, with a few exceptions, polygynous Pied Flycatcher males normally have their two females more than about 100 m apart. By contrast, different pairs may have their nests as close as 20 m apart.

To sum up, many Pied Flycatcher males try to attract a second female because this will increase their reproductive success. Apparently the best way to achieve this goal is to take up separate distant territories. The main benefit gained by

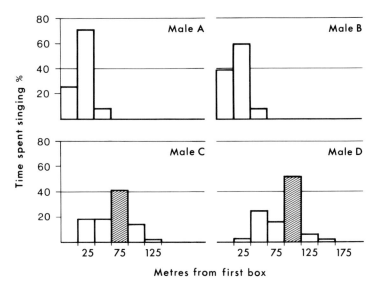

Fig. 92. Distribution of singing activity by Pied Flycatcher males at empty nest boxes at different distances from the first female's nest. Shaded bars indicate the distance at which already-mated males attracted a secondary female. The two males singing close to their original box failed to attract a second female.

males from being polyterritorial is, in our view, that they can thereby conceal their true mating status, making it difficult for prospecting females to use male mating status as a criterion when choosing a breeding situation.

That females indeed have difficulties in separating already-mated males from unmated males will be dealt with in more detail below. As previously stated, already-mated males in secondary territories are often males that arrived early, and they are therefore also old and dark. Likewise, they are less often present in their secondary territories than are unmated males in their first territories. Thus, it would be possible for females to use, for example, age, colour, and time present in the territory as cues for assessing male mating status.

If and how these cues are used by females was studied by us in a nest-box experiment, in which we created nearby territories (≈100 m) for duos of already-mated and unmated males (Fig. 93; Alatalo *et al.*, 1990d; see also pp. 188–190). The distance between the 'pair' of males of different mating status was so little that song from one territory could be heard in the other. Thus, females searching for a mate should become aware of the presence of both males and be able to visit and compare them; both males had similar new nest boxes so as to reduce the difference in territory quality between the two sites. To check whether females were aware of the two males we released marked females on two occasions near a male duo, and indeed both females visited the two males before mating. In this experiment, as in more natural situations, already-mated males in secondary

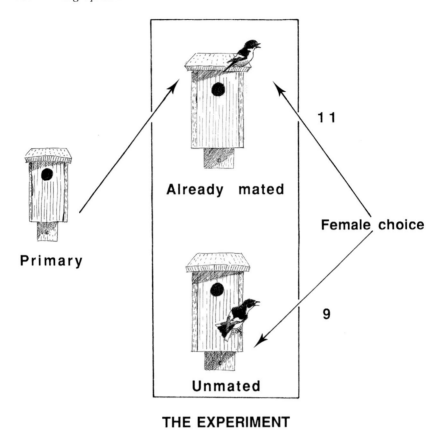

THE EXPERIMENT

Fig. 93. Design of a mate choice experiment, in which we created nearby territories (≈100 m apart) for duos of already-mated and unmated males. Among the 20 cases of paired comparisons the already-mated male was chosen first on 11 occasions.

territories were on average darker (71% of the dorsal area being black) than were unmated males (31%). Already-mated males also sang less persistently, mainly because they were less often present in their territories (73% of the time) than were unmated males (85%). Thus, in this experimental situation, females searching for a mate would be able to compare at a low cost an already-mated and an unmated male, the former on average being darker and less persistent in the territory. By choosing the unmated male she would have received full male help in feeding the nestlings, while if she chose the already-mated male she would later be partly abandoned since males direct their main feeding efforts towards the brood of the primary female (Fig. 47). Thus, if male mating status influences female reproductive success, and if females were able to discriminate between different types of males, one should expect the first female arriving at each of our male 'duos' (we had 20 replicates) to have mated with the unmated male. This was, however, not the case. Among the 20 cases of paired comparisons, the unmated male was chosen first on 9 occasions while on 11 occasions the already-mated male was chosen first (Fig. 93; one-tailed binomial test, $P = 0.75$). Thus, females seemed to have selected males randomly with respect to their mating status. With respect to male characteristics, other than mating status, the male in the duo singing more than the other male became mated first in 8 out of 14 possible comparisons ($P = 0.40$; in 6 cases one of the males was already paired when we sampled the song and thus did not sing). In relation to male plumage coloration, again there was no significant preference for dark or brown males. In 3 cases 'pairs' of males were of the same colour, but in the other comparisons females first mated with the browner one in 10 cases and with the blacker male in 7 ($P = 0.32$). Moreover, the reproductive success of females choosing the already-mated male was significantly reduced, both counted as number of fledged young and as estimated number of recruits, compared to females mating with the unmated male. Secondary females also raised young of lower fledging weight. Thus, females mating with the already-mated male would have done far better if they had chosen the alternative unmated male.

It has been suggested by Järvi *et al.* (1982) and Alatalo *et al.* (1984d) that to avoid already-mated males, Pied Flycatcher females could select brown males since, especially late in the season, these are normally the unmated ones. However, in all the experiments we have done so far, we have never found a clear female preference for any particular male colour. Nor have we found any changes in female mating preferences with regard to male plumage coloration over the breeding season (e.g. Alatalo *et al.*, 1990e).

In fact, it is relatively easy for humans familiar with the mating system of the Pied Flycatcher to distinguish between already-mated and unmated males, and even more so if we use multivariate statistical methods. By contrast, Pied Flycatcher females seem to make no distinction between already-mated and unmated males. One reason might be because mated males move away from their first territory and behave in many ways like unmated males in their secondary territory, especially in the presence of a female.

However, at some point, the secondary female must 'realize' that she will obtain reduced male assistance, and the question then becomes why she does not abandon the breeding attempt after having become aware of her situation. As previously discussed, searching for breeding opportunities is probably very costly, and may be even more so following a desertion. As the season progresses, the risk increases of encountering already-mated males in secondary territories, since more and more males can leave their first female which no longer needs to be guarded. Thus, if she gives up a secondary situation, the female might easily end up as secondary again, and then she has wasted valuable time. A delay in the start of breeding will cause a reduction in the expected number of young produced (-0.10 young per day; see Chapter 6). Moreover, delayed breeding might lead to reduced survival prospects for the offspring and, also, late breeding parents have to moult while still feeding young which might lead to decreased ability to feed them. Therefore, secondary females although in a sticky position probably cut their losses best by proceeding with the breeding.

One can also imagine that because of some constraint females may stay in their chosen breeding situation even if the prospect of success suddenly diminishes. Analogously, Cuckoo hosts stay and feed the Cuckoo chick once they have accepted the foreign egg although they suffer a very costly deterioration in the breeding situation. To examine if this might also be applicable to Pied Flycatcher females, we carried out an experiment at Uppsala and at Konnevesi in Finland. Since it is very difficult to manipulate males' mating status directly, we instead modified nest-hole quality to see if and when females would desert a breeding situation that suddenly deteriorates. As discussed earlier, inhabiting an unsafe nest-hole might lead to predation; one component of safety is hole entrance size, and unsurprisingly Pied Flycatcher females prefer narrow entrances.

In our experiment we put up normal boxes with a 30 mm hole in the front. Either 1 h or 24 h after female settlement, we exchanged the original fronts for fronts having entrances of either 45 or 60 mm; a nest-hole with a 60 mm opening would seldom be accepted by a prospecting female. We also had control boxes from which we removed the front and then replaced it by another with identical entrance size. Female settlement was considered to have occurred when a female had entered the original box several times, and was calmly perching outside it. In our view, the design of the experiment is not unduly unrealistic because in nature there are occasions when nest-hole quality suddenly changes, for example, when females have to switch to another nest-hole within a territory because of interference from tits, or when hole openings become enlarged by woodpeckers.

When the change of front was made 1 h after pair formations, 50% of the 22 females rejected the male whose nest front had been altered, whereas none of the control females left. This difference is statistically significant (Fisher exact test, two-tailed $P = 0.0012$, Fig. 94). There was a tendency ($P < 0.10$) for rejection to be more frequent (64% of 14 cases) when the 60 mm entrance was used than when the smaller (45 mm) was used (25% of 8 cases). When the opening size was changed 24 h after pairing, one (4.8%) of the 21 females deserted the nest-site, which is a significant difference from the 1 h manipulation ($P = 0.002$, Fig. 94).

This experiment illustrates that females may change their mating decision if they perceive a change in the quality of the breeding situation very soon after settlement. However, very few females did so after having spent a day on the territory. Their reaction may be similar when females perceive that they are secondary females of polygynous males, which means that males may not have to stay very long in their secondary territory after having attracted a female to ensure that she does not leave.

The behaviours of already-mated males and of prospecting females, as de-scribed above, quite consistently suggest to us that Pied Flycatcher females are unaware of the male's status at the moment of mating. The contest between male and female Pied Flycatchers seems in this respect to have been won by the male because if males can conceal their true mating status, even for a relatively short

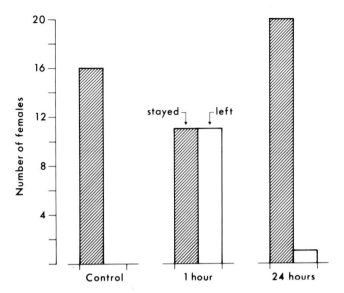

Fig. 94. *Number of females that left their mates (open bars) or stayed (shaded) after the nest box front (entrance size 30 mm) of the chosen box had been exchanged for a front with larger entrance size (either 45 or 60 mm). Redrawn from Alatalo and Lundberg (1990).*

time, females will probably not subsequently abandon their breeding situation. Polyterritoriality helps males to conceal that they are already mated. Thus, the deception hypothesis can explain both why males are polyterritorial and why secondary (and primary) females suffer reduced breeding success.

THE SEARCH COST HYPOTHESIS

Other than the deception hypothesis the most plausible alternative explanation for polyterritorial polygyny in the Pied Flycatcher and reduced breeding success among secondary females is the 'search cost hypothesis' (Stenmark *et al.*, 1988). According to this hypothesis there are sufficient behavioural differences between mated and unmated males (e.g. time present in territory, song rate, but see pp. 188–190) for females to be able to identify already-mated males. None the less, some females choose already-mated males because they cannot afford the high cost of searching for an unmated male (see also pp. 192–193); and this cost is argued to exceed the cost of being a secondary female. We have some cause to doubt the search cost hypothesis. First, it predicts that a female will choose an already-mated male only when she has not previously encountered an unmated one, or cannot do so at a low cost. This was clearly not the case in the experiment reported on pp. 188–189 where females were given a choice between an unmated and a mated male which were within earshot of each other, so that both could be inspected at low costs; and, indeed, released marked females were seen to visit both males. Yet in about half of our 20 comparisons already-mated males were chosen in preference to unmated males (Fig. 93; Alatalo *et al.*, 1990d). Hence, polygyny in this case cannot be explained by lack of opportunity of mating with an unmated male at a low cost. Rather, females selected males randomly with respect to their mating status.

Our second reason for doubting the search cost hypothesis is as follows. Studies by Stenmark *et al.* (1988) and Dale *et al.* (1990) suggest that female Pied Flycatchers search for mates for about one to two days. If this is correct, which we have no reason to doubt, our experience from studies in nest box areas and natural deciduous habitats around Uppsala suggests that unmated males are usually abundant enough that it would be easy for a human to locate several unmated males within such a period of time (if mating status was easy to determine). Pied Flycatcher females are more mobile than humans and, thus, it would be easier for them to locate singing males than it is for us. If Pied Flycatcher females can easily tell mated and unmated males apart (as assumed by the search cost hypothesis), it should not be very difficult for them to locate an unmated male within a day or two. However, females obviously do not have this power of discrimination, and that suggests to us that the unveiling of male mating status is the most difficult and costly step in female choice, which is the assumption of the deception hypothesis rather than of the search cost hypothesis.

The third point is that the search cost hypothesis cannot explain why males are polyterritorial. To counter this objection, it has been suggested that the spacing out of males' territories is caused by aggression between females. In accordance with this, Breiehagen and Slagsvold (1988) observed that during nest building and laying, females were aggressive towards caged females that were presented to them close to the nest-site. Males might thus be forced to take up separate distant territories to be able to attract additional females without interference between primary and secondary females. We ourselves have observed aggression between females close to the nests, and it has also been reported by von Haartman (1951b, 1956). On the other hand, there are also reports that females can be amicable towards each other, and as mentioned earlier two females can some-times even breed in the same nest box. In any case, while female aggression may play some role in polyterritoriality, it is not a sufficient explanation for the poor choices made by the secondary females. For the three reasons discussed we believe that the deception hypothesis is more plausible than the search cost hypothesis for explaining why some Pied Flycatcher females mate with already-mated males.

OTHER HYPOTHESES

After the deception hypothesis was advanced in 1981, a plethora of alternative hypotheses were proposed to explain polyterritorial polygyny in this species.

Examples of such other hypotheses are 'female retention' (Slagsvold and Lifjeld, 1986), 'spreading the risk of nest predation' (Winkel and Winkel, 1984), and 'avoiding food competition' (Alatalo and Lundberg, 1984a). Some more are derived from data on other species, and may therefore not be fully applicable to the Pied Flycatcher.

The female retention hypothesis suggests that males are polyterritorial so as to be able to have a second territory to offer their female and thus quickly restart breeding in case of predation of the first nest. The nest predation hypothesis suggests that clumping of nests increases the risk of predation, and hence males should be polyterritorial. It could also be argued that males take up separate distant territories to avoid competition for food between their two females. We have several objections to these hypotheses and present them in various chapters of this book and in Alatalo and Lundberg (1990). Our major objection, however, to all these other alternative hypotheses is that they cannot explain both why secondary females should accept a situation leading to reduced reproductive success and why males are polyterritorial; at most they can explain one or the other.

SUMMARY

Pied Flycatcher males are polyterritorial and polygynous. After having attracted a first female, many males move away to defend a separate distant territory. About 10–15% of all males succeed in attracting a second female into their second territory. This secondary female is more or less abandoned by the male and has to raise her brood with reduced male help in the feeding of young. A few males may even attract a third female. Males clearly gain by attracting more than one female since they then sire more offspring, whereas secondary females lose. It is likely that polyterritoriality might also lead to some costs for the male,

such as other males taking over the first territory, or the first female copulating with neighbouring males causing extra-pair paternity. If possible a female should in most cases choose an unmated male over a mated one. However, prospecting females are probably unable to separate unmated males from already-mated ones in secondary territories. We suggest that polyterritoriality is a deceptive male behaviour which increases his chances of attracting a second female, at the expense of the reproductive success of such secondary females. This is facilitated by the behaviour of already-mated males in secondary territories, which is very like that of unmated males, and to the fact that females are in a hurry to mate and, also, that they do not readily change a mating decision.

CHAPTER 13

Hybridization

The Pied and Collared Flycatchers are very similar in plumage coloration and ecology: males of both species are black and white while females are brownish, they have the same foraging techniques, both species prefer deciduous forest, and they nest in holes in trees. However, their songs are different, and in breeding plumage males can easily be separated because Collared Flycatchers have a conspicuous white collar and rump. Over a large part of their range the two

213

species occur together (see Fig. 5), and despite clear differences in song and plumage, hybridization does take place where they overlap. In general, hetero-specific pairings often lead to the production of unfit hybrids, and selection against hybrids usually leads to prezygotic (i.e. before fertilization of an egg cell) isolation and divergence in species recognition systems. Species recognition is known to involve characters such as plumage coloration, courtship displays, song and morphology. In the present chapter we shall provide information on the frequency of heterospecific matings among flycatchers, on which birds become involved in mixed pairs, on what happens to hybrids, and on characteristics that might be important in species recognition.

CHARACTERISTICS OF HYBRIDS AND THE FREQUENCY OF HYBRIDIZATION

Hybrids between Pied and Collared Flycatchers have been known in the literature since the 18th century. The earliest record we know of is a drawing in Louis Leclerc de Buffon's *Histoire Naturelle des Oiseaux* from the middle of the 18th century. This drawing shows three flycatchers, one of which is clearly a male hybrid (we have seen it reproduced in Rosvall, 1982, p. 37). More recent reports on observations of hybrids come from Germany (Löhrl, 1950), Sweden (Järbäck and Järbäck, 1972; Alerstam et al., 1978) and Finland (Vepsäläinen and Järvinen, 1977), and hybrids have also been found breeding. Male hybrids are most easily recognized by their incomplete neck collar, but females are more difficult to identify. Pied and Collared Flycatcher females differ in the amount of white on the outer webs at the base of the primaries and in the colour of the light patch on the feathers on the back of the neck (Svensson, 1984), and hybrid females are often intermediate between the two pure species in these characters.

We have studied hybridization between Pied and Collared Flycatchers on the islands of Gotland and Öland in the Baltic (Alatalo et al., 1982a, 1990b) where both species occur in sympatry. The islands have probably been colonized quite recently by the two species since the Collared Flycatcher was not seen by Linnaeus on his visit to Gotland in 1741 nor by an ornithological expedition in 1824 (Rosvall, 1982). It was not until 1846 that the Collared Flycatcher was first described from Gotland (Sundevall, 1846), and on Öland it was first seen in 1867 (Rosvall, 1982). We have no records on when the Pied Flycatcher first colonized these islands, but our guess would be some time during the 19th century (see Chapter 2). The nearest Collared Flycatcher population is found about 600 km to the south of these islands while the Pied Flycatcher breeds abundantly in all countries surrounding the Baltic Sea. On Gotland, the Collared Flycatcher is the more numerous of the two species, making up 80–90% of the total combined population. On northern Öland, where we studied them, the proportion of Collared Flycatchers is about 60%, while Pied Flycatchers predominate on the southern part of the island.

On the basis of the relative abundance of the two species in the study areas on the islands, and if individuals of the two species mated randomly, we would have expected about 11% of the pairs on southern Gotland and 39% on northern Öland to be heterospecific. However the observed frequencies were 3.2% and 5.3%, respectively, which is significantly less (chi-square test, $P < 0.001$ in both cases) than expected from random mating. Thus, there is an overrepresentation of conspecific matings, which shows that a species recognition system has developed. Nevertheless, some individuals do fail to mate with a conspecific. Of the 64 heterospecific pairs found over the years 1980 to 1986, 29 involved a Collared Flycatcher male and a Pied Flycatcher female whereas 35 were the opposite mating combination. Thus, there was no bias with respect to gender in mixed pairs (binomial test, $P > 0.50$).

We can now ask whether birds that failed to mate with members of their own species were a random sample from the population or differed from other individuals in some respect. Females were mostly caught on the nest during incubation, while males were caught when they were feeding nestlings. Some flycatcher nests lack a male, usually because the father is polygynous and mainly feeds the nestlings in the primary nest (see Chapter 7), and in some of these cases we failed to catch the male. In nests where no eggs hatched, which mainly happens when one parent is a hybrid (see below), we added nestlings from nearby nests and thereby made it possible to catch the parents. Males and females were weighed and we also measured wing and tarsus length. For Pied Flycatcher males we scored the blackness of the back (see Chapter 10), and in males of both species we measured the size of the white forehead patch, which is much larger in the Collared Flycatcher. We then compared the morphology of males and females that became involved in heterospecific pairs with those that mated with a conspecific. Of 16 comparisons involving male and female morphology between different mating combinations, only one was significant at the 0.05 level; Pied Flycatcher females mated to Collared Flycatcher males had shorter wings than had Pied Flycatcher females mated to conspecifics. This could be interpreted as an age effect since wing length increases with age (see Table 4), though one significant difference is to be expected by pure chance when so many comparisons have been made.

Natal dispersal is low on the islands of Gotland and Öland, especially in the Collared Flycatcher (Pärt and Gustafsson, 1989). Since all nestlings were ringed we knew the exact age of many of the birds that bred. When looking only at birds of known age, we found no significant difference ($P > 0.30$ in all cases) in age group (one-year-old versus older) between males and females in conspecific and heterospecific pairs, indicating that young birds did not become involved in mixed pair matings more often than old birds, though our sample for Pied Flycatcher females was rather small ($n = 13$).

In Chapter 10 we dealt with the geographical variation in male colour and suggested that the brown plumage coloration in male Pied Flycatchers could be related to avoidance of hybridization with the Collared Flycatcher (for

Table 18.   Back colour of male Pied Flycatchers in mixed and pure pairs in sympatry
(Gotland and Öland), and on the mainland in allopatry (Uppsala). Colour types (I–
VII) refer to Drost's (1936) scale. From Alatalo et al. (1990b).

| Colour type | Sympatry | | Allopatry |
	Mixed (%)	Pure (%)	Pure (%)
Black (I–II)	14.8	29.5	24.0
Medium (III–IV)	70.4	45.3	52.2
Brown (V–VII)	14.8	25.3	23.8
n =	27	95	404

flycatchers this idea was proposed by Røskaft et al., 1986), but on Gotland and
Öland we found little evidence favouring the idea that dark Pied Flycatcher males
were involved more often in heterospecific matings (Table 18). However, the
distribution of Pied Flycatcher males of different colours was not random in
relation to habitat and breeding density of the Collared Flycatcher: dark Pied
Flycatcher males were mainly found in areas with few breeding Collared
Flycatcher pairs while brown Pied Flycatcher males were more often in areas
preferred by the Collared Flycatcher, suggesting the colour might be important
in interspecific relations (see Chapter 10 for further details).

Thus, neither male or female size characters or age seem to influence the risk of
hybridization very much. Yet another feature, however, appeared to be important, and that is what we call 'mixed singing' among Pied Flycatcher males. The
songs and alarm calls of Pied and Collared Flycatchers are highly species-specific
and a human listener can easily distinguish them from each other (Fig. 95). On
Öland, where most singing males were tape recorded, it was found that about
65% of the Pied Flycatcher males sang a song which much resembled that of the
Collared Flycatcher (mixed song; Eriksson, 1991). Among 32 males recorded
singing the mixed song, 26 mated with a conspecific, 4 mated with the wrong
species, one mated with a female of unknown species identity (the nest was
predated), and one remained unmated. In contrast, none of the male Pied
Flycatchers singing a pure song became involved in heterospecific matings. One
could argue that the Pied Flycatchers singing a mixed song were not pure-bred.
However, they were morphologically indistinguishable from allopatric Pied
Flycatcher males (characters measured were wing and tarsus length, colour type,
and amount of white on the forehead and on the primaries). Though successful
hybridization seems possible (see below), we do not believe that all these males
were hybrids in some generation. This mixed singing might explain why some
Collared Flycatcher females mated with Pied Flycatcher males. It can also explain
why some Pied Flycatcher females mated with Collared Flycatcher males,
provided that Collared Flycatcher song is included in the mate recognition
system of Pied Flycatcher females.

Some evidence in favour of these ideas comes from a laboratory experiment
with oestradiol-implanted Pied Flycatcher females which were captured outside

Uppsala where no Collared Flycatchers occur. Each was presented with a nest box, from which different types of song were played after each other in a random order (Pied and Collared Flycatcher, and Willow Warbler song; see Chapter 11 for details of the experiment), and then we measured the number of nest-box visits the birds made during different play-backs. Fourteen out of 15 females visited the box during the song of the Pied Flycatcher, 10 also the box with Collared Flycatcher song, and 5 the box when Willow Warbler song was played back. A box with Willow Warbler song, however, was only visited if the song was played after flycatcher song, but never when it was played beforehand, perhaps indicating that females responding to Willow Warbler song were so stimulated by the preceding flycatcher song that they also responded to the song of an unrelated species. Alternatively they did not care about the Willow Warbler song but only responded to the presence of the nest box.

In total, the box broadcasting Pied Flycatcher song was visited by the 14 females 110 times. When broadcasting Collared Flycatcher song the box was inspected 26 times, while 11 nest-box visits were made when Willow Warbler song was played. Clearly, Pied Flycatcher song was the main attractant, but the Collared Flycatcher song also gave rise to female willingness to visit the nest box. One of the females clearly preferred Collared Flycatcher song to Pied Flycatcher song, and in another case it was a draw. It is possible that the Collared Flycatcher song is included in the mate recognition system of female Pied Flycatchers to some degree.

As for Pied Flycatcher males singing the 'mixed song' many hybrid males also sang a song similar to that of the Collared Flycatcher. Gelter (1987) analysed 740 song strophes from 11 hybrid males on the island of Öland and found, from a discriminant function analysis based on seven song variables, that 87% of the song strophes could be classified as Collared Flycatcher song. This could be compared to 63% of the strophes of Pied Flycatcher males singing a 'mixed song', 18% of those singing a 'pure song', and 97% of the strophes sung by Collared Flycatcher males.

So, why do so many Pied Flycatcher males sing a Collared-like song in areas of sympatry? This subject has been studied by Dag Eriksson (of Uppsala University) on the island of Öland. In brief, his arguments for the occurrence of mixed singing are as follows. The song of the Pied Flycatcher is very variable, and in areas of sympatry males are known to pick up notes from other males, and even from other species (see e.g. Fig. 61), which possibly makes the song more complex. The benefits to Pied Flycatcher males of having complex songs are so far largely unknown, though some of our data indicate that complex song is more attractive to females than is simple song (see Chapter 11). Support for complex songs being more attractive also comes from studies on other species of songbirds, for example *Acrocephalus* warblers (Catchpole, 1987). Thus, intra- and interspecific song copying might in many cases be adaptive because it increases song repertoire size. However, copying the song of Collared Flycatcher males in areas of sympatry appears to be maladaptive since it increases the risk of heterospecific mating. Since the two flycatcher species are closely related, it could even be that Collared Flycatcher song is included in the innate song template of the Pied Flycatcher, making it easier to copy. Some support for this last suggestion is that hybrid males sing a song more similar to Collared Flycatcher song than to Pied Flycatcher song (Fig. 95). We have never heard a Collared Flycatcher male sing a Pied-like song.

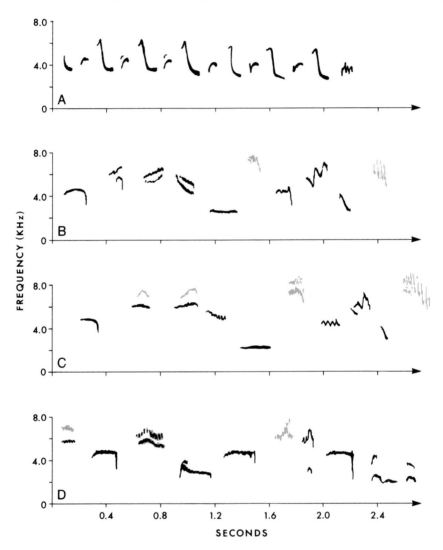

Fig. 95.   *Sonograms of a male Pied Flycatcher singing a pure song (A) and a mixed song (B). The Collared Flycatcher song is reproduced in (C), while (D) shows a song strophe from a hybrid male. All were recorded on the northern part of the island of Öland in the Baltic.*

MATING AND BREEDING SUCCESS OF HYBRIDS

The first Pied and Collared Flycatchers arrive on their breeding grounds in late April or early May. From Öland we have data on arrival and mating time (defined as start of nest-building) for the whole population. These data show that Pied Flycatcher males, as a whole, arrive significantly earlier than Collared Flycatcher males. This observed difference, however, could be spurious for the following reason. Collared Flycatcher males are dominant over Pied Flycatcher males (e.g. Löhrl, 1955; Alerstam *et al.*, 1978), and thereby they can probably take up the best territories. Therefore some late arriving Pied Flycatcher males might be prevented from taking up territories in our study areas, giving the impression that, among 'stationary' males (i.e. as opposed to 'floaters'), Pied Flycatchers arrive earlier than Collared Flycatchers. Hybrid males arrived at about the same time as Collared Flycatcher males.

Collared Flycatcher males mated significantly sooner, in relation to time of arrival, than Pied Flycatcher males. Again, this result must be accepted with caution. Since the Collared Flycatcher is the commoner of the two species in northern Öland, and probably also occupies the best parts of our study area, it might be easier and take shorter time for Collared Flycatcher males to attract a mate. The relative time between arrival and mating for hybrid males was intermediate between those recorded for the pure species pairs, but not significantly different from either species. Thus, hybrids do not seem to be at a disadvantage with respect either to arrival time or to time needed to attract females, compared with the pure species.

Both clutch size and fledging success in flycatchers decline as the breeding season progresses (see Chapter 6), and it is therefore advantageous to start breeding early. Looking at the mean start of egg-laying for different mating combinations on Gotland and Öland, we found that on average pure pairs of both the Pied and Collared Flycatcher started laying 26 May ($n = 135$ and 1670, respectively). The corresponding figure for heterospecific pairs was 27 May ($n = 65$) and that for pairs with one hybrid involved was 25 May ($n = 76$). None of these breeding dates differ significantly from the others (U-tests, $P > 0.10$ in all cases). Thus, hybrids do not start breeding later than pure pairs.

Turning to clutch size and fledging success, Pied Flycatchers lay significantly larger clutches (6.5 eggs) than Collared Flycatchers (6.0 eggs) on these Baltic islands. Pied Flycatcher females mated to Collared Flycatcher males laid a clutch of approximately the same size (6.3 eggs) as those mated with a conspecific. Likewise, Collared Flycatcher females laid the same clutch size (6.0 eggs) when mated with Pied Flycatcher males as when mated with conspecifics. Thus, it seems that clutch size is only determined by the female parent. Since mating combinations with Pied Flycatcher females paired with Collared Flycatcher males were as common as mixed pairs the other way around, clutch size of heterospecific pairs fell in between (6.2 eggs) that of pure pairs. If the female parent was a hybrid, clutch size (6.3 eggs) was significantly larger than if the

Table 19.   Clutch size, fledging success and proportion of fledged young recruited of pure flycatcher pairs, of heterospecific pairs, and of hybrids. n = *number of clutches. From Alatalo* et al. *(1990b).*

Male × female	Clutch size			Fledged young			Proportion of fledged young recruited		
	$\bar{x}$	SD	n	$\bar{x}$	SD	n	$\bar{x}$	SD	n
PF × PF	6.49	0.75	131	5.47	1.77	121	4.31	8.38	75
CF × CF	6.02	0.73	1662	4.78	1.95	1659	11.99	15.80	1605
CF × PF	6.34	0.61	29	4.86	2.07	29	10.82	15.53	62
PF × CF	6.03	0.75	35	4.91	1.90	34			
CF or PF × hybrid	6.28	1.13	40	1.79	2.67	38	11.22	13.02	31
Hybrid × CF or PF	6.28	0.73	43	4.20	2.81	40			

female was a Collared Flycatcher but not significantly different from that of pure Pied Flycatcher females (Table 19). Again, with regard to the size of the clutch, hybrids do not seem to do less well than pure pairs.

So, what about hatching success? Less than one per cent of the pure species pairs failed to hatch any incubated eggs at all, and the figure for heterospecific pairs was 1.6%. Of all eggs laid by each mating combination, Pied Flycatcher pairs hatched 96% of them, while the hatching success of Collared Flycatcher pairs and of mixed pairs was 95% in both cases. However, if hybrids were involved the hatching success was significantly lowered. In 26% of the clutches where the male was a hybrid no eggs hatched at all. The proportion of total hatching failures was even larger when the female parent was a hybrid (65%), and of all eggs laid by pairs involving one hybrid (male or female) 49% failed to hatch. Thus, with respect to hatching success, pairs involving one hybrid were at a clear selective disadvantage, especially if the female was a hybrid (Fig. 96). It thus seems quite clear that hybrids have reduced fertility, but why is there a difference between the sexes? Haldane (1922) suggested that the heterogametic sex should be more likely to be sterile, and in birds this is the female. Additionally, another explanation could be that hybrid males are infertile as often as hybrid females, but the observed difference in hatching success is an effect of extra-pair copulations. Extra-pair copulations, leading to multiple paternity, are probably not uncommon among flycatchers (see Chapter 12). Thus, if the female is a hybrid and sterile, no eggs will hatch irrespective of whom she was inseminated by. However, if the male is a sterile hybrid, while the female is 'pure', extra-pair copulations with other 'pure' males would probably result in enhanced hatching success. If this were the case, one would expect higher hatching success if the male is a hybrid than if the female is a hybrid. A recent study using DNA-fingerprinting (Gelter, 1989) showed that hybrid males were true fathers to some offspring, but also that some other offspring resulted from extra-pair copulations.

The reduced hatching success of hybrids also leads to reduced fledging success,

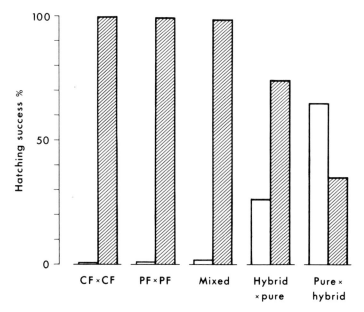

Fig. 96. Proportion of clutches with complete hatching failure (open bars) and clutches where at least one egg hatched in pure Collared Flycatcher pairs (CF × CF), pure Pied Flycatcher pairs (PF × PF), heterospecific pairs (CF male × PF female or PF male × CF female), and pairs involving one hybrid (hybrid male × a pure CF or PF female and a pure CF or PF male × hybrid female). Data from the Baltic islands of Gotland and Öland (see Alatalo et al., 1990c).

especially if the female parent was a hybrid. When the male was a hybrid, a pair produced an average of 4.2 fledglings compared to 1.8 if the female was a hybrid; pairs with a hybrid female produced significantly fewer fledglings than pure pairs of either species (Mann–Whitney U-test, P < 0.01). If the male was a hybrid, fledging success was reduced only in comparison with pure Pied Flycatcher pairs (P = 0.01), though again the reason for better reproductive success could be that hybrid males are not the true fathers of all the offspring.

Among offspring fledged, however, we could not find any difference in recruitment rate between pure Collared Flycatcher pairs and 'hybrid pairs'. Natal dispersal in the Pied Flycatcher is much greater in terms of distance than in the Collared Flycatcher, and we recovered 4.3% of the fledged Pied Flycatcher nestlings in later years. The corresponding figure for Collared Flycatcher nestlings was 12.0%, while those for heterospecific pairs or for pairs involving one hybrid parent were 10.8% and 11.2%, respectively (Table 19). Thus, fledglings from hybrid parents seem to return to their natal area in the same proportion as do offspring from pure Collared Flycatcher pairs and mixed pairs.

The main selective disadvantage of being a hybrid seems to be that hatching success is clearly reduced. In other reproductive aspects hybrids obviously do as well as conspecific pairs and, in conclusion, the relatively frequent occurrence of heterospecific pairings, in spite of the highly reduced fitness of hybrid offspring, is likely to persist because of difficulties in species recognition. Many female Pied Flycatchers breeding on Gotland and Öland are likely to be immigrants from allopatric regions, where there has been little selection for recognizing Collared Flycatcher males. Also, female flycatchers choose mates on the basis of territory quality rather than on male characteristics (see Chapter 11). Similarly, males of both species might not have been able to evolve a perfect faculty of distinguishing females of the two species since the females are very similar in appearance, and males are less choosy than females. All these factors may reduce the possibility of rapid evolution of perfect species recognition.

SUMMARY

Heterospecific matings frequently occur between Pied and Collared Flycatchers in areas of sympatry, such as the Baltic islands of Gotland and Öland. However, the observed frequencies of mating with the wrong species were much lower on both islands than would be expected if individuals mated randomly with respect to species identity; this indicates that a species recognition system has developed. Individuals that paired with the wrong species were no different in morphology or age from those mating with a conspecific. However, Pied Flycatcher males that sang a Collared-like song, which are common on these islands, ran a higher risk of mating with a Collared Flycatcher female than did males singing a typical Pied Flycatcher song. Hybrids were at a selective disadvantage because they hatched fewer eggs, and this was especially the case if the female parent was a hybrid. In all other aspects that could be measured, hybrids performed as well as the 'pure' species. Immigration of Pied Flycatchers from allopatric regions to the islands might be one explanation as to why perfect species recognition has not yet evolved, despite marked differences in song and the presence of a conspicuous white neck collar on the male Collared Flycatcher.

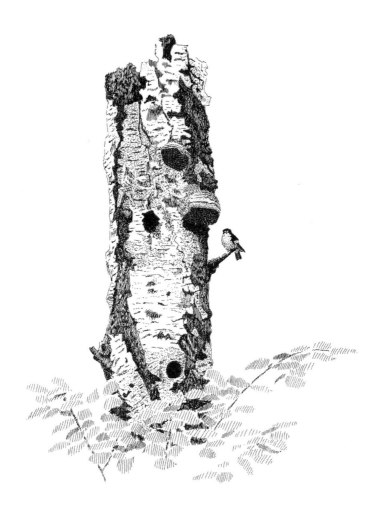

CHAPTER 14

Breeding in Natural Cavities

The Pied Flycatcher is probably the easiest bird to attract to nest boxes. If good quality boxes are put up in a woodland before the birds' arrival on spring migration, most, if not all, pairs can be attracted to them. Hence, most of our knowledge about the breeding biology and population dynamics of this species comes from nest box studies. One could thus argue that much of what we believe we know about the Pied Flycatcher, especially concerning male polyterritoriality, may result from the artificial situation with nest boxes, and our previous conclusions might in some cases be erroneous. In this chapter, therefore, we look at the reproductive performance and behaviour of birds breeding in natural nest-holes, to see whether they are less successful or behave differently under natural circumstances.

ORIGIN AND CHARACTERISTICS OF NATURAL CAVITIES

Suitable nesting holes for Pied Flycatchers are without doubt more scarce in the managed forests of today than they were in the primeval forests of the past. Likewise, natural holes are, and most likely always have been, scarcer in coniferous than in deciduous habitats, and in young compared to old forests.

The main study that we will refer to in this chapter was carried out from 1983 to 1985 in a more-or-less natural deciduous forest (Andersby) north of Uppsala (Alatalo *et al.*, 1990a). The total study area consisted of 59 ha of forest. In the first year (1983), however, we only searched 39 ha of the area. Dominant trees in this forest are silver and downy birch, aspen, pedunculate oak, rowan, small-leaved lime and Norway maple, often with an understorey of hazel. A small part (1 ha) of the forest has an admixture of Norway spruce (Fig. 97). The area was used in the past mainly for grazing cattle and horses (Hytteborn, 1975). This ceased in the 1920s when the open parts became overgrown. To re-create the former forest structure, 31 ha was thinned in 1967–8, and parts of this are now grazed by cattle. Twenty-seven hectares of the forest are untouched, and this area became a nature reserve in 1987. No nest boxes exist in or near this 'natural' area – our nest box study areas are situated about 30 km to the south.

During the three years of study we found a total of 105 nest-holes used for breeding or defended by unmated Pied Flycatcher males. Such natural cavities can arise from a variety of causes. Out of 81 natural nest-sites found by us, and classified as to origin, 68% were the result of falling branches or some similar form of damage to the trunk, such that the trunk had become hollowed out either through decay or by excavation by tits. The second most common nest-type, in relation to origin, were old woodpeckers' nests. In our study 21% were Great Spotted Woodpecker and 10% Lesser Spotted Woodpecker nests. In the Białowieża Forest in eastern Poland, Wesołowski (1989) found 47.4% of Pied Flycatcher nests to be located in woodpecker-made nests while the rest were classified as 'natural holes'.

A parallel study, on the availability of nest-holes (Allan Carlson and Ulf Sandström, pers. comm.), revealed that the density of natural cavities in our Swedish study area (woodpecker holes and fallen-branch holes) was 41 per ha, and if other types of holes were included it came to 52 per ha. Of the 338 cavities examined by Carlson and Sandström, 32.5% were made by woodpeckers, 58.5% were caused by fallen branches, and 9% were due to other damage to the

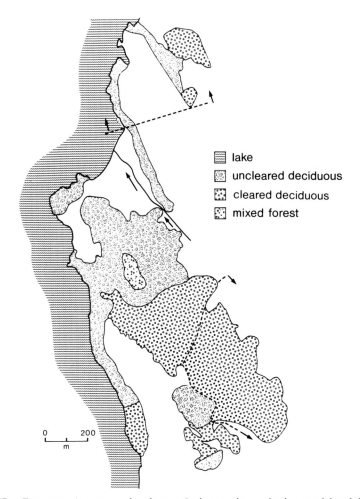

Fig. 97.   Forest types in our natural study area. In the west the area borders on a lake while to the east, south and north there are clear-cuttings or fields with a few scattered trees. A small stream surrounded by meadows runs through the area. Areas north and south of the broken lines were not studied in the first year (1983).

lake

uncleared deciduous

cleared deciduous

mixed forest

trunk. The above figures are based on a sample of seven subplots within the wood, each being 0.5 ha in size. These plots were chosen so as to represent the different forest types in the wood, since there was a large variation in the density of nest-holes between different parts of the forest. The area with the lowest density had 24 holes/ha while that with the highest had 224 holes/ha. However, not all these potential natural nesting cavities were suitable for the Pied Fly-catcher, mainly because the entrance hole was too large. The tree species with

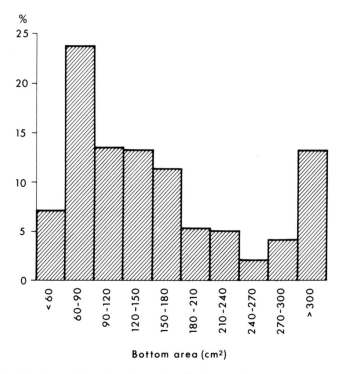

Fig. 98.   Distribution of size of nest bottom (considered as an ellipse) in natural cavities used by the Pied Flycatcher. Taken from Alatalo et al. (1988b).

most holes were aspen and oak. Aspens often grow in clumps, thus creating a patchy distribution of nest-holes. The majority of nest-holes in aspens (59.2%) were due to excavation by woodpeckers. In oaks, on the other hand, only 7.1% of the holes were of woodpecker origin, while 63.8% were due to fallen branches.

Mean breeding density of Pied Flycatchers in this wood was 0.6 pairs/ha, though in the most natural parts the density was slightly above one pair/ha. This could be compared with the mean of 1.8 pairs/ha (range 0.4–3.1) found in our nest box areas in deciduous forest which hold about 5 boxes/ha. The higher breeding density in nest box areas suggests that most of the natural cavities were of poorer quality than our nest boxes. In semi-natural deciduous forests elsewhere nest-hole density values range approximately from 5 to 15 holes/ha (Edington and Edington, 1972; Ludescher, 1973).

Natural cavities vary greatly in size. Our standard nest boxes have a bottom area of 100 cm^2 and a volume of approximately 1550 cm^3, measured from the rim of the nest to the top of the entrance hole. On average, the natural cavities we measured were larger than our boxes, with a median bottom area of 123 cm^2 and a median volume of 2035 cm^3. The variation, however, was huge; the smallest

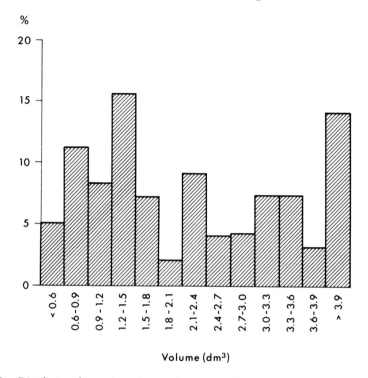

Fig. 99.   *Distribution of nest volumes in natural cavities used by the Pied Flycatcher. Volume was measured by multiplying the bottom area by the sum of hole depth and entrance height. Taken from Alatalo et al. (1988b).*

cavity had a bottom area of 33 cm^2 and a volume of 210 cm^3 while the largest had a bottom area of 735 cm^2 and a volume of 12 725 cm^3 (Figs 98 and 99). Natural nest cavities of about the same size were also found in a study in the Netherlands by van Balen *et al.* (1982). The mean bottom area of natural nest-holes occupied by tits, Nuthatches and Redstarts in the Dutch study was 127 cm^2, and the range was 33 to 491 cm^2. Thus, these data conflict with the usual statement that natural cavities are smaller than standard boxes. However, cavities made by woodpeckers are rather different from those having been caused by a fallen branch – the former have more the shape of a nest box while holes of the latter type are often shallow and oriented horizontally rather than vertically.

LAYING DATE, CLUTCH SIZE AND BREEDING SUCCESS IN NATURAL CAVITIES

Since nest boxes are usually preferred to holes in trees one would expect birds using natural sites to start breeding later and perhaps also to reproduce less well, than those breeding in boxes. A second reason to expect this is the routine procedure of cleaning nest boxes after each season, which reduces the number of parasites in nests (Møller, 1989). The median laying date of the first egg for Pied Flycatchers breeding in natural cavities in the years 1983 to 1985 in the Andersby forest was 27 May ($n = 84$) while nest-box breeders in the same years were slightly earlier (24 May, $n = 166$). This difference is significant and somewhat larger than that found for southern Sweden, where median laying date in boxes was 26–27 May and in natural holes 28 May (Nilsson, 1984). We do not know whether this difference in timing is due to the fact that natural cavities are more difficult to find than boxes or that natural holes are of lower average quality. Since predation on natural cavities is higher than on boxes (see below) the later average breeding in natural holes might also be due to there being more repeat clutches, after predation in the early nesting stage. However, we can rule out any possibility that birds using natural holes are different from those breeding in boxes. As an example, if we compare male plumage colour according to Drost's (1936) scale, the mean plumage score ($\pm$ SD) of males breeding in natural cavities was 3.5 ± 1.0 ($n = 31$) while in nest box areas in the same years they had a colour score of 3.4 ± 1.2 ($n = 250$; $z = 0.35$, $P > 0.10$).

Turning to clutch size, in two of the three years of study it was larger in nest box areas than in natural cavities (in 1985 the difference was statistically significant) while in one year it was larger in natural cavities. Combining all years we found that the average clutch size ($\pm$SD) for birds breeding in boxes was 6.62 eggs $\pm$ 0.77 ($n = 194$) while for birds breeding in natural cavities it was 6.45 eggs $\pm$ 0.74 ($n = 74$; $t = 1.63$, $P > 0.10$). The small difference observed could largely be explained by the difference in laying dates. Clutch size in the Pied Flycatcher decreases by about 0.07 eggs per day over the breeding season (see Chapter 6). Thus, correcting for median time of laying we should subtract 0.21 eggs from the number of eggs laid by nest box breeding pairs, and we will end up with a very similar clutch size for Pied Flycatchers breeding in natural holes and in boxes.

Comparing clutch size with female mating status – i.e. monogamous, primary and secondary females – we found them to lay clutches ($\pm$ SD) of 6.63 ± 0.56 ($n = 57$), 6.50 ± 0.84 ($n = 6$) and 5.50 ± 0.53 ($n = 8$) eggs, respectively. Secondary females started laying considerably later (35.8, $1 = 1$ May, $n = 9$) than primary and monogamous females (25.6, $n = 7$ against 26.4, $n = 65$). The smaller clutch size of secondary females, however, was not only due to their later start of breeding because monogamous females laying at the same time as secondary females laid on average 6.11 eggs $\pm$ 0.33 ($n = 9$; $P = 0.012$). This is the same pattern as found for nest box breeding populations (see Chapter 6).

For several hole-nesting species, including the Pied Flycatcher, it has been reported that clutch size decreases with cavity size (e.g. Karlsson and Nilsson, 1977). Most of these studies have been performed by the use of nest boxes of various sizes. In another study on Pied Flycatchers breeding in natural holes in southern Sweden (Nilsson, 1984), clutch size was significantly smaller (6.00 eggs) than in nearby control boxes (6.48 eggs), and the author suggested that the

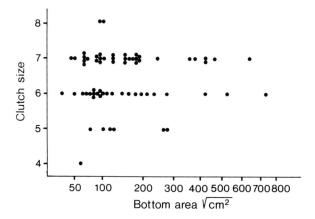

Fig. 100. Relationship between Pied Flycatcher clutch size and areas of nest bottom (measured as an ellipse) in natural breeding cavities. r = 0.038, P = 0.76. Taken from Alatalo et al. (1988b).

difference was probably due to the small size of natural holes. This is contrary to our findings (see above), where clutch sizes were about the same and natural holes were larger than boxes. However, we also analysed our clutch size data in relation to different cavity measures. We found no correlations between these measurements and clutch size, that for bottom area was $r = 0.038$ ($P = 0.76$; Fig. 100) and for volume $r = 0.021$ ($P = 0.87$).

In all years pairs breeding in natural cavities produced fewer fledglings than pairs breeding in boxes, though the difference was only significant in one year. When all years were combined, pairs in natural holes raised ($\pm$SD) 3.79 fledglings $\pm$ 3.12 ($n = 84$) which is significantly less ($P < 0.001$, Mann–Whitney U-test) than pairs in boxes (5.61 $\pm$ 1.92, $n = 194$) in the same years. The main reason for the reduction in breeding success in natural cavities was the much higher predation rate. Predation rate varied greatly between years, and was in natural holes 23.8%, 34.3% and 57.1% for the three years, giving an overall mean of 39.3%. The corresponding figures for nest box areas in the same years were 2.1%, 18.4% and 0%, with a mean of 5.7%. These figures are similar to those found by Nilsson (1984), who reported predation rates of 22.6% for natural holes and 4.5% for boxes. Dividing according to female mating category, primary females had on average 28.5%, monogamous females 38.4%, and secondary females a 44.4% predation rate. Secondary females produced ($\pm$ SD) on average 2.67 $\pm$ 2.55 ($n = 9$) nestlings which can be compared with simultaneous monogamous females which produced 3.33 $\pm$ 3.20 ($n = 9$) nestlings. The data are few and this difference is not statistically significant (U-test, $P = 0.63$), while if we compare only nests that gave rise to at least one fledgling, the proportion (80%) remained the same, but the difference was significant (4.80 $\pm$ 0.45, $n = 5$ against 6.00 $\pm$ 0.71, $n = 5$, $P = 0.012$). Furthermore, since secondary females have less male help in feeding the young (Chapter 7), the young might beg more for food in such nests, a behaviour that might attract predators. In our wood the main predators were probably mustelids.

If comparing only successful nests of monogamous females (i.e. nests from which at least one young fledged), we found no significant difference in final brood size between natural cavities and boxes (6.35 ± 0.70, $n = 40$, against 6.21 ± 1.01, $n = 171$), indicating that cavity-nesting pairs did not suffer considerable additional losses to those caused by predation. However, we have not been able to weigh and measure nestlings from natural holes, so we do not know if they are in poorer condition at fledging than are fledglings from boxes.

PREDATION AND NEST-SITE CHARACTERISTICS

Predation was the main factor reducing reproductive success in natural cavities as compared to boxes. The main predators are probably mustelids, but woodpeckers might also depredate Pied Flycatcher nests. To find out which holes are the safest in relation to predation risk, we inspected all nest-holes using a dentist's mirror and measured 15 variables related to the nest-hole and the nesting tree. These variables included size of cavity, height of cavity, height of tree, tree species and condition of tree. If we first consider the origin of nest-holes, those made by the Lesser Spotted Woodpecker were most unsafe while fallen-branch holes were the safest (Table 20). Other single variables that affected predation rate were tree height, distance of entrance from ground, angle of opening, and distance from entrance to nest-cup. This means that high nests in tall trees are safer than those lower down in small trees, an entrance hole pointing upwards is better than one pointing downwards, and a long distance between entrance and nest-cup is better than a short one. The distribution of nest heights for successful and depredated nests is shown in Figure 101. It is likely that tree height entered as a significant character because many nests in dead tree stumps were depredated. Also, high nests are probably more difficult for mustelids to climb, and if the nest-hole is pointing upwards it will make it less visible from the ground. The results from the nest-box experiments described in Chapter 4 also showed that Pied Flycatcher females prefer high sites to low ones. It is somewhat less clear

Table 20.   *Type of nest-hole and associated rates of predation (chi square = 6.62, d.f. = 2, P < 0.05). Entrance-hole size is given as the mean of height and width.*

Type of hole	Predation (%)	Entrance-hole size (mm)	n
Lesser Spotted Woodpecker nest	72.7	35.6	11
Great Spotted Woodpecker nest	41.4	45.8	17
Fallen-branch hole	30.9	33.6	55

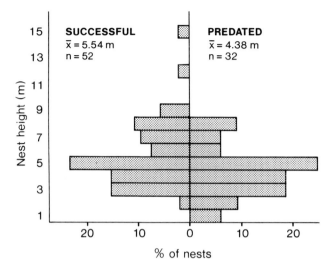

Fig. 101.   Nest height for successful and predated Pied Flycatcher nests located in natural cavities.

why nests located far from the opening are safer, though weasels seem more often to prey on the female than on the eggs and nestlings, and perhaps the female has a better chance of escape when she is further away from the entrance. From the Białowieża study referred to earlier it was further found that Pied Flycatchers to a large extent used thin trees for nesting, and for some reason nests in such trees also seem to be safer than nests in stouter trees (see below).

We also applied a discriminant function analysis to the nest–site measurements. This is a statistical method that computes a new variable from several measured variables, such that the new variable maximally separates the two samples. In our case we looked for a combination of variables that separated depredated from non-depredated nests. The analysis showed that a model including the variables tree height (coefficient = 1.21), angle of opening (0.67) and tree circumference at 2 m (−0.77) could classify 78.6% of all nests correctly as to whether or not they were depredated. In plain language, this means that safe holes were those situated in tall, thin, living trees, and where the hole had been caused by the falling of a branch. By using the above three variables we further calculated a standardized canonical discriminant function coefficient, with a mean of zero and a standard deviation of one, as a measure of nest-hole quality for each individual nest. In Figure 102 we show the location of all active Pied Flycatcher nests in the 'natural' area together with their nest-hole quality value. From the figure one can see that nest cavities are often clumped, and so also are good quality nest-sites. We can assign territory quality values to nests occupied by females of different mating status or by unmated males (Table 21). Primary nests of polygynous males had a higher quality value than second nests or secondary territories where the male failed to attract a female. Similarly, monogamous females laying at the same time

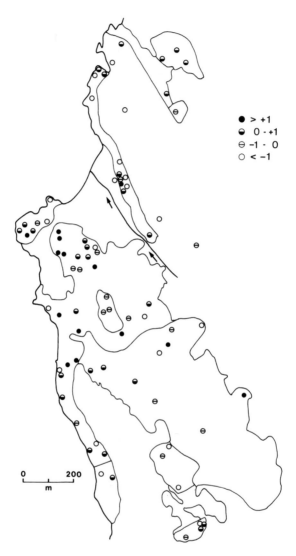

Fig. 102.   Distribution of natural nest-holes of different quality. Quality was categorized by a discriminant function coefficient. Dots with a positive sign indicate nest-holes that are better than average while dots with negative signs show nest-holes of poorer than average quality.

Table 21. *Nest-hole quality scores of natural cavities for Pied Flycatcher males of different mating status. The differences between categories are not significant (F = 1.35, P = 0.25). Monogamous nests simultaneous in time to secondary nests are given in italics (test between these two groups: t = 1.03, P = 0.32, d.f. = 16).*

	Discriminant scores		
	Mean	SD	*n*
Primary nest	+0.30	1.21	7
Monogamous nest	−0.02	1.17	65
Monogamous nest	*+0.33*	*0.87*	*9*
Secondary nest	−0.19	1.25	9
Secondary territory	−0.27	1.25	15
Unmated	+0.13	1.01	7

as secondary females had a higher quality score than the latter category. Though the differences are not statistically significant, the analyses clearly show that secondary females of polygynous males cannot compensate for the reduction in male assistance by acquiring higher quality nesting sites.

Another factor that intuitively ought to influence the safety of the nest is entrance size. More species of predators should be able to enter large openings than small, and our nest-box experiments on entrance size (described in Chapter 4) clearly showed that female Pied Flycatchers indeed prefer small openings. However, in the analysis of natural cavities this character did not enter as a significant variable. There is a tendency for early nesting females to have smaller nest openings than either later breeding females or males that failed to attract females (Table 22). Nesting cavities made by woodpeckers had a higher predation rate than fallen-branch holes, and they also had larger entrance holes (Table 20). However, old Lesser Spotted Woodpecker nests suffered higher predation than did Great Spotted Woodpecker nests despite the larger entrance size of the latter. One explanation for this might be that many Lesser Spotted Woodpecker nests were situated rather low in tree stumps, and such nests often became depredated.

Predation on Pied Flycatcher nests in natural cavities was not related to time of egg-laying; the mean laying time (±SD) for successful nests was 27.1 ± 6.3 (1 = 1 May) while for predated nests it was 28.9 ± 5.7 ($t = 1.32$, d.f. = 82, $P = 0.19$). In general most instances of predation occurred early in the nesting phase. In 27 cases we could establish the time of predation, and in 78% of these events it occurred during laying or incubation. Of six certain cases of predation during incubation, in five instances the female was killed but the eggs were left. Moreover, we could not find any relationship between nest density and risk of predation. We analysed the incidence of predation in relation to the number of

Table 22.   *Nest-hole entrance size of natural cavities for Pied Flycatcher males of different mating status. The differences between categories are significant (F = 2.75, P < 0.05). Entrance size is given as the mean of height and width in mm. Monogamous nests simultaneous in time to secondary nests are given in italics (test between these two groups:* t = 0.15, P > 0.50, d.f. = 16).*

	Entrance size		
	Mean	SD	*n*
Primary nest	36.4	8.5	7
Monogamous nest	35.9	7.4	68
Monogamous nest	*39.6*	*10.5*	*9*
Secondary nest	39.2	6.4	9
Secondary territory	41.7	6.8	12
Unmated	40.4	9.1	7

neighbours within 100 m (0, 1, 2, 3, or >4) but found no significant relationship between probability of predation and breeding density (Kolmogorov–Smirnov two-sample test, $D = 0.17$, $P > 0.10$; Alatalo and Lundberg, 1990). However, it is possible that proximity to other hole-nesting species might have affected rates of predation. It is also possible that areas with many holes include holes of high quality while dispersed holes are of poor quality, for example, those located in stumps. We will then fail to find any effects of density on predation risks. Nest-hole quality is certainly the most important factor reducing risks of predation.

MALE BEHAVIOUR

In total, during the three years, we individually colour-ringed 31 Pied Flycatcher males in order to follow their activities. The majority of unringed males could also be recognized by the plumage patterns on their backs (see Chapter 10) and by the shape of the white patch on the forehead (Fig. 1). The less recognizable males, in particular if they were suspected of holding two territories, were carefully checked several times. This allowed us to determine the mating status of most males and females in the area. However, during the last year (1985) the degree of polyterritoriality was not followed up with the same accuracy as in the two preceding years.

Among mated males, 12.5% attracted a second female, while 8.9% of all males remained unmated. In 1983, 67% of all mated males were polyterritorial but the corresponding figure for 1984 was 45%, which might be an underestimate because during that year we searched a larger area and might therefore have overlooked some polyterritorial males. The raw data are shown in Table 23. Our estimate that 12.5% of males attract a second female in a 'natural' forest can be

Table 23. *Number of Pied Flycatcher males of different mating status in a forest where birds bred in natural cavities. Polyterritorial males were those that took up distant secondary territories; thus they include polygynous males and monogamous males that tried but failed to attract a second female. A larger area (59 ha) was searched in 1984 and 1985 than in 1983 (39 ha). Degree of polyterritoriality was not well studied in 1985, and was probably less accurate in 1984 than in 1983.*

Year	Polygamous	*Polyterritorial*	Monogamous	Unmated
1983	3	*12*	15	1
1984	3	*10*	28	5
1985	3	*?*	20	1

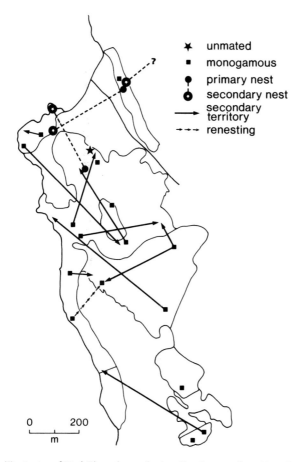

Fig. 103. *Territories of Pied Flycatcher males breeding in natural cavities. Arrows indicate the positions of secondary territories, and broken lines combine nests of males that attracted more than one female. Data from 1983.*

compared with our figures from nest box areas. In deciduous forest we found polygyny frequency to vary between 6.8% and 11.3%, depending on whether boxes were in short supply or in excess. Corresponding figures from coniferous forest are 6.3% and 39.4%, respectively (Alatalo and Lundberg, 1984a; see also Appendix 8 for data from other areas).

The median distance between a male's two territories in our 'natural' forest was 250 m ($n = 17$, range 80–540 m), while the distance between the first and second nests of polygynous males was 230 m ($n = 9$, range 120–>300 m); for an example from 1983 see Figure 103 (see also Appendix 7). These distances are greater than those we found in nest box areas 30–40 km away from Andersby, where the median was 150 m (Appendix 7). It seems that by providing boxes in excess, natural polyterritorial distances will be sightly underestimated. The longer inter-nest distances in natural forests probably cannot be explained by scarcity of nest-holes. High quality holes were often clumped (Fig. 102), so there would have been ample opportunities for males to attract secondary females close to the first nest, if distance were not important for the prospects of attracting additional females. Since most males seemed to move further away than necessary when taking up a good quality secondary territory (Figs 102 and 103), this suggests to us that males take up distant secondary territories to hide the fact that they are already mated.

SUMMARY

Nest-holes in natural forest were plentiful, but presumably many were of poor quality, leading to lower breeding density than in nest box areas. Most components of female reproductive success were similar in the natural situation compared to those nesting in boxes. The same holds for females of different status, for example, secondary females produced fewer offspring than concurrently nesting monogamous females. The major difference between natural cavities and boxes, with regard to breeding success, was the much higher predation rate on natural cavities, leading to lower fledging success. Most of the depredation took place during laying or incubation, and the main predators were probably weasels and woodpeckers. Properties of the nesting tree and the nest-hole influenced predation risks, such that holes located high up in tall, thin, living trees, and nest-holes derived from fallen branches were the safest. Low cavities originally made by woodpeckers, or situated in tree stumps, on the other hand, were very often depredated. Also secondary Pied Flycatcher females did not have better quality territories than concurrently laying monogamous females, and therefore were not able to compensate for their lower status.

In the 'natural' forest, males were polyterritorial to about the same degree (10–15%) as in nest box areas and about two-thirds of the males took up secondary territories. The distance between a male's two territories was slightly greater in the natural forest than in nest box areas with boxes in excess. Polyterritoriality in natural forests is not due to a lack of nest-holes close to the first nest.

Appendices

Morphology of the Collared Flycatcher and four subspecies of the Pied Flycatcher, as measured from museum collections (means ± SD). All hypoleuca *are from Scandinavia. Shape of white patch in forehead: R = rectangular, V = variable.*

	Collared Flycatcher	Pied Flycatcher			
	albicollis	*hypoleuca*	*semitorquata*	*iberiae*	*speculigera*
$n =$	9	14	22	12	7
Bill length (mm)	12.6 ± 0.6	12.9 ± 0.5	12.5 ± 0.6	12.7 ± 0.6	12.9 ± 0.7
Wing length (mm)	81.6 ± 1.6	79.9 ± 1.6	81.6 ± 1.6	78.5 ± 2.3	78.3 ± 2.0
Tarsus length (mm)	16.6 ± 0.5	17.0 ± 0.5	16.6 ± 0.5	16.4 ± 0.7	17.0 ± 0.5
White on wing (mm)					
3rd primary	3.4 ± 3.4	0.0	0.9 ± 1.9	0.3 ± 0.9	0.8 ± 1.3
4th primary	4.9 ± 3.8	0.0	2.5 ± 2.9	1.3 ± 1.8	2.5 ± 2.9
5th primary	6.2 ± 3.0	0.0	3.7 ± 2.7	2.2 ± 2.3	3.2 ± 2.9
6th primary	7.0 ± 3.0	3.0 ± 1.2	4.7 ± 2.3	4.0 ± 2.4	4.2 ± 4.0
7th primary	7.0 ± 3.0	3.6 ± 1.2	5.1 ± 2.4	3.7 ± 1.9	1.8 ± 3.5
Plumage colour					
(% non-black feathers)	2.3	38.2	20.5	6.3[1]	12.9
(range)	1–5	5–95	1–70	0–25	1–40
Forehead	R	V	V	R	R

(1) Curio (1960a) found *iberiae* males to be of mean colour type 1.7 according to Drost's (1936) score, which is quite similar to our estimate. Potti and Montalvo (1991a), however, found Spanish males to be much browner (mean score = 3.4, which corresponds to a plumage colour value of 32.5%). These differences could be due to true inter-population differences or caused by different researchers' appreciation of colour. For further details on plumage colour assessment see Chapter 10.

APPENDIX 2: DIET OF THE PIED FLYCATCHER

Diet (in % of prey items given to nestlings) of the Pied Flycatcher in different countries and habitats.

	Lepi-doptera	Dip-tera	Arach-nida	Hymen-optera	Coleop-tera	Homop-tera	Others	*n*
Sweden[1]	32.2	22.8	13.1	6.7	4.4	8.4	12.4	298
Finland[2]	24.8	22.4	19.5	11.0	10.2	4.1	8.0	246
Norway[3]	23.2	9.9	8.2	38.6	16.3	–	3.8	586
Norway[4]	50.2	12.1	1.6	11.2	8.9	4.1	11.9	992
Germany[5]	37.7	9.4	17.7	14.4	13.2	0.5	7.1	1725
Germany[6]	9.4	17.1	14.3	9.6	19.7	19.4	10.5	20 499
Germany[7]	19.7	10.3	24.2	15.2	16.8	2.1	11.7	6436
Germany[8]	20.7	36.3	11.6	7.9	11.5	8.4	3.6	9811
Germany[9]	37.4	17.4	13.4	4.8	9.2	13.9	3.9	12 672

1 = Alatalo *et al.* (1988c); deciduous and coniferous forest.
2 = Von Haartman (1954); deciduous and spruce forest.
3 = Meidell (1961); coniferous and mountain birch forest.
4 = Lifjeld and Slagsvold (1988a); deciduous forest.
5 = Mansfeld (1942), Creutz (1953); from von Haartman (1954); various habitats.
6 = Dornbusch (1981); pine forest.
7 = Bösenberg (1964); pine forest.
8 = Bösenberg (1964); beech forest.
9 = Bösenberg (1964); oak forest.

APPENDIX 3: BREEDING DATA FOR THE PIED FLYCATCHER

Average breeding data from different study sites. We have included all clutches, and laying date is the mean or the median depending on the value given. We have attempted to estimate number of fledged young and breeding success for all nests including those with total losses. Habitats are: Con = coniferous, Mix = mixed, Dec = deciduous, Mou = mountainous habitat (>300 m). Column abbreviations: Lat = latitude °N, Hab = habitat, Lay = laying date, Clu = clutch size, Fle = number of fledged young, BrS = breeding success as the % of eggs producing fledged young, n = number of nests.

Site	Lat	Hab	Lay	Clu	Fle	BrS	n	Source
Finland								
Kilpisjärvi	69	Mou	13/6	5.55	3.43	61.8	663	A
Värriö	67	Mou	11/6	5.75	4.05	70.8	110	B
Hyytiälä	62	Con	31/5	5.91	4.34	73.4	167	C
Siuntio	60	Con	29/5	6.35	4.48	74.5	866	D
Sweden								
Ammarnäs	66	Mou	11/6	5.41	4.43	81.9	309	E
Uppsala	60	Dec	26/5	6.53	5.21	79.8	679	F
Uppsala	60	Con	27/5	6.31	4.06	64.3	170	F
Tärnsjö	60	Con		6.26	5.56	88.9	1795	G
Värmland	60	Mix	27/5	6.25	4.74★	75.8	838	H
Göteborg	58	Con		6.08	4.26	70.1	297	I
Skåne	56	Dec	21/5	6.41	4.97★	77.5	549	J
Skåne	56	Con	26/5	6.16	3.58★	58.1	148	J
Skåne	56	Dec	27/5	6.49	5.55	85.5	319	K
Skåne	56	Con	27/5	6.16	4.79	77.8	31	K
Norway								
Suldal	59	Mou	3/6	5.98	5.00★	83.6	85	L
UK								
Cumbria	55	Dec	15/5	6.79	5.50	81	205	F
Forest of Dean	51	Dec	13/5	6.92★★	5.06	78.0★★	1108	M
Belgium								
Peerdsbos	51	Dec	13/5	5.92	4.97	84.0	35	N
Germany								
Berlin	53	Con		6.29	4.55★	72.3	169	O
Dresden	51	Dec	12/5	6.31	4.30	68.1	590	P
Harz	51	Mou	19/5	5.65	2.94	52.0	257	Q
Spain								
La Hiruela	41	Mou	3/6	5.31	4.45	83.8	49	R

★ Estimated by us to include total nest losses during incubation and nestling stages.
★★ Excluding late replacement clutches.

Sources: (A) Järvinen (1989); (B) Pulliainen (1977); (C) Tompa (1967); (D) Virolainen (1984); (E) Svensson (1987); (F) this study; (G) Johansson (1977); (H) Borgström (1990); (I) Askenmo (1982); (J) Källander *et al.* (1987); (K) Källander (1975); (L) Meidell (1961); (M) Harvey *et al.* (1988); (N) Dhondt *et al.* (1987); (O) Curio (1959c); (P) Creutz (1955); (Q) Zang (1975); (R) Potti *et al.* (1987).

APPENDIX 4: RETURN RATES IN DIFFERENT PARTS OF EUROPE

Return rates of males, females and nestlings in different parts of Europe. The main sources for this compilation are Curio (1959c), von Haartman (1960), Røskaft et al. (1986) and Slagsvold and Lifjeld (1990).

Country	Latitude °N	Males %	Males n	Females %	Females n	Nestlings %	Nestlings n	Source
Sweden	66	24	786	8	1165	1.1	6459	A, B
Sweden	60	20	323	7	393	0.1	2189	C
Sweden	59			14	154	0.0	155	D
Sweden	58	28	73					E
Finland	62	33	36	15	46	1.6	192	F
Finland	60	36	379	14	576	1.8	2842	F
Finland	60	29	34					G
Norway	63	37	149					H
Norway	63	34	110					G
Norway[1]	60	31	124					I
Norway[2]	60	49	293					I
USSR	56			27	363	5.9	653	F, J
UK	55	44	214	44	176	13.8	1239	C
UK	52	39	95	41	216	2.8	2222	K
UK	52	24	374	23	646	3.8	4086	L
Netherlands	52			28	198			F
Germany	53	45	121	30	120	10.4	710	J
Germany	53					8.8	11 018	M
Germany	52	40	359			5.2	1500	G, N, O
Germany	52	22	44					G, P
Germany	51	28	160	27	340	2.6	2406	Q
Germany	51	35	37	38	40	0.4	229	R
Germany	50	22	51	23	115	5.6	1277	S

Sources: (A) Nyholm and Myhrberg (1983); (B) Nyholm (1986); (C) this study; (D) Enemar (1948); (E) Askenmo (1979); (F) von Haartman (1960); (G) Røskaft *et al.* (1986); (H) Slagsvold and Lifjeld (1988a); (I) Slagsvold and Lifjeld (1990); (J) Curio (1959c); (K) Campbell (1955); (L) Campbell (1959); (M) Sternberg (1989); (N) Winkel and Winkel (1984); (O) Winkel (1982); (P) Zang (1975); (Q) Creutz (1955); (R) Trettau (1952); (S) Trettau and Merkel (1943).

1 = Females removed from the study area.
2 = Females added to the study area.

APPENDIX 5: PLUMAGE COLOUR OF PIED FLYCATCHER MALES

Mean plumage colour (according to Drost's 1936 score) of Pied Flycatcher males of different ages and at different places in Europe. Numbers refer to places shown in Fig. 66.

	Site	Latitude °N	All males	Adult males	Yearling males	n	Source
1	Sweden	66	3.2			403	A
2	Sweden	60		3.0	4.2	408	B
3	Norway	63	3.9			166	C
4	Finland	60		3.2	4.5	213	D
5	Finland	60	3.8			117	C
	Scandinavia[1]			3.0	4.2	84	E
6	USSR	55		4.4	6.0	148	C
7	UK	55		2.7	3.6	489	B
8	Netherlands	53	6.2			77	F
9	Germany	53		5.5	6.9	24	G
10	Germany	52		6.1	6.8	416	C, H
11	Germany	52		5.9	6.8	536	I
12	Germany	52	5.7			44	J
13	Germany	51	6.5			49	K
14	Germany	50		5.5	6.5	105	L
15	Switzerland	47	3.6			34	M
16	Switzerland	47	3.5			75	N

Sources: (A) Nyholm and Myhrberg (1983); (B) this study; (C) Røskaft *et al.* (1986); (D) von Haartman (1985); (E) Drost (1936); (F) Haverschmidt (1973); (G) Curio (1959c); (H) Winkel and Winkel (1984); (I) Winkel *et al.* (1970); (J) Zang (1975); (K) Trettau (1952); (L) Trettau and Merkel (1943); (M) Sternberg (1964); (N) Eggenberger (1964).

(1) Based on museum skins and birds caught on northward migration on Heligoland, Germany.

APPENDIX 6: POLYTERRITORIAL BIRD SPECIES IN EUROPE

List of European bird species which are regularly or occasionally polyterritorial. Mainly based on Møller (1986).

Regularly	Occasionally
Kestrel	Meadow Pipit
Tengmalm's Owl	Tree Pipit
Redstart	Dipper
Wood Warbler	Stonechat
Pied Flycatcher	Wheatear
Collared Flycatcher	Blyth's Reed Warbler
	Marsh Warbler
	Barred Warbler
	Whitethroat
	Willow Warbler
	Penduline Tit
	Reed Bunting
	Common Rosefinch

APPENDIX 7: POLYTERRITORIALITY DISTANCES

Distances between the first nest and secondary territory, and between first and secondary nests in the Pied Flycatcher. Expanded from Alatalo and Lundberg (1990).

Locality	Mean	Median	Range	n	Remarks	Source
Distance between first nest and secondary territory (m)						
Sweden	266	295	71–578	17	1	A
Finland	326		c. 100–1300	85	2	B
Distance between first and secondary nest (m)						
Sweden	c. 240	150	40–1000	27	2	C
Sweden	220	230	120–350	9	1	A
Sweden			40, 100	2	2	D
Finland	217		c. 100–400	23	2	B
Finland	155	150	60–500	35	2, 3	E
Finland	582	480	140–1300	19	2, 4	E
Norway	228		57–631	41	2, 5	F
UK	c. 200	112		19	2	G
UK	149	130	40–900	32	2	H
Belgium	117		26–232	7	2	I
Germany			100, 225	2	2	J
Germany	258		20–750	51	2	K

Remarks: (1) Natural cavities; (2) nest boxes; (3) high breeding density; (4) low breeding density; (5) female-biased sex ratio experimentally induced.
Sources: (A) Alatalo and Lundberg (1990); (B) von Haartman (1956a); (C) Alatalo and Lundberg (1984a); (D) Nyholm (1984); (E) Rätti and Alatalo (pers. comm.); (F) Stenmark *et al.* (1988); (G) Harvey *et al.* (1984); (H) this study; (I) Dhondt *et al.* (1987); (J) Trettau and Merkel (1943); (K) Winkel and Winkel (1984).

APPENDIX 8: FREQUENCY OF POLYGYNY

The frequency of polygyny in the Pied Flycatcher. Expanded from Alatalo and Lundberg (1990).

Locality	Polygynous males (%)	Secondary females (%)	Females paired with polygynous males (%)	Habitat	Remarks	Source
Sweden	5.7	8.7		D	1, 4, 5	A
Sweden		6.8		D	1, 3, 6	B
Sweden		11.3		D	1, 4, 6	B
Sweden		6.3		C	1, 3, 6	B
Sweden		39.4		C	1, 4, 6	B
Sweden		14.3		D	2, 5	B
Sweden	18.5			C	1, 4, 5	C
Sweden	39.3			C	1, 4, 6	C
Sweden	13.8			C	1, 4, 5	D
Finland	*c.* 7.0		12.8	C	1, 3, 5	E
Norway	27.9		47.5	M	1, 4, 5, 7	F
UK		7.7		D	1, 4, 5	G
UK		16.7		D	1, 4, 6	G
Belgium	22.5			D	1, 4, 5	H
Germany	3.0			M	1, 3, 5	I
Germany	13.2		20.7	C	1, 4, 5	J
Germany	6.6			D	1, 4, 8	K

Habitat: D = Deciduous, C = Coniferous, M = Mixed deciduous and coniferous forest.
Remarks: (1) Nest boxes; (2) natural cavities; (3) boxes in shortage; (4) boxes in excess; (5) based on polygynous males actually observed; (6) based on polygynous males observed plus broods belonging to males which did not participate in feeding young in late nests; (7) female biased sex ratio experimentally induced; (8) of males studied throughout their lives.
Sources: (A) Nyholm (1984); (B) Alatalo and Lundberg (1984a); (C) Askenmo (1977a); (D) Silverin (1980); (E) von Haartman (1951b); (F) Stenmark *et al.* (1988); (G) Alatalo and Lundberg (1990); (H) Dhondt *et al.* (1987); (I) Curio (1959b); (J) Winkel and Winkel (1984); (K) Sternberg (1989).

APPENDIX 9: LIST OF LATIN NAMES

Birds

Blackbird	*Turdus merula*
Blackbird, Red-winged	*Agelaius phoeniceus*
Blackcap	*Sylvia atricapilla*
Brambling	*Fringilla montifringilla*
Bunting, Corn	*Miliaria calandra*
Indigo	*Passerina cyanea*
Ortolan	*Emberiza hortulana*
Reed	*E. schoeniclus*
Buzzard, Common	*Buteo buteo*
Honey	*Pernis apivorus*
Chaffinch	*Fringilla coelebs*
Cuckoo	*Cuculus canorus*
Dipper	*Cinclus cinclus*
Dunnock	*Prunella modularis*
Falcon, Eleonora's	*Falco eleonorae*
Flycatcher, Collared	*Ficedula albicollis*
Damar	*F. henrici*
Pied	*F. hypoleuca*
Spotted	*Muscicapa striata*
Kestrel	*Falco tinnunculus*
Magpie	*Pica pica*
Nuthatch	*Sitta europaea*
Owl, Tengmalm's	*Aegolius funereus*
Pipit, Meadow	*Anthus pratensis*
Tree	*A. trivialis*
Redstart	*Phoenicurus phoenicurus*
Redwing	*Turdus iliacus*
Rosefinch, Common	*Carpodacus erythrinus*
Ruff	*Philomachus pugnax*
Sparrow, Song	*Melospiza melodia*
Tree	*Passer montanus*
White-crowned	*Zonotrichia leucophrys*
Sparrowhawk	*Accipiter nisus*
Starling	*Sturnus vulgaris*
Stonechat	*Saxicola torquata*
Tit, Blue	*Parus caeruleus*
Coal	*P. ater*
Great	*P. major*
Marsh	*P. palustris*
Penduline	*Remiz pendulinus*
Sombre	*P. lugubris*
Willow	*P. montanus*
Warbler, Barred	*Sylvia nisoria*
Blyth's Reed	*Acrocephalus dumetorum*
Marsh	*A. palustris*

Warbler, Willow	*Phylloscopus trochilus*
Wood	*Ph. sibilatrix*
Wheatear	*Oenanthe oenanthe*
Whinchat	*Saxicola rubetra*
Whitethroat	*Sylvia communis*
Woodpecker, Great Spotted	*Dendrocopus major*
Lesser Spotted	*D. minor*
Wren, Long-billed Marsh	*Cistothorus palustris*
Wryneck	*Jynx torquilla*

MAMMALS

Marten, Pine	*Martes martes*
Stoat	*Mustela erminea*
Weasel	*M. nivalis*

PLANTS

Alder	*Alnus glutinosa*
Ash	*Fraxinus excelsior*
Aspen	*Populus tremula*
Beech	*Fagus silvatica*
Bilberry	*Vaccinium myrtillus*
Birch, Downy	*Betula pubescens*
Silver	*B. verrucosa*
Bracken	*Pteridium aquilinum*
Hazel	*Corylus avellana*
Hornbeam	*Carpinus betulus*
Lime, Small-leaved	*Tilia cordata*
Maple, Norway	*Acer platanoides*
Oak, Cork	*Quercus suber*
Pedunculate	*Q. robur*
Sessile	*Q. petraea*
Pine, Scots	*Pinus silvestris*
Rowan	*Sorbus aucuparia*
Spruce, Norway	*Picea abies*

References

ALATALO, R. V. 1978. Varpuslintujen munaluvusta Oulussa. Suomenselän Linnut 13: 114–119. (In Finnish).

ALATALO, R. V. & ALATALO, R. H. 1979. Resource partitioning among a flycatcher guild in Finland. Oikos 23: 46–54.

ALATALO, R. V. & LUNDBERG, A. 1984a. Polyterritorial polygyny in the pied flycatcher *Ficedula hypoleuca* – evidence for the deception hypothesis. Annales Zoologici Fennici 21: 217–228.

ALATALO, R. V. & LUNDBERG, A. 1984b. Density dependence in breeding success of the pied flycatcher *Ficedula hypoleuca*. Journal of Animal Ecology 53: 969–977.

ALATALO, R. V. & LUNDBERG, A. 1986a. Heritability and selection on tarsus length in the pied flycatcher (*Ficedula hypoleuca*). Evolution 40: 574–583.

ALATALO, R. V. & LUNDBERG, A. 1986b. The sexy son hypothesis: data from the pied flycatcher (*Ficedula hypoleuca*). Animal Behaviour 34: 1454–1462.

ALATALO, R. V. & LUNDBERG, A. 1989. Clutch size of the Pied Flycatcher (*Ficedula hypoleuca*) – an experiment. Ornis Fennica 66: 15–23.

ALATALO, R. V. & LUNDBERG, A. 1990. Polyterritorial polygyny in the pied flycatcher. In:

Slater, P. J. B., Rosenblatt, J. S. & Beer, C. (eds). Advances in the study of behavior. Vol. 19: 1–27. San Diego, Calif.: Academic Press.

ALATALO, R. V., CARLSON, A., LUNDBERG, A. & ULFSTRAND, S. 1981. The conflict between male polygamy and female monogamy: the case of the pied flycatcher *Ficedula hypoleuca*. American Naturalist 117: 738–753.

ALATALO, R. V., GUSTAFSSON, L. & LUNDBERG, A. 1982a. Hybridization and breeding success of the Collared and the Pied Flycatcher on the island of Gotland. Auk 99: 285–291.

ALATALO, R. V., LUNDBERG, A. & BJÖRKLUND, M. 1982b. Can the song of male birds attract other males? An experiment with the pied flycatcher *Ficedula hypoleuca*. Bird Behaviour 4: 42–45.

ALATALO, R. V., LUNDBERG, A. & STÅHLBRANDT, K. 1982c. Why do pied flycatcher females mate with already-mated males? Animal Behaviour 30: 585–593.

ALATALO, R. V., CARLSON, A., LUNDBERG, A. & ULFSTRAND, S. 1984a. Male deception or female choice in the pied flycatcher *Ficedula hypoleuca*: a reply. American Naturalist 123: 282–285.

ALATALO, R. V., GUSTAFSSON, L. & LUNDBERG, A. 1984b. Why do young passerine birds have shorter wings than older birds? Ibis 126: 410–415.

ALATALO, R. V., GUSTAFSSON, L. & LUNDBERG, A. 1984c. High frequency of cuckoldry in pied and collared flycatchers. Oikos 42: 41–47.

ALATALO, R. V., LUNDBERG, A. & STÅHLBRANDT, K. 1984d. Female mate choice in the pied flycatcher *Ficedula hypoleuca*. Behavioral Ecology and Sociobiology 14: 253–261.

ALATALO, R. V., LUNDBERG, A. & ULFSTRAND, S. 1985. Habitat selection in the pied flycatcher *Ficedula hypoleuca*. In: Cody, M. (ed.), Habitat selection in birds: 59–83. New York: Academic Press.

ALATALO, R. V., GUSTAFSSON, L. & LUNDBERG, A. 1986a. Do females prefer older males in polygynous bird species? American Naturalist 127: 241–245.

ALATALO, R. V., LUNDBERG, A. & GLYNN, C. 1986b. Female pied flycatchers choose territory quality and not male characteristics. Nature 323: 152–153.

ALATALO, R. V., GOTTLANDER, K. & LUNDBERG, A. 1987. Extra-pair copulations and mate guarding in the polyterritorial pied flycatcher *Ficedula hypoleuca*. Behaviour 101: 139–155.

ALATALO, R. V., CARLSON, A. & LUNDBERG, A. 1988a. The search cost in mate choice of the Pied Flycatcher. Animal Behaviour 36: 289–291.

ALATALO, R. V., CARLSON, A. & LUNDBERG, A. 1988b. Nest cavity size and clutch size of Pied Flycatchers *Ficedula hypoleuca* breeding in natural tree-holes. Ornis Scandinavica 19: 317–319.

ALATALO, R. V., GOTTLANDER, K. & LUNDBERG, A. 1988c. Conflict or cooperation between parents in feeding nestlings in the Pied Flycatcher *Ficedula hypoleuca*. Ornis Scandinavica 19: 31–32.

ALATALO, R. V., GUSTAFSSON, L. & LUNDBERG, A. 1989. Extra-pair paternity and heritability estimates of tarsus length in pied and collared flycatchers. Oikos 56: 54–58.

ALATALO, R. V., CARLSON, A. & LUNDBERG, A. 1990a. Polygyny and breeding success of Pied Flycatchers nesting in natural cavities. In: Blondel, J., Gosler, A., Lebreton, J.-D. & McCleery, R. (eds). Population biology in passerine birds. An integrated approach: 323–330. Berlin: Springer.

ALATALO, R. V., ERIKSSON, D., GUSTAFSSON, L. & LUNDBERG, A. 1990b. Hybridization between Pied and Collared Flycatchers – sexual selection and speciation theory. Journal of Evolutionary Biology 3: 375–389.

ALATALO, R. V., GLYNN, C. & LUNDBERG, A. 1990c. Singing rate and female attraction in the pied flycatcher: an experiment. Animal Behaviour 39: 601–603.

ALATALO, R. V., LUNDBERG, A. & RÄTTI, O. 1990d. Male polyterritoriality and imperfect female choice in the pied flycatcher Ficedula hypoleuca. Behavioral Ecology 1: 171–177.

ALATALO, R. V., LUNDBERG, A. & SUNDBERG, J. 1990e. Can female preference explain sexual dichromatism in the pied flycatcher Ficedula hypoleuca? Animal Behaviour 39: 244–252.

ALERSTAM, T. 1982. Fågelflyttning. Lund: Signum.

ALERSTAM, T. 1985. Breeding birds in a deciduous woodland: effects of providing supernumerary nest-boxes in a high-density bird community. Anser 24: 213–234. (In Swedish with English summary).

ALERSTAM, T. & HÖGSTEDT, G. 1983. The role of the geomagnetic field in the development of birds' compass sense. Nature 306: 463–465.

ALERSTAM, T., EBENMAN, B., SYLVÉN, M., TAMM, S. & ULFSTRAND, S. 1978. Hybridization as an agent of competition between two bird allospecies: Ficedula albicollis and F. hypoleuca on the island of Gotland in the Baltic. Oikos 31: 326–331.

ASHMOLE, N. P. 1963. The regulation of numbers of tropical oceanic birds. Ibis 103: 458–473.

ASKENMO, C. 1977a. Some aspects of the reproduction strategy of the pied flycatcher Ficedula hypoleuca (Pallas). Doctoral dissertation, University of Gothenburg, Gothenburg.

ASKENMO, C. 1977b. Effects of addition and removal of nestlings on nestling weight, nestling survival, and female weight loss in the Pied Flycatcher Ficedula hypoleuca (Pallas). Ornis Scandinavica 8: 1–8.

ASKENMO, C. 1979. Reproductive effort and return rate of male pied flycatchers. American Naturalist 114: 748–753.

ASKENMO, C. 1982. Clutch size flexibility in the Pied Flycatcher Ficedula hypoleuca. Ardea 70: 189–196.

ASKENMO, C. E. H. 1984. Polygyny and nest site selection in the pied flycatcher. Animal Behaviour 32: 972–980.

BAKER, R. R. & PARKER, G. A. 1979. The evolution of bird coloration. Philosophical Transactions of the Royal Society of London, Series B, 287: 63–130.

BAPTISTA, L. F. & PETRINOVICH, L. 1986. Song development in the white crowned sparrow: social factors and sex differences. Animal Behaviour 34: 1359–1371.

BARROWCLOUGH, G. F. 1978. Sampling bias in dispersal studies based on a finite area. Bird Banding 49: 333–341.

BARROWCLOUGH, G. F. & SIBLEY, F. C. 1980. Feather pigmentation and abrasion: test of a hypothesis. Auk 97: 881–883.

BERGMAN, S. 1934. Iakttagelser över den svart och vita flugsnapparens, Muscicapa atricapilla, uppfödning av sina ungar. Fauna och Flora 29: 161–166. (In Swedish).

BERNDT, R. 1960. Zur Dispersion der Weibschen von Ficedula hypoleuca im nördlichen Deutschland. Proceedings of the XII International Ornithological Congress, Helsinki 1958, pp. 85–96.

BERNDT, R. & STERNBERG, H. 1969. Alter- und Geschelchtsunterschiede in der Dispersion des Trauerschnäppers (Ficedula hypoleuca). Journal für Ornithologie 110: 22–26.

BERNDT, R. & WINKEL, W. 1967. Die Gelegegrösse des Trauerschnäppers (Ficedula hypoleuca) in Beziehung zu Ort, Zeit, Biotop und Alter. Vogelwelt 88: 97–136.

BERNDT, R. & WINKEL, W. 1979. Verfrachtungs-Experimente zur Frage der Geburtsortsprägung beim Trauerschnäpper (Ficedula hypoleuca). Journal für Ornithologie 120: 41–53.

BERNDT, R., WINKEL, W. & ZANG, H. 1981. Über Legebeginn und Gelegestärke des Trauerschnäppers (*Ficedula hypoleuca*) in Beziehung zur geographischen Lage des Brutortes. Vogelwarte 31: 101–110.

BIBBY, C. J. & GREEN, R. E. 1980. Foraging behaviour of migrant pied flycatchers, *Ficedula hypoleuca*, on temporary territories. Journal of Animal Ecology 49: 507–521.

BIRKHEAD, T. R. 1988. Behavioural aspects of sperm competition in birds. In: Slater, P. J. B., Rosenblatt, J. S. & Beer, C. (eds). Advances in the study of behavior. Vol. 18: 35–72. San Diego, Calif.: Academic Press.

BJÖRKLUND, M. & WESTMAN, B. 1983. Extra-pair copulations in the Pied Flycatcher (*Ficedula hypoleuca*). Behavioral Ecology and Sociobiology 13: 271–275.

BORGSTRÖM, E. 1990. Breeding data for the Pied Flycatcher, *Ficedula hypoleuca*, in Central Sweden. Vår Fågelvärld 49: 140–146. (In Swedish with English summary).

BÖSENBERG, K. 1964. Vergleichende Feststellung zur Nestlingsnahrung von Trauerschnäpper (*Ficedula hypoleuca* (Pall.)), Kohlmeise (*Parus major* L.) und Blaumeise (*Parus caeruleus* L.) in verschiedenen Waldbiotopen. Beiträge zur Vogelkunde 9: 249–262.

BREIEHAGEN, T. & SLAGSVOLD, T. 1988. Male polyterritoriality and female–female aggression in pied flycatchers *Ficedula hypoleuca*. Animal Behaviour 36: 604–605.

BRISSON, M. J. 1760. Ornithologie ou méthode content la Division des Oiseaux. Book II. Paris.

BURTT, E. H., Jr. 1979. Tips on wings and other things. In: Burtt, E. H., Jr. (ed.), The behavioral significance of color: 75–110. New York: Garland STPM Press.

BUSSE, P. 1984. Key to sexing and ageing of European Passerines. Hanover: Beiträge zur Naturkunde Niedersachsens, 37 Jahrgang. Sonderheft 1984.

CAMPBELL, B. 1955. A population of Pied Flycatchers (*Muscicapa hypoleuca*). Acta XI Congressus Internationalis Ornithologici, Basle 1954, pp. 428–434.

CAMPBELL, B. 1959. Attachment of Pied Flycatchers *Muscicapa hypoleuca* to nest-sites. Ibis 101: 445–448.

CAMPBELL, B. 1968. The Dean nestbox study. Forestry 41: 27–46.

CATCHPOLE, C. K. 1987. Bird song, sexual selection and female choice. Trends in Ecology & Evolution 2: 94–97.

CHARNOV, E. L. & KREBS, J. R. 1974. On clutch-size and fitness. Ibis 116: 217–219.

CREUTZ, G. 1953. Ernährungsweise und wirtschaftliche Bedeutung des Trauerschnäppers. Anzeiger für Schädlingskunde 26: 17–23.

CREUTZ, G. 1955. Der Trauerschnäpper (*Muscicapa hypoleuca*) (Pallas). Eine Populationsstudie. Journal für Ornithologie 96: 241–326.

CURIO, E. 1959a. Beobachtungen am Halbringschnäpper, *Ficedula semitorquata*, im mazedonischen Brutgebiet. Journal für Ornithologie 100: 176–209.

CURIO, E. 1959b. Verhaltenstudien am Trauerschnäpper. Supplement 3 to Zeitschrift für Tierpsychologie, pp. 1–118.

CURIO, E. 1959c. Beiträge zur Populationsökologie des Trauerschnäppers (*Ficedula h. hypoleuca* Pallas). Zoologische Jahrbücher 87: 185–230.

CURIO, E. 1960a. Die systematishe Stellung des spanischen Trauerschnäppers. Vogelwelt 81: 113–121.

CURIO, E. 1960b. Lebensertwartung und Brutgrösse beim Trauerschnäpper (*Muscicapa h. hypoleuca*). Proceedings of the XII International Ornithological Congress, Helsinki 1958, pp. 158–161.

CURRY-LINDAHL, K. 1981. Bird migration in Africa. London: Academic Press.

DALE, S., AMUNDSEN, T. LIFJELD, J. T. & SLAGSVOLD, T. 1990. Mate sampling behaviour of female pied flycatchers: evidence for active mate choice. Behavioral Ecology and Sociobiology 27: 87–91.

DARWIN, C. 1871. The descent of man, and selection in relation to sex. London: John Murray.

DAVIES, N. B. 1989. Sexual conflict and the polygamy threshold. Animal Behaviour 38: 226–234.

DHONDT, A. A. 1977. Interspecific competition between great and blue tits. Nature 268: 521–523.

DHONDT, A. A. & EYCKERMAN, R. 1980. Competition and the regulation of numbers in great and blue tit. Ardea 68: 121–132.

DHONDT, A. A., FIERENS, F., LAMBRECHTS, M., ADRIAENSEN, F., MATTHYSEN, E., DE LAET, J. & BIJNENS, L. 1987. The establishment of a breeding population of the Pied Flycatcher, *Ficedula hypoleuca*, in the Peerdsbos, near Antwerp. Le Gerfaut 77: 333–339.

DORNBUSCH, M. 1981. Die Ernährung einiger Kleinvogelarten in Kiefernjungbestockungen. Beiträge zur Vogelkunde 27: 73–99.

DOWSETT, R. J., BACKHURST, G. C. & OATLEY, T. B. 1988. Afrotropical ringing recoveries of Palaearctic migrants 1. Passerines (Turdidae to Oriolidae). Tauraco 1: 29–63.

DRENT, R. H. & DAAN, S. 1980. The prudent parent: energetic adjustments in avian breeding. Ardea 68: 225–252.

DROST, R. 1936. Über das Brutkleid männlicher Trauerfliegenfänger, *Muscicapa hypoleuca*. Vogelzug 6: 179–186.

DROST, R. 1951. Kennzeichen für Alter und Geschlecht bei Sperlingsvögeln. Wilhelmshafen: Ornithologische Merkblätter No. 1.

DROST, R. & SCHILLING, L. 1940. Über den Zug des Trauerfliegenschnäppers, *Muscicapa hypoleuca* (Pall). Vogelzug 11: 71–85.

DUNAJEWSKI, A. 1938. Beitrag zur individuellen und geographischen Farbenvariation des Trauerfliegen(schnäppers)fängers, *Ficedula hypoleuca* (Pall). Acta Ornithologica Musei Zoologici Polonici 2: 413–419.

EDINGTON, J. M. & EDINGTON, M. A. 1972. Spatial patterns and habitat partition in the breeding birds of an upland wood. Journal of Animal Ecology 41: 331–357.

EGGENBERGER, H. 1964. Über die Farbtypen der männlichen Trauerschnäpper, *Ficedula hypoleuca*, in der Ost-schweiz. Ornithologische Beobachter 61: 95–99.

ENEMAR, A. 1948. Några erfarenheter från fem års holkstudier. Vår Fågelvärld 7: 105–117. (In Swedish).

ENEMAR, A. & ARHEIMER, O. 1989. Developmental asynchrony and onset of incubation among passerine birds in a mountain birch forest of Swedish Lapland. Ornis Fennica 66: 32–40.

ENEMAR, A. & SJÖSTRAND, B. 1972. Effects of the introduction of Pied Flycatchers *Ficedula hypoleuca* on the composition of a passerine bird community. Ornis Scandinavica 3: 79–89.

ENEMAR, A., NYHOLM, E. & PERSSON, B. 1972. The influence of nest-boxes on the passerine bird community of Fågelsångdalen, Southern Sweden. Vår Fågelvärld 31: 263–268. (In Swedish with English summary).

ERIKSSON, D. 1991. The significance of song for species recognition and mate choice in the pied flycatcher (*Ficedula hypoleuca*). Doctoral dissertation, Uppsala University, Uppsala.

ERIKSSON, D. & WALLIN, L. 1986. Male bird song attracts females – a field experiment. Behavioral Ecology and Sociobiology 19: 297–299.

FOLLOWS, G. W. 1982. Some aspects of the breeding biology of the Pied Flycatcher *Ficedula hypoleuca* in a North Yorkshire woodland. Naturalist 107: 31–35.

FRANCIS, G. W. 1986. Melanin. Naturen 1986: 193–196. (In Norwegian).

FRETWELL, F. D. 1972. Populations in a seasonal environment. Princeton, NJ: Princeton University Press.

FRETWELL, F. D. & LUCAS, Jr., H. L. 1969. On territorial behavior and other factors influencing habitat distribution in birds. I. Theoretical development. Acta Biotheoretica 19: 16–36.

GELTER, H. 1987. Song differences between the Pied Flycatcher *Ficedula hypoleuca*, the Collared Flycatcher *F. albicollis*, and their hybrids. Ornis Scandinavica 18: 205–215.

GELTER, H. 1989. Genetic and behavioural differentiation associated with speciation in the flycatchers *Ficedula hypoleuca* and *F. albicollis*. Doctoral dissertation, Uppsala University, Uppsala.

GEZELIUS, L., GRAHN, M., KÄLLANDER, H. & KARLSSON, J. 1984. Habitat-related differences in clutch size of the Pied Flycatcher *Ficedula hypoleuca*. Annales Zoologici Fennici 21: 209–212.

GINN, H. B. & MELVILLE, D. S. 1983. Moult in birds. BTO guide no. 19: Tring.

GLUTZ von BLOTZHEIM, U. 1962. Die Brutvögel der Schweiz. Aarau.

GOTTLANDER, K. 1987. Variation in the song rate of the male pied flycatcher *Ficedula hypoleuca*: causes and consequences. Animal Behaviour 35: 1037–1043.

GRANT, P. R. 1979. Ecological and morphological variation of Canary Island Blue Tits *Parus caeruleus* (Aves: Paridae). Biological Journal of the Linnean Society 11: 103–129.

GRIMES, L. G. 1987. The birds of Ghana. BOU Check-list No. 9. British Ornithologists Union.

GUSTAFSSON, L. 1985. Fitness factors in the collared flycatcher *Ficedula albicollis* Temm. Doctoral dissertation, Uppsala University, Uppsala.

GUSTAFSSON, L. 1986. Lifetime reproductive success and heritability: empirical support for Fisher's fundamental theorem. American Naturalist 128: 761–764.

GUSTAFSSON, L. 1987. Interspecific competition lowers fitness in Collared Flycatchers *Ficedula albicollis*: an experimental demonstration. Ecology 68: 291–296.

GUSTAFSSON, L. 1989. Collared Flycatcher. In: Newton, I. (ed.), Lifetime reproduction in birds: 75–88. London: Academic Press.

GUSTAFSSON, L. & NILSSON, S. G. 1985. Clutch size and breeding success of Pied and Collared Flycatchers *Ficedula* spp. in nest-boxes of different sizes. Ibis 127: 380–385.

GUSTAFSSON, L. & SUTHERLAND, W. J. 1988. Measuring the costs of reproduction in birds; the case of the Collared Flycatcher *Ficedula hypoleuca*. Nature 335: 813–815.

HAFTORN, S. 1971. Norges fugler. Oslo: Universitetsforlaget. (In Norwegian).

HAFTORN, S. 1988. Incubating female passerines do not let the egg temperature fall below the 'physiological zero temperature' during their absences from the nest. Ornis Scandinavica 19: 97–110.

HAFTORN, S. & REINERTSEN, R. E. 1990. Thermoregulatory and behavioral responses during incubation of free-living female Pied Flycatchers *Ficedula hypoleuca*. Ornis Scandinavica 21: 255–264.

HAFTORN, S. & YTREBERG, N.-J. 1988. Incubation rhythm in the Pied Flycatcher *Ficedula hypoleuca*. Fauna Norvegica Series C, Cinclus 11: 71–88.

HALDANE, J. B. S. 1922. Sex-ratio and unisexual sterility in hybrid animals. Journal of Genetics 12: 101–109.

HALLIDAY, T. R. 1978. Sexual selection and mate choice. In: Krebs, J. R. & Davies, N. B. (eds). Behavioural ecology: an evolutionary approach: 180–213. Oxford: Blackwell.

HANNILA, J. & JÄRVINEN, A. 1987. Feeding activity of hole-nesting passerines during the nestling period in northern Lapland. Acta Regiae Societatis Scientiarum et Litterarum Gothoburgensis. Zoologica 14: 102–108.

HANSEN, L. 1954. Birds killed at lights in Denmark 1886-1939. Videnskablige Meddelelser fra Dansk Naturhistorisk Forening 116: 269–368.

HARTERT, E. 1910. Die Vögel der paläarktischen Fauna. Vol. I. Berlin: Friedländer.

HARVEY, P. H., GREENWOOD, P. J. & PERRINS, C. M. 1979. Breeding area fidelity of great tits (*Parus major*). Journal of Animal Ecology 48: 305–313.

HARVEY, P. H., GREENWOOD, P. J., CAMPBELL, B. & STENNING, M. J. 1984. Breeding dispersal of the pied flycatcher (*Ficedula hypoleuca*). Journal of Animal Ecology 53: 727–736.

HARVEY, P. H., STENNING, M. J. & CAMPBELL, B. 1985. Individual variation in seasonal breeding success of pied flycatchers (*Ficedula hypoleuca*). Journal of Animal Ecology 54: 391–398.

HARVEY, P. H., STENNING, M. J. & CAMPBELL, B. 1988. Factors influencing reproductive success in the pied flycatcher. In: Clutton-Brock, T. H. (ed.). Reproductive success. Studies of individual variation in contrasting breeding systems: 189–200. Chicago: University of Chicago Press.

HAVERSCHMIDT, F. 1973. Waarnemingen aan een populatie Bonte Vliegenvangers *Ficedula hypoleuca*. Limosa 46: 1–20.

HEIDENSTRÖM, A., BENSCH, S., HASSELQUIST, D. & OTTOSSON, U. 1990. Observations on Palaearctic migrants rare to Ghana. Bulletin of the British Ornithologists Club 110: 194–195.

HELLE, P. & PULLIAINEN, E. 1983. On the efficiency of the line transect method: a study based on nest searching. Ornis Fennica 60: 35–41.

HENWOOD, K. & FABRICK, A. 1979. A quantitative analysis of the dawn chorus: temporal selection for communicatory optimization. American Naturalist 114: 260–274.

HIEBERT, S. H., STODDARD, P. K. & ARCESE, P. 1989. Repertoire size, territory acquisition and reproductive success in the song sparrow. Animal Behaviour 34: 266–273.

HINGSTON, R. W. G. 1933. The meaning of animal colour and adornment. London: Edward Arnold.

HÖGSTEDT, G. 1980. Evolution of clutch size in birds: adaptive variation in relation to territory quality. Science 210: 1148–1150.

HÖGSTEDT, G. 1981. Should there be a positive or negative correlation between survival of adults in a bird population and their clutch size? American Naturalist 118: 568–571.

HOPE JONES, P., MEAD, C. J. & DURMAN, R. F. 1977. The migration of the Pied Flycatcher from and through Britain. Bird Study 24: 2–14.

HOWARD, R. & MOORE, A. 1980. A complete checklist of the birds of the world. Oxford: Oxford University Press.

HOWARD, R. & MOORE, A. 1991. A complete checklist of the birds of the world. London: Academic Press. (2nd ed.).

HUXLEY, J. 1942. Evolution, the modern synthesis. London: Allen and Unwin.

HYTTEBORN, H. 1975. Deciduous woodland at Andersby, Eastern Sweden. Above-ground tree and shrub production. Acta Phytogeographica Suecica 61: 1–96.

HYYTIÄ, K. & VIKBERG, P. 1973. Autumn migration and moult of the Spotted Flycatcher *Muscicapa striata* and the Pied Flycatcher *Ficedula hypoleuca* at the Signilskär bird station. Ornis Fennica 50: 134–143.

ISENMANN, P. & MOALI, A. 1987. Clutch-size reduction in the Pied Flycatcher *Ficedula hypoleuca* in North-West Africa. Ornis Fennica 64: 119.

JANETOS, A. C. 1980. Strategies of female mate choice: a theoretical analysis. Behavioral Ecology and Sociobiology 7: 107–112.

JÄRBÄCK, A. & JÄRBÄCK, N. 1972. Bastardering mellan hane av svartvit flugsnappare och hona av halsbandsflugsnappare. Vår Fågelvärld 31: 129. (In Swedish).

JÄRVI, T., RØSKAFT, E. & SLAGSVOLD, T. 1982. The conflict between male polygamy and female monogamy: some comments on the 'cheating hypothesis'. American Naturalist 120: 689–691.

JÄRVI, T., RØSKAFT, E., BAKKEN, M. & ZUMSTEG, B. 1987. Evolution of variation in male secondary sexual characteristics. A test of eight hypotheses applied to pied flycatchers. Behavioral Ecology and Sociobiology 20: 161–169.

JÄRVINEN, A. 1980. Population dynamics in the Pied Flycatcher *Ficedula hypoleuca* at subarctic Kilpisjärvi, Finnish Lapland. Ornis Fennica 57: 17–25.

JÄRVINEN, A. 1983. Breeding strategies of hole-nesting passerines in northern Lapland. Annales Zoologici Fennici 20: 129–149.

JÄRVINEN, A. 1989. Clutch-size variation in the Pied Flycatcher *Ficedula hypoleuca*. Ibis 131: 572–577.

JÄRVINEN, A. 1990. Incubation and nestling periods in hole-nesting passerines in Finnish Lapland. Ornis Fennica 67: 65–72.

JÄRVINEN, A. 1991. A meta-analytic study of the effects of female age on laying-date and clutch-size in the Great Tit *Parus major* and the Pied Flycatcher *Ficedula hypoleuca*. Ibis 133: 62–67.

JÄRVINEN, A. & LINDÉN, H. 1980. Timing of breeding and the clutch size in the pied flycatcher *Ficedula hypoleuca* in Finnish Lapland. Ornis Fennica 57: 112–116.

JÄRVINEN, A. & VÄISÄNEN, R. A. 1983. Egg size and related reproductive traits in a southern passerine *Ficedula hypoleuca* breeding in an extreme northern environment. Ornis Scandinavica 14: 253–262.

JÄRVINEN, A. & YLIMAUNU, J. 1986. Growth of nestling Pied Flycatchers *Ficedula hypoleuca* in northern Lapland. Ornis Fennica 63: 17–25.

JOHANSSON, H. 1974. Clutch size and breeding success in some hole nesting passerines in Central Sweden 1972–1974 (1952–1963). Fauna och Flora 69: 212–218. (In Swedish with English summary).

JOHANSSON, H. 1977. Kullstorlek och häckningsframgång hos några holkhäckande småfågelarter i nordvästra Uppland 1975–1977. Fauna och Flora 72: 257–264. (In Swedish).

KACELNIK, A. & KREBS, J. R. 1982. The dawn chorus in the Great Tit (*Parus major*): proximate and ultimate causes. Behaviour 83: 287–309.

KÄLLANDER, H. 1975. Breeding data for the Pied Flycatcher *Ficedula hypoleuca* in southern-most Sweden. Ornis Fennica 52: 134–143.

KÄLLANDER, H. & SMITH, H. G. 1990. Manipulation of the brood size of Pied Flycatchers. In: Blondel, J., Gosler, A., Lebreton, J.-D. & McCleery, R. (eds). Population biology of passerine birds. An integrated approach: 257–268. Berlin: Springer.

KÄLLANDER, H., KARLSSON, J., ROSENLUND, N. & SVENSSON, S. 1987. Clutch-size and breeding success of the Pied Flycatcher *Ficedula hypoleuca* in two contrasting habitats in South Sweden. Acta Regiae Societatis Scientiarum et Litterarum Gothoburgensis. Zoologica 14: 76–83.

KARLSSON, J. 1984. För fångst eller fägnad? Bruket av starholkar på Gotland och Öland under 1700- och 1800-talen. Vår Fågelvärld 43: 35–40. (In Swedish).

KARLSSON, J. & NILSSON, S. G. 1977. The influence of nest-box area on clutch size in some hole-nesting passerines. Ibis 119: 207–211.

KARLSSON, L., PERSSON, K. & WALLINDER, G. 1986. Ageing and sexing in Pied Flycatchers, *Ficedula hypoleuca*. Vår Fågelvärld 45: 131–146. (In Swedish with English summary).

KLOMP, H. 1970. The determination of clutch size in birds. A review. Ardea 58: 1–124.

KLUIJVER, H. N. 1951. The population ecology of the Great Tit, *Parus m. major* L. Ardea 40: 123–141.

KRAL, M., JÄRVI, T. & BICIK, V. 1988. Inter-specific aggression between the Collared Flycatcher and the Pied Flycatcher: the selective agent for the evolution of light-coloured male Pied Flycatcher populations? Ornis Scandinavica 19: 287–289.

KREBS, J. R. 1970. Regulation of numbers in the Great Tit (Aves: Passeriformes). Journal of Zoology, London 162: 317–333.

KREBS, J. R. 1979. Bird colours. Nature 282: 14–16.

KROODSMA, D. E. & PICKERT, R. 1980. Environmentally dependent sensitive periods for avian vocal learning. Nature 288: 477–479.

LACK, D. 1940. Courtship feeding in birds. Auk 57: 169–178.

LACK, D. 1947. The significance of clutch-size Part I-II. Ibis 89: 302–352.

LACK, D. 1948. The significance of clutch-size Part III. Some interspecific comparisons. Ibis 90: 25–45.

LACK, D. 1954. The natural regulation of animal populations. London: Oxford University Press.

LACK, D. 1966. Population studies of birds. Oxford: Clarendon.

LACK, D. 1968. Ecological adaptations for breeding in birds. London: Methuen.

LACK, D. 1971. Ecological isolation in birds. Oxford: Blackwell.

LAVEE, D., SAFRIEL, U. N. & MEILIJSON, I. 1991. For how long do trans-Saharan migrants stop over at an oasis? Ornis Scandinavica 22: 33–44.

LENNERSTEDT, I. 1969. Night rest and nest-visit frequency at five nests of Pied Flycatcher, *Ficedula hypoleuca* (Pall.), in Swedish Lapland. Arkiv för Zoologi 22: 279–287.

LENNERSTEDT, I. 1987. Feeding rhythm in three passerines under subarctic conditions in Lapland. Acta Regiae Societatis Scientiarum et Litterarum Gothoburgensis. Zoologica 14: 109–117.

LEVERTON, R. 1989. Wing length changes in individually-marked Blackbirds *Turdus merula* following moult. Ringing & Migration 10: 17–25.

LIFJELD, J. T. & SLAGSVOLD, T. 1986. The function of courtship feeding during incubation in the pied flycatcher *Ficedula hypoleuca*. Animal Behaviour 34: 1441–1453.

LIFJELD, J. T. & SLAGSVOLD, T. 1988a. Effects on energy costs on the optimal diet: an experiment with Pied Flycatchers *Ficedula hypoleuca* feeding nestlings. Ornis Scandinavica 19: 111–118.

LIFJELD, J. T. & SLAGSVOLD, T. 1988b. Female pied flycatchers *Ficedula hypoleuca* choose male characteristics in homogeneous habitats. Behavioral Ecology and Sociobiology 22: 27–36.

LIFJELD, J. T. & SLAGSVOLD, T. 1989a. Allocation of parental investment by polygynous Pied Flycatcher males. Ornis Fennica 66: 3–14.

LIFJELD, J. T. & SLAGSVOLD, T. 1989b. Female nutritional state influences the allocation of incubation feeding by polygynous pied flycatcher males. Animal Behaviour 38: 903–904.

LIFJELD, J. T. & SLAGSVOLD, T. 1990. Manipulations of male parental investment in polygynous pied flycatchers, *Ficedula hypoleuca*. Behavioral Ecology 1: 48–54.

LIFJELD, J. T., SLAGSVOLD, T. & STENMARK, G. 1987. Allocation of incubation feeding in a polygynous mating system: a study on pied flycatchers *Ficedula hypoleuca*. Animal Behaviour 35: 1663–1669.

LIFJELD, J. T., SLAGSVOLD, T. & LAMPE, H. M. 1991. Low frequency of extra-pair paternity in pied flycatchers revealed by DNA fingerprinting. Behavioral Ecology and Sociobiology 29: 95–101.

LINDÉN, M. & MØLLER, A. P. 1989. Cost of reproduction and covariation in life history traits in birds. Trends in Ecology & Evolution 4: 367–371.

LÖHRL, H. 1950. Ein Bastard Halbandschnäpper-Trauerschnäpper (*Muscicapa albicollis* × *M. hypoleuca*). Ornithologische Berichte 3: 126–130.

LÖHRL, H. 1955. Beziehungen zwischen Halsband- und Trauerfliegenschnäpper (*Muscicapa albicollis* und *M. hypoleuca*) in demselben Brutgebiet. Acta XI Congressus Internationalis Ornithologici, Basel 1954: 202–203.

LÖHRL, H. 1959. Zur Frage des Zeitpunktes einer Prägung auf die Heimatregion beim Halsbandschnäpper (*Ficedula albicollis*). Journal für Ornithologie 100: 132–140.

LUDESCHER, F. B. 1973. Sumpfmeise (*Parus p. palustris*) und Weidenmeise (*Parus montanus salicarius* Br.) als sympatrische Zwillingsarten. Journal für Ornithologie 114: 3–56.

LUNDBERG, A. & EDHOLM, M. 1982. Earlier and later arrivals of migrants in central Sweden. British Birds 75: 583–585.

LUNDBERG, A., ALATALO, R. V., CARLSON, A. & ULFSTRAND, S. 1981. Biometry, habitat distribution and breeding success in the Pied Flycatcher *Ficedula hypoleuca*. Ornis Scandinavica 12: 68–79.

LYNES, H. 1934. Contribution to the ornithology of southern Tanganyika Territory. Journal für Ornithologie 82: 1–147.

MACE, R. 1987. Why do birds sing at dawn? Ardea 75: 123–132.

MANSFELD, K. 1942. Zur Ernährung des Trauerfliegenschnäppers (*Muscicapa hypoleuca* Pall.) in Wald und Obstgarten. Anzeiger für Schädlingskunde 18: 66–70.

MEAD, C. J. & CLARK, J. A. 1987. Report on Bird-Ringing for 1987. Ringing & Migration 8: 135–200.

MEARNS, B. & MEARNS, R. 1988. Biographies for birdwatchers. London: Academic Press.

MEIDELL, O. 1961. Life history of the Pied Flycatcher and the Redstart in a Norwegian mountain area. Nytt Magasin for Zoologi 10: 5–47.

MESCH, J. A. 1845. Upsalatraktens fauna. Öfversigt af Kongl. Vetenskaps-Akademiens Förhandlingar 1: 83–91. (In Swedish).

MØLLER, A. P. 1986. Mating systems among European passerines: a review. Ibis 128: 234–250.

MØLLER, A. P. 1989. Parasites, predators and nest boxes: facts and artefacts in nest box studies of birds? Oikos 56: 421–423.

MONTGOMERIE, R. D. 1985. Why do birds sing at dawn? Abstracts of spoken and poster papers at the 19th International Ethological Conference, Toulouse, p. 242.

MOREAU, R. E. 1972. The Palaearctic–African bird migration systems. London: Academic Press.

MORENO, J. 1989. Strategies of mass change in breeding birds. Biological Journal of the Linnean Society 37: 297–310.

MORENO, J. & CARLSON, A. 1989. Clutch size and the cost of incubation in the Pied Flycatcher. Ornis Scandinavica 20: 123–128.

MURPHY, E. C. & HAUKIOJA, E. 1986. Clutch size in nidicolous birds. In: Johnston, R. F. (ed.). Current ornithology, Vol. 4: 141–180. New York: Plenum Press.

NICE, M. M. 1957. Nesting success in altricial birds. Auk 74: 305–321.

NILSSON, S. 1824. Skandinavisk fauna, foglarna. Lund.

NILSSON, S. 1835. Skandinavisk fauna, foglarna. Lund. (2nd edn)

NILSSON, S. 1858. Skandinavisk fauna, foglarna. Lund. (3rd edn)

Nilsson, S. G. 1979. Density and species richness of some forest bird communities in South Sweden. Oikos 33: 392–401.

Nilsson, S. G. 1984. Clutch size and breeding success of the Pied Flycatcher *Ficedula hypoleuca* in natural tree-holes. Ibis 126: 407–410.

Nisbet, I. C. T. 1973. Courtship-feeding, egg-size and breeding success in common terns. Nature 241: 141–142.

Noordwijk, A. J. van, Balen, J. H. van & Scharloo, W. 1981. Genetic and environmental variation in clutch size of the Great Tit *Parus major*. Netherlands Journal of Zoology 31: 342–372.

Nyholm, N. E. I. 1984. Polygyny in the pied flycatcher *Ficedula hypoleuca* at Ammarnäs, Swedish Lapland. Annales Zoologici Fennici 21: 229–232.

Nyholm, N. E. I. 1986. Birth area fidelity and age at first breeding in a northern population of Pied Flycatcher *Ficedula hypoleuca*. Ornis Scandinavica 17: 249–252.

Nyholm, N. E. I. & Myhrberg, H. E. 1983. Breeding area fidelity of the Pied Flycatcher *Ficedula hypoleuca* at Ammarnäs, Swedish Lapland. Ornis Fennica 60: 22–27.

Ödmann, S. 1792. Specimen ornithologiæ Wermdöensis ex observationibus propriis. Nova Acta Regiæ Societatis Scientiarum Upsaliensis 5: 50–84.

Ojanen, M. 1982. Var övervintrar den svartvita flugsnapparen *Ficedula hypoleuca*? Kommentar till Sten Österlöfs artikel i Vår Fågelvärld 1979. Vår Fågelvärld 41: 29–31. (In Swedish with English summary).

Ojanen, M. 1983. Significance of variation in egg traits in birds, with special reference to passerines. Doctoral dissertation, University of Oulu, Oulu.

Ojanen, M. 1987. A method for age determination of Pied Flycatchers *Ficedula hypoleuca* in spring. Acta Regiae Societatis Scientiarum et Litterarum Gothoburgensis. Zoologica 14: 95–101.

Ojanen, M. & Orell, M. 1982. Onset of moult among breeding Pied Flycatchers (*Ficedula hypoleuca*) in northern Finland. Vogelwarte 31: 445–451.

Olofsson, F. 1939. Svart och vit flugsnappare (*Muscicapa hypoleuca*) bigamist. Fauna och Flora 34: 190. (In Swedish).

Olsson, V. 1947. Results of a bird census in the province of Uppland 1947. Vår Fågelvärld 6: 93–125. (In Swedish with English summary).

Orians, G. H. 1969. On the evolution of mating systems in birds and mammals. American Naturalist 103: 589–603.

Österlöf, S. 1979. Var övervintrar den svartvita flugsnapparen *Ficedula hypoleuca*? Vår Fågelvärld 38: 247–250. (In Swedish with English summary).

Palmgren, P. 1930. Quantitative Untersuchungen über die Vogelfauna in den Wäldern Südfinnlands, mit besonderer Berucksichtigung Ålands. Acta Zoologica Fennica 7: 1–218.

Pärt, T. 1990. Natal dispersal in the collared flycatcher: possible causes and reproductive consequences. Ornis Scandinavica 21: 83–88.

Pärt, T. 1991. Philopatry and age as factors influencing reproductive success in the collared flycatcher (*Ficedula albicollis*). Doctoral dissertation, Uppsala University, Uppsala.

Pärt, T. & Gustafsson, L. 1989. Breeding dispersal in the collared flycatcher (*Ficedula albicollis*): possible causes and reproductive consequences. Journal of Animal Ecology 58: 305–320.

Pasanen, S. 1977. Breeding biology of the Pied Flycatcher *Ficedula hypoleuca* in eastern Finland. Ornis Fennica 54: 119–122.

PENNYCUICK, C. J. 1975. Mechanics of flight. In: Farner, D. S. and King, J. R. (eds), Avian biology: 1–75. New York: Academic Press.

PERRINS, C. M. 1965. Population fluctuations and clutch-size in the Great Tit, *Parus major* L. Journal of Animal Ecology 34: 601–647.

PERRINS, C. M. 1970. The timing of birds' breeding season. Ibis 112: 242–255.

PERRINS, C. M. 1979. British tits. London: Collins.

PETTIFOR, R. A., PERRINS, C. M. & McCLEERY, R. H. 1988. Individual optimization of clutch size in great tits. Nature 336: 160–162.

PFEIFER, S. & KEIL, W. 1962. Untersuchungen über die Fütterungsfrequenz einiger Singvogelarten. Ornithologische Mitteilungen 14: 21–26.

PFEIFER, S. & RUPPERT, K. 1953. Versuche zur Steigerung der Siedlungsdichte höhlen- und buschbrütender Vogelarten. Biologische Abhandlungen 6: 1–28.

POTTI, J. & MONTALVO, S. 1991a. Male colour variation in Spanish Pied Flycatchers *Ficedula hypoleuca*. Ibis 133: 293–299.

POTTI, J. & MONTALVO, S. 1991b. Male arrival and female mate choice in Pied Flycatchers *Ficedula hypoleuca* in Central Spain. Ornis Scandinavica 22: 45–54.

POTTI, J., AGUADO, F. J. S., BLANCO, D. & MONTALVO, S. 1987. Breeding data for a population of Pied Flycatchers *Ficedula hypoleuca* in Central Spain. Ardeola 34: 105–110.

PULLIAINEN, E. 1977. Habitat selection and breeding biology of box-nesting birds in northeastern Finnish Forest Lapland. Aquilo Ser. Zoologica 17: 2–22.

RABØL, J. 1978. One-direction orientation versus goal area navigation in migratory birds. Oikos 36: 216–223.

RADESÄTER, T., JACOBSSON, S., ANDBJER, N., BYLIN, A. & NYSTRÖM, K. 1987. Song rate and pair formation in the willow warbler (*Phylloscopus trochilus*). Animal Behaviour 35: 1645–1651.

RALPH, C. L. 1969. The control of color in birds. American Zoologist 9: 521–530.

REAL, L. 1990. Search theory and mate choice. I. Models of single-sex discrimination. American Naturalist 136: 376–404.

RENDAHL, H. & VESTERGREN, M. 1961. Die Zugverhältnisse der schwedischen Fliegenschnäpper. Mit Berücksichtigung der Ergebnisse von den finnischen und norwegischen Brutgebieten. Arkiv för Zoologi 13: 113–154.

RICKLEFS, R. E. 1980. Geographical variation in clutch size among passerine birds: Ashmole's hypothesis. Auk 97: 38–49.

ROSENFELD, J. & FAGERSTRÖM, T. 1980. Vårflyttningens förlopp över Örskär hos tretton nattflyttande småfåglar. Vår Fågelvärld 39: 217–224. (In Swedish with English summary).

RØSKAFT, E. & JÄRVI, T. 1983. Male plumage colour and mate choice of female Pied Flycatchers *Ficedula hypoleuca*. Ibis 125: 396–400.

RØSKAFT, E., JÄRVI, T., NYHOLM, N. E. I., VIROLAINEN, M., WINKEL, W. & ZANG, H. 1986. Geographic variation in secondary sexual plumage colour characteristics of the male Pied Flycatcher. Ornis Scandinavica 17: 293–298.

ROSVALL, S. 1982. Halsbandsflugsnappare och skärfläcka. Visby: Hanseproduktion (In Swedish).

ROYAMA, T. 1966. A re-interpretation of courtship feeding. Bird Study 13: 116–129.

SANDBERG, R., PETTERSSON, J. & PERSSON, K. 1991. Migratory orientation of free-flying Robins *Erithacus rubecula* and Pied Flycatchers *Ficedula hypoleuca*: release experiments. Ornis Scandinavica 22: 1–11.

SAUROLA, P. 1988. Bird ringing in Finland 1913–1987. Lintumies 23: 234–248.

SCOPOLI, J. A. 1769. 'Annus I. Historico-naturalis. Descriptiones avium musei proprii earunque rariorum, quas vidit in vivario Augustiss. Imperatoris, et in museu excell. comitis Francisci Annib'. Turriani. Lipsiæ.

SEARCY, W. A., ERIKSSON, D. & LUNDBERG, A. 1991. Deceptive behavior in pied flycatchers. Behavioral Ecology and Sociobiology 29: 167–175.

SILVERIN, B. 1975. Reproductive organs and breeding behaviour of the male Pied Flycatcher *Ficedula hypoleuca* (Pallas). Ornis Scandinavica 6: 15–26.

SILVERIN, B. 1980. Effect of long-acting testosterone treatment on free-living pied flycatchers, *Ficedula hypoleuca*, during the breeding period. Animal Behaviour 28: 906–912.

SILVERIN, B. 1981. Reproductive effort, as expressed in body and organ weights, in the Pied Flycatcher. Ornis Scandinavica 12: 133–139.

SILVERIN, B. & ANDERSSON, G. 1984. Food composition of adult and nestling Pied Flycatchers, *Ficedula hypoleuca*, during the breeding period. Vår Fågelvärld 43: 517–525. (In Swedish with English summary).

SKUTCH, A. F. 1949. Do tropical birds rear as many young as they can nourish? Ibis 91: 430–455.

SLAGSVOLD, T. 1975. Competition between the Great Tit *Parus major* and the Pied Flycatcher *Ficedula hypoleuca* in the breeding season. Ornis Scandinavica 6: 179–190.

SLAGSVOLD, T. 1976. Annual and geographical variation in the time of breeding in the Great Tit *Parus major* and the Pied Flycatcher *Ficedula hypoleuca* in relation to environmental phenology and spring temperature. Ornis Scandinavica 7: 127–145.

SLAGSVOLD, T. 1986a. Nest site settlement by the Pied Flycatcher: does the female choose her mate for the quality of his house or himself? Ornis Scandinavica 17: 210–220.

SLAGSVOLD, T. 1986b. Asynchronous versus synchronous hatching in birds: experiments with the pied flycatcher. Journal of Animal Ecology 55: 1115–1134.

SLAGSVOLD, T. 1987. Nest site preference and clutch size in the Pied Flycatcher *Ficedula hypoleuca*. Ornis Scandinavica 18: 189–197.

SLAGSVOLD, T. 1989. Experiments on clutch size and nest size in passerine birds. Oecologia 80: 297–302.

SLAGSVOLD, T. & LIFJELD, J. T. 1986. Mate retention and male polyterritoriality in the pied flycatcher *Ficedula hypoleuca*. Behavioral Ecology and Sociobiology 19: 25–30.

SLAGSVOLD, T. & LIFJELD, J. T. 1988a. Plumage colour and sexual selection in the pied flycatcher *Ficedula hypoleuca*. Animal Behaviour 36: 395–407.

SLAGSVOLD, T. & LIFJELD, J. T. 1988b. Pied Flycatchers *Ficedula hypoleuca* prefer dry nest cavities. Fauna norvegica Series C. Cinclus 11: 67–70.

SLAGSVOLD, T. & LIFJELD, J. T. 1988c. Ultimate adjustment of clutch size to parental feeding capacity in a passerine bird. Ecology 69: 1918–1922.

SLAGSVOLD, T. & LIFJELD, J. T. 1989a. Constraints on hatching asynchrony and egg size in pied flycatchers. Journal of Animal Ecology 58: 837–849.

SLAGSVOLD, T. & LIFJELD, J. T. 1989b. Hatching asynchrony in birds: the hypothesis of sexual conflict over parental investment. American Naturalist 133: 239–253.

SLAGSVOLD, T. & LIFJELD, J. T. 1990. Return rates of male Pied Flycatchers: an experimental study manipulating breeding success. In: Blondel, J., Gosler, A., Lebreton, J.-D. & McCleery, R. (eds). Population biology in passerine birds. An integrated approach: 441–452. Berlin: Springer.

SLAGSVOLD, T., LIFJELD, J. T., STENMARK, G. & BREIEHAGEN, T. 1988. On the cost of searching for a mate in female pied flycatchers *Ficedula hypoleuca*. Animal Behaviour 36: 433–442.

SMITH, K. D. 1965. On the birds of Morocco. Ibis 107: 493–526.

SMITH, V. W. 1966. Autumn and spring weights of some Palaearctic migrants in central Nigeria. Ibis 108: 492–512.

SNOW, D. W. 1954. The habitats of Eurasian tits *Parus* spp. Ibis 96: 565–585.

SONERUD, G. A. 1985. Nest hole shift in Tengmalm's owl *Aegolius funereus* as defence against nest predation involving long-term memory in the predator. Journal of Animal Ecology 54: 179–192.

SOVERI, J. 1940. Die Vogelfauna von Lammi, ihre regionale Verbreitung und Abhängigkeit von den ökologischen Faktoren. Acta Zoologica Fennica 118: 1–176.

STAAV, R. 1989. Åldersrekord för fåglar ringmärkta i Sverige – Aktuell lista 1989. Vår Fågelvärld 48: 251–275 (In Swedish with English summary).

STEARNS, S. C. 1976. Life-history tactics: a review of the ideas. Quarterly Review of Biology 51: 3–47.

STENMARK, G., SLAGSVOLD, T. & LIFJELD, J. T. 1988. Polygyny in the pied flycatcher, *Ficedula hypoleuca*: a test of the deception hypothesis. Animal Behaviour 36: 1646–1657.

STERNBERG, H. 1964. Untersuchungen über die Farbtypenzugehörigkeit der männlichen Trauerschnäpper, *Ficedula hypoleuca*, im schweizerischen Mittelland. Ornithologische Beobachter 61: 90–94.

STERNBERG, H. 1989. Pied Flycatcher. In: Newton, I. (ed.), Lifetime reproduction in birds: 56–74. London: Academic Press.

STJERNBERG, M. 1974. Nest-building by the Pied Flycatcher *Ficedula hypoleuca*. Ornis Fennica 51: 85–109.

STRESEMANN, E. 1926. Die systematische Stellung von *Muscicapa semitorquata* E. v. Homeyer. Ornithologische Monatsberichte 34: 4–9.

STRÖM, H. 1774. Om et par rare fugle. Konglige Norske Videnskabers Selskabs Skrifter D. 5: 539–546. (In Norwegian).

SUNDEVALL, C. J. 1846. Ny svensk fogel, Gottlands fogelfauna. Om namnet *Muscicapa*. Öfversigt af Konglige Vetenskaps-Akademiens Förhandlingar 2: 222–225. (In Swedish).

SVENSSON, L. 1984. Identification guide to European passerines. Stockholm.

SVENSSON, S. 1987. Nesting density and breeding performance of the Pied Flycatcher *Ficedula hypoleuca* near the tree line in Swedish Lapland. Acta Regiae Societatis Scientiarum et Litterarum Gothoburgensis. Zoologica 14: 84–94.

TENGMALM, P. G. 1783. Ornithologiska anmärkningar gjorde vid Almare-Stäk i Upland. Konglige Vetenskaps Academiens nya Handlingar 4: 43–55. (In Swedish).

TIAINEN, J., SAUROLA, P. & SOLONEN, T. 1984. Nest distribution of the Pied Flycatcher *Ficedula hypoleuca* in an area saturated with nest-boxes. Annales Zoologici Fennici 21: 199–204.

TOMIALOJĆ, L., WESOŁOWSKI, T. & WALANKIEWICZ, W. 1984. Breeding bird community of a primaeval temperate forest (Białowieża National Park, Poland). Acta Ornithologica 20: 241–310.

TOMPA, F. S. 1967. Reproductive success in relation to breeding density in pied flycatchers, *Ficedula hypoleuca* (Pallas). Acta Zoologica Fennica 118: 1–28.

TRETTAU, W. 1952. Planberingung des Trauerfliegenschnäppers (*Muscicapa hypoleuca*) in Hessen. Vogelwarte 16: 89–95.

TRETTAU, W. & MERKEL, F. 1943. Ergebnisse einer Planberingung des Trauerfliegenfängers (*Muscicapa hypoleuca* Pallas) in Schlesien. Vogelzug 14: 77–90.

TRIVERS, R. L. 1972. Parental investment and sexual selection. In: Campbell, B. G. (ed.), Sexual selection and the descent of man, 1871–1971: 135–179. Chicago: Aldine.

ULFSTRAND, S. & HÖGSTEDT, G. 1976. How many birds breed in Sweden. Anser 15: 1–32. (In Swedish with English summary).

VAN BALEN, J. H. 1979. Observations on the post-fledging dispersal of the Pied Flycatcher, *Ficedula hypoleuca*. Ardea 67: 134–137.

VAN BALEN, J. H., BOOY, C. J. H., VAN FRANEKER, J. A. & OSIECK, E. R. 1982. Studies on hole-nesting birds in natural nest sites. 1. Availability and occupation of natural nest sites. Ardea 70: 1–24.

VAN OORT, E. D. 1911. On the catalogue of the collection of birds brought together by A. Vroeg. Notes from the Leyden Museum 34: 66–69.

VAURIE, C. 1959. The birds of the Palearctic fauna. Passeriformes. London: Witherby.

VEPSÄLÄINEN, K. & JÄRVINEN, O. 1977. Ein Bastard-Männchen Halsband-Trauerschnäpper (*Ficedula albicollis* × *F. hypoleuca*) brütet in Finnland. Journal für Ornithologie 118: 436–437.

VERNER, J. 1964. Evolution of polygamy in the long-billed marsh wren. Evolution 18: 252–261.

VERNER, J. & WILLSON, M. F. 1966. The influence of habitats on mating systems of North American passerine birds. Ecology 47: 143–147.

VIROLAINEN, M. 1984. Breeding biology of the Pied Flycatcher *Ficedula hypoleuca* in relation to population density. Annales Zoologici Fennici 21: 187–197.

VON HAARTMAN, L. 1945. Some cases of polygamy of the Pied Flycatcher (*Muscicapa h. hypoleuca* Pall.). Vår Fågelvärld 4: 27–32. (In Swedish with English summary).

VON HAARTMAN, L. 1949. Der Trauerfliegenschnäpper. I. Ortstreue und Rassenbildung. Acta Zoologica Fennica 56: 1–104.

VON HAARTMAN, L. 1951a. Der Trauerfliegenschnäpper. II. Populationsprobleme. Acta Zoologica Fennica 67: 1–60.

VON HAARTMAN, L. 1951b. Successive polygamy. Behaviour 3: 256–274.

VON HAARTMAN, L. 1954. Der Trauerfliegenschnäpper. III. Die Nahrungsbiologie. Acta Zoologica Fennica 83: 1–96.

VON HAARTMAN, L. 1956a. Territory in the pied flycatcher *Muscicapa hypoleuca*. Ibis 98: 460–475.

VON HAARTMAN, L. 1956b. Der Einfluss der Temperatur auf den Brutrhytmus experimentell nachgewiesen. Ornis Fennica 33: 100–107.

VON HAARTMAN, L. 1958. The incubation rhythm of the female Pied Flycatcher (*Ficedula hypoleuca*) in the presence and absence of the male. Ornis Fennica 35: 71–76.

VON HAARTMAN, L. 1960. The Ortstreue of the Pied Flycatcher. Proceedings of the XII International Ornithological Congress, Helsinki 1958: 266–273.

VON HAARTMAN, L. 1967a. Geographical variations in the clutch-size of the pied flycatcher. Ornis Fennica 44: 89–98.

VON HAARTMAN, L. 1967b. Clutch-size in the pied flycatcher. Proceedings of the XIV International Ornithological Congress, Oxford, pp. 155–164.

VON HAARTMAN, L. 1969. The nesting habits of Finnish birds I. Passeriformes. Commentationes Biologicae 32: 1–187.

VON HAARTMAN, L. 1971. Population dynamics. In: Farner, D. S. and King, J. R. (eds), Avian biology, Vol I: 391–459. London: Academic Press.

VON HAARTMAN, L. 1982. Two modes of clutch size determination in passerine birds. Journal of the Yamashina Institute for Ornithology 14: 214–219.

VON HAARTMAN, L. 1985. The biological significance of the nuptial plumage of the male Pied Flycatcher. Acta XVIII Congressus Internationalis Ornithologicus, Moscow 1982: 34–60.

VON HAARTMAN, L. 1988. The biological significance of the nuptial plumage of the male Pied Flycatcher. Corrected second print from Acta XVIII Congressus Internationalis Ornithologicus, Moscow 1982. Helsinki: L. von Haartman.

VON HAARTMAN, L. 1990. Breeding time of the Pied Flycatcher *Ficedula hypoleuca*. In: Blondel, J., Gosler, A., Lebreton, J.-D. & McCleery, R. (eds). Population biology in passerine birds. An integrated approach: 1–16. Berlin: Springer.

VON HAARTMAN, L. & LÖHRL, H. 1950. Die Lautäusserungen des Trauer- und Halsband-fliegenschnäppers, *Muscicapa h. hypoleuca* (Pall.) und *M. a albicollis* Temminck. Ornis Fennica 27: 85–97.

VON HAARTMAN, L., HILDÉN, O., LINKOLA, P., SUOMALAINEN, P. & TENOVUO, R. 1963–72. Pohjolan linnut värikuvin. Helsinki: Otava. (In Finnish).

WALLIN, L. 1986. Divergent character displacement in the song of two allospecies: the Pied Flycatcher *Ficedula hypoleuca*, and the Collared Flycatcher *Ficedula albicollis*. Ibis 128: 251–259.

WALTER, H. 1968. Zur Abhängigkeit des Eleonorafalken (*Falco eleonorae*) vom mediterranen Vogelzug. Journal für Ornithologie 109: 323–365.

WALTER, H. 1979. Eleonora's falcon. Chicago: University of Chicago Press.

WEATHERHEAD, P. J. & ROBERTSON, R. J. 1979. Offspring quality and the polygyny threshold: 'the sexy son hypothesis'. American Naturalist 113: 201–208.

WESOŁOWSKI, T. 1989. Nest-sites of hole-nesters in a primaeval temperate forest (Białowieża National Park, Poland). Acta Ornithologica 25: 321–351.

WESTNEAT, D. F. 1987. Extra-pair fertilizations in a predominantly monogamous bird: genetic evidence. Animal Behaviour 35: 877–886.

WINKEL, W. 1982. Zum Ortstreu-Verhalten des Trauerschnäppers (*Ficedula hypoleuca*) im westlichen Randbereich seines mitteleuropäischen Verbreitungsgebietes. Journal für Ornithologie 123: 155–173.

WINKEL, W. 1989. Langfristige Bestandsentwicklung von Kohlmeise (*Parus major*) und Trauerschnäpper (*Ficedula hypoleuca*): Ergebnisse aus Niedersachsen. Journal für Ornithologie 130: 335–343.

WINKEL, W. & WINKEL, D. 1974. Brutbiologische Untersuchungen am Trauerschnäpper (*Ficedula hypoleuca*) während seiner Legeperiode. Vogelwelt 95: 60–70.

WINKEL, W. & WINKEL, D. 1984. Polygynie des Trauerschnäppers (*Ficedula hypoleuca*) am Westrand seines Areals in Mitteleuropa. Journal für Ornithologie 125: 1–14.

WINKEL, W., RICHTER, D. & BERNDT, R. 1970. Über Beziehungen zwischen Farbtyp und Lebensalter männlicher Trauerschnäpper (*Ficedula hypoleuca*). Vogelwelt 91: 161–170.

WITTENBERGER, J. F. 1979. The evolution of mating systems in birds and mammals. In: Marler, P. & Vandenbergh, J. (eds). Handbook of behavioral neurobiology, vol. 3, Social behavior and communication. New York: Plenum Press.

WITTENBERGER, J. F. 1983. Tactics of mate choice. In: Bateson, P. (ed.), Mate choice: 435–447. Cambridge: Cambridge University Press.

YLIMAUNU, J. & JÄRVINEN, A. 1987. Do Pied Flycatchers *Ficedula hypoleuca* have a brood-survival or brood-reduction strategy? Ornis Fennica 64: 10–15.

ZANG, H. 1975. Populationsstudien am Trauerschnäpper (*Ficedula hypoleuca*) im Bergwald des Harzes also einem suboptimalen Habitat. Vogelwelt 96: 161–184.

ZANG, H. 1980. Der Einfluss der Höhenlage auf Siedlungsdichte und Brutbiologie höhlenbrütender Singvögel im Harz. Journal für Ornithologie 121: 371–386.

ZANG, H. 1985. Hangexposition und Brutbiologie von Wasseramsel (*Cinclus cinclus*), Trauerschnäpper (*Ficedula hypoleuca*), Kohl- und Tannenmeise (*Parus major, P. ater*). Journal für Ornithologie 126: 73–84.

Index

Age
  at first breeding, 114–116
  determination, 30–34
  importance for female choice, 170, 171
Alarm calls, 136
Altitude, and clutch size, 71, 72
Ashmole's hypothesis, 70
Autumn migration, *see* Migration

Basal metabolic rate, 93
Bill size, 47, 238
Blackbird, 33
Blackbird, Red-winged, 2, 163, 182
Blackcap, 8, 9, 14
Body mass
  female, 47, 48, 57, 78, 92, 102
  male, 47, 57, 92, 163, 177
  nestling, 49, 51, 76, 80, 81, 83, 93, 96,
    106–108, 121, 122, 146, 170, 171, 201
Body temperature, 89
Brambling, 51, 168, 169
Breeding
  age at first, 114–116, 148
  density, *see* Density
  phenology, 61–69
  success, 48–50, 57, 76, 81, 83, 84,
    104–106, 193–203, 207, 219–222, 229,
    240
  time, 62–69, 74–77, 228
Brood reduction, 94
Bunting
  Corn, 182
  Indigo, 197
  Ortolan, 130
  Reed, 130, 243
Buzzard
  Common, 154
  Honey, 154

Calendar effect, 74, 75, 77
Calls, *see* Song
Catching flycatchers, 5, 134, 215
Chaffinch, 130
Clutch-size, 48, 50, 51, 60–87, 89, 219,
    220, 228, 229, 240
  manipulations, 82–85, 94
  optimization, 80–86
  reduction with time, 74–77, 228
  variation, 60, 69–80
Coloration, *see* Male colour
Competition
  interspecific, 50–52, 55, 151, 152, 154
  intraspecific, 48–51, 176–179
Copulations, 194–198
Courtship feeding, *see* Incubation feeding
Cuckoo, 208

Dawn chorus, 132, 133
Deception hypothesis, 182, 203–210, 212
Density
  at stop-over areas, 23
  breeding, 40–46, 48–53, 73, 121, 152,
    185, 187, 195, 226, 233, 234, 244
  winter, 23
Diet
  of adults, 55, 56, 58, 59, 63
  of nestlings, 58, 59, 63, 98, 239
Dipper, 243
Dispersal
  adult, 82
  causes and consequences, 119–122
  female, 118–120, 241
  male, 116–118, 120, 241
  natal, 77, 121–123, 241
Distances between territories, 186, 187,
    204, 205, 236, 244

Distribution
  breeding time, 10–14
  winter, 13, 16, 17
DNA-fingerprinting, 197, 198, 220
Doubly labelled water, 93
Drost's score, 139–143, 148, 168, 238, 242
Dunnock, 129, 130

Egg
  dumping, 197
  formation, 64–66
  laying time, *see* Breeding
  size, 89
  temperature, 91
Egg-laying, 46, 56, 62–68, 89, 219, 233
Extra-pair copulations, 186, 194–197, 220
Extra-pair fertilizations, 186, 194,
  196–198, 220

Falcon, Eleonora's, 23
Feeding rate, 97–104, 172, 201
Female choice of mate, 132, 154, 160–175,
  190–193, 203–211
Female–female aggression, 204, 210
Female pairing status
  monogamous, 57, 76, 79, 98, 102–105,
    170, 182, 198–203, 228–230, 233, 234
  primary, 57, 79, 101–104, 186, 188,
    198–202, 209, 215, 228, 229, 233, 234
  secondary, 57, 76, 79, 100–104, 170,
    182, 187, 198–203, 207–209, 212, 228,
    229, 233, 234, 236
  tertiary, 103, 185
  unmated, 114–116, 201
Female search costs, 192, 193, 209, 210
Fertile period, 186, 194, 195
Fidelity
  to breeding site of females, 118, 119
  to breeding site of males, 116, 117
  to natal area, 121–123
Fledging success, *see* Breeding
Fledgling weight, *see* Body mass
Flight speed, 23, 24, 171
Flycatcher
  Collared, 1, 4, 10–14, 32, 41, 51, 55, 73,
    74, 80–83, 85, 106, 117, 119–121,
    123, 133, 141, 144, 146, 147,

  150–155, 197, 198, 202, 204, 213–222,
    238, 243
  Damar, 8
  Spotted, 55, 56
Food, *see* Diet
Food abundance, 84, 164, 174, 175, 200
Foraging techniques, 55, 56
Forehead patch, 3, 12, 171, 215, 234

Gonads, seasonal changes in, 92
Good genes, 160

Habitat preferences, 46–50
Hatching
  asynchrony, 93, 94
  pattern, 93, 94
  success, 95, 96, 220, 221
Heritability, 67, 69, 85, 86, 145, 197, 202,
  203
Heterospecific matings, 150, 152, 154,
  214–222
Hormones, 65, 163, 167, 190
Hybridization, 213–222
  avoidance of, 150–152, 154, 215–217
  fitness of hybrids, 198, 219–222
  frequency of, 152, 215, 216

Incubation, 56, 57, 89–93, 233
  feeding, 56, 57
Infertile eggs, 89, 90, 95, 96, 220, 221
Intra-pair copulations, 194–196

Kestrel, 243

Latitude, and clutch size, 69–72
Lifespan, 112, 113
Lifetime reproductive success, 61, 80, 108,
  109, 194

Magpie, 82
Male colour
  classification, 139, 148
  heritability, 145, 146

Male colour—*cont.*
  importance for female choice, 163,
    165–170, 206, 207
  importance in male–male competition,
    177–179
  variation with age, 139–143, 148, 149
  variation between populations, 140,
    141, 144–147, 150, 153, 215, 216,
    228, 238, 242
  variation within populations, 47,
    144–147, 152, 153, 216, 228
  variation between subspecies, 12, 238
Male–male competition, 134, 151, 152,
    165, 166, 176–179
Male pairing status
  monogamous, 57, 98, 120, 169–171,
    193, 194, 233, 234
  polygynous, 57, 100–104, 120, 135,
    136, 169, 170, 181–190, 194, 201,
    202, 204–210, 212, 215, 231, 233–235
  unmated, 114–116, 135, 136, 187–190,
    202, 206, 207, 209, 210, 212, 224,
    233, 234
Mate guarding, 195
Maternal effects, 69, 197
Mate-searching behaviour, 191–193
Mating system, 180–211
Melanin, 144
Migration
  autumn, 18–24
  speed of, 23, 24
  spring, 24–26
  time of, 16–26, 46, 153
Mixed matings, *see* Heterospecific matings
Mixed paternity, *see* Extra-pair
    fertilizations
Mixed singing, 216, 217
Monoterritoriality, 181, 182
Morphology, 33, 46–48, 163, 172, 202,
    238
Mortality
  females, 83, 114, 233
  males, 83, 114, 147, 148
Moult, 29, 30, 34, 35, 139, 144, 148, 165,
    207

Name and history, 8–18

Natural cavities, 38, 74, 184, 233–237,
    244, 245
Nest
  bottom area, 73, 74, 226, 227, 229
  entrance size, 38, 39, 174, 192, 208, 209,
    233, 234
  height, 38, 39, 174, 192, 193, 230, 231
  structure, 40, 74
  volume, 226, 227, 229
Nest-building, 40
Nestling
  care, 97–104
  growth, 96, 97
Non-breeding birds, *see* Male, and Female
    pairing status, unmated
Nuthatch, 50, 117, 227

Owl, Tengmalm's, 243

Pair formation, 157–160
Parasites, 1, 39, 238
Paternal care quality, 171, 172
Pipit
  Meadow, 243
  Tree, 243
Plumage, *see* Male colour
Polygyny, 49, 57, 100, 105, 120, 181–188,
    193–211, 233, 236, 245
Polygyny threshold model, 182, 183
Polyterritoriality, 2, 79, 135, 136, 181,
    182, 184–186, 188, 190, 191, 194,
    203–212, 234–236, 244
Predation, 23, 38, 39, 70, 147, 148, 166,
    173–175, 200, 203, 208, 211, 228–234

Random territories, 161–166, 170, 173,
    174
Recruitment, 51, 61, 63, 76, 77, 80–84,
    106–109, 115, 146, 220, 221, 246
Redstart, 4, 40, 51, 55, 56, 117, 227, 243
Redwing, 51
Repeatability, 202
Reproductive success, *see* Breeding
    success
Ringing recoveries, 16–18, 20–22, 25
Rosefinch, Common, 243

Ruff, 154

Sex determination, 34–35
Sex ratio, 113–114
Sexual conflict, 182, 203
Sexual dichromatism, 8, 147, 148
Sexual selection, 126, 165, 166, 169, 170,
    176, 178
Sexy sons, 202, 203
Song, 44, 45, 125–137, 163–165
    copying, 128–130, 217, 218
    function, 133–135, 153, 157, 191, 217
    intensity, 130–132, 163–165, 189, 190,
        204–206
    learning, 127, 128, 217
    repertoire, 126–130, 134, 162, 163, 164,
        217
    structure, 11, 13, 14, 126, 127, 216
    versatility, 126, 127, 163
Sonograms of vocalizations, 126, 127,
    129, 135, 218
Sparrow
    Song, 126, 128, 163
    Tree, 4
    White-crowned, 127
Sparrowhawk, 114, 147, 148
Spring
    arrival, 26–29, 45, 46, 162, 163
    migration, *see* Migration
Starling, 74
Stonechat, 243
Subspecies, 10–14, 29, 141, 146, 170, 238
Survival
    adult, 82, 112
    female, 76, 77, 80, 81, 83, 112, 113, 116
    male, 83, 102, 103, 112, 113, 116, 148,
        149
    nestling, 108, 112, 201

Tail length, 47

Tarsus length, 47, 50, 77–79, 94, 108, 121,
    163, 170, 171, 177, 196, 197, 201, 238
Taxonomy, 8–10
Territory
    intrusions, 153
    quality, 160, 164–166, 172–175, 179,
        188, 190, 203, 222, 231–233
    size, 41, 173, 187
Timing of breeding, *see* Breeding time
Tit
    Blue, 2, 4
    Coal, 4
    Great, 2, 4, 39, 48, 50–52, 80, 82, 114,
        126, 163
    Marsh, 4, 10
    Penduline, 243
    Sombre, 10
    Willow, 51

Vocalizations, *see* Song

Warbler
    Barred, 243
    Blyth's Reed, 243
    Marsh, 243
    Willow, 51, 129, 130, 217, 243
    Wood, 243
Weight, *see* Body mass
Wheatear, 243
Whinchat, 9, 14
Whitethroat, 243
Wing length, 26, 32–34, 47, 48, 97, 163,
    170, 177, 215, 238
Wintering areas, 16, 17
Woodpecker
    Great Spotted, 224, 230, 233
    Lesser Spotted, 224, 230, 233
Wren, Long-billed Marsh, 127, 128
Wryneck, 4